PENGUIN BOOKS

COLLEGES THAT CHANGE LIVES

LOREN POPE, a Washington newspaperman who led the fight for better schools in rural Loudoun County, Virginia, first began writing about education in a column for the *Gannett Newspapers* in 1952. His column led to his position as education editor of *The New York Times* during the height of the college-going chaos of the late '50s started by the GI Bill. As an education journalist, and later a top administrator of what is now Oakland University in Michigan, he became deeply concerned with the lack of information on colleges that was available to consumers. He believed that uninformed choices could account for heavy dropout, transfer, and failure rates. His interest was triggered by the poor advice he got for his own son from friends in the then Office of Education.

In 1965, he opened the College Placement Bureau in Washington, D.C., to help families make informed, fruitful choices. Out of his reporting and research came a book, *The Right College: How to Get In, Stay In, Get Back In* (Macmillan, 1970), and several magazine articles, including the nationally syndicated "Twenty Myths That Can Jinx Your College Choice," first published in *The Washington Post Magazine*. *Reader's Digest* has sold a half-million reprints of its condensation, titled "Facts to Know in Picking a College."

These articles inspired his second book, *Looking Beyond the Ivy League: Finding the College That's Right for You*, which is now available from Penguin in a fully revised and updated edition.

Pope contributes to professional journals and speaks at meetings of the National Association of College Admissions Counselors. He has also appeared on radio and television.

COLLEGES THAT CHANGE LIVES

40 Schools That Will
Change the Way You Think
About Colleges

LOREN POPE

PENGUIN BOOKS

PENGUIN BOOKS
Published by the Penguin Group
Penguin Group (USA) Inc., 375 Hudson Street, New York, New York
10014, U.S.A.
Penguin Group (Canada), 90 Eglinton Avenue East, Suite 700, Toronto,
Ontario, Canada M4P 2Y3 (a division of Pearson Penguin Canada Inc.)
Penguin Books Ltd, 80 Strand, London WC2R 0RL, England
Penguin Ireland, 25 St Stephen's Green, Dublin 2, Ireland
(a division of Penguin Books Ltd)
Penguin Group (Australia), 250 Camberwell Road, Camberwell, Victoria
3124, Australia (a division of Pearson Australia Group Pty Ltd)
Penguin Books India Pvt Ltd, 11 Community Centre, Panchsheel Park,
New Delhi – 110 017, India
Penguin Group (NZ), cnr Airborne and Rosedale Roads, Albany, Auckland
1310, New Zealand (a division of Pearson New Zealand Ltd)
Penguin Books (South Africa) (Pty) Ltd, 24 Sturdee Avenue, Rosebank,
Johannesburg 2196, South Africa

Penguin Books Ltd, Registered Offices:
80 Strand, London WC2R 0RL, England

First published in Penguin Books 1996
First revised edition published 2000
This second revised edition published 2006

5   7   9   10   8   6

Copyright © Loren Pope, 1996, 2000, 2006
All rights reserved

ISBN 0 14 30.3736 6
CIP data available

Printed in the United States of America
Set in Fairfield Light
Designed by Mia Risberg

To Virginia Buege, the very able young mother who had the idea for the Colleges That Change Lives book tours when she was on the Beloit College admissions staff, and who has smoothly coordinated them since their beginning in 1998.

Without her help, and sometimes her direction, this book would not have been possible.

Her high school classmates in Wylie, Texas were right on the mark when they voted her "most likely to succeed."

Acknowledgments

This second edition would not have been possible without the perceptive help and counsel of Virginia Buege, former Beloit admissions officer who had the idea for the annual CTCL book tours, and who as their coordinator has helped make them into SRO events in twenty-two cities as of 2005. She has done all the leg work and the job of getting the colleges to provide the necessary updating material as well as the Ten Years Later surveys.

In the first edition I wrote that for a book such as this to be valid, the faculty members have to be, as an academic friend once observed, "stoop-shouldered with honesty." Professors, deans, provosts, and occasional presidents constituted a principal source of information at each college. I am indebted to them for their kindnesses and for their willingness to discuss their colleges with candor. Their breadth of view was also crucial. Having been graduate assistants or faculty members at all the leading universities and many top colleges, they could make invaluable comparisons. At all these forty colleges they are demonstrating daily that teaching is an act of love.

I am equally indebted to the many students I talked with at each of the colleges whose opinions were equally candid and who in their enthusiasm often went beyond the faculty claims about nurturing or sense of belonging.

Able admissions staffs did much to make my visits more effective, provided accurate data, and often arranged special interviews or meetings at my request.

A friend used to say: Behind every good man stands a good woman. In my case it took two: My very able Penguin editor, Alicia Bothwell Mancini, and Virginia Buege, to whom this book is dedicated.

Contents

SOUTH

MIDWEST

SOUTHWEST

NORTHWEST

Introduction

This book, along with its companion, *Looking Beyond the Ivy League,* will help youths of many levels of academic aptitude find catalytic colleges that will change their lives, help them find themselves, raise their aspirations, and empower them. In doing so it will free them from our system's obscene obsession with academic aptitude, which does not determine achievement, satisfaction with life, or the merit of a human being.

Some of the greatest minds of the twentieth century have been hopeless cases in school. Nevertheless one of them said that being dyslexic had made his achievements possible, as you can read in the chapter, "Today's Learning Disabled Will Be Tomorrow's Gifted."

America's educational system, the envy of the world, is the only one that enables everyone to realize his or her potential. This, rather than our physical resources, has been the force behind America's great achievements in its first two centuries.

Its continuing health depends also on its people having moral compasses, and as one dean said, these colleges "are incubating the continuity of democratic values."

Events Demand
a Second Edition

A new edition is needed to report several important facts. The most dramatic is the Ivy confirmation that "liberal education in the research universities is a project in ruins," but is "alive and well" in such colleges as these. In other words, the Ivies, like the emperor, have no clothes.

Another is additional evidence that the "learning disabled" of today will be the gifted of tomorrow.

A new feature is a "Ten Years Later" section at the end of each college profile to show that the profound influence these colleges exert is not just a flash in the pan. Students and graduates alike testify that their college experiences continue to influence the course of their lives as much as ever.

New curricular emphases, in particular the growing importance of foreign study, are adding exciting new breadth to the college experience, and many new state-of-the-art physical facilities reflect advances in science and technology as well as in student unions and plush new dorms.

This edition will prove to teenagers that the colleges depicted in 1995 or 2000 are not ancient history. They live.

A MISSIONARY FOR CTCL

The message of this book has been so great a force in freeing families from the college bugaboo, that many high school counselors and college admissions officers have helped me spread the good news. At the forefront has been Martha (Marty) O'Connell. After twenty-eight years in admissions she resigned as vice president for enrollment and financial aid at McDaniel College out of a sense of mission to carry on the Colleges That Change Lives torch.

COLLEGES THAT
CHANGE LIVES

Relax! Your Future Is Assured!

You don't have to be one of the jittery millions of wannabees anxiously fattening resumes to impress some high-status school that won't do nearly as much for you as one of the catalytic colleges that really wants you.

That is a guarantee. And it has been cosigned by a leading Ivy savant. In what was, for him, a dramatic exposé, he wrote in the April 1, 2005 *Chronicle of Higher Education*, "I fear that liberal education in the research universities, despite the recent hoopla, is a project in ruins." It is so bad, he said, that it threatens the "vitality" of our democracy. The author is Dr. Stanley N. Katz, director of Princeton's Center for Arts and Cultural Policy Studies. He is also president emeritus of the American Council of Learned Societies, and both a Harvard University alum and a former faculty member.

But liberal education, he added, is alive and well in the four-year liberal-arts colleges.

What he could also have said was that you don't have to be an A student to have a better-than-Ivy-college experience that will make you a smarter, better, and more confident and effective person. These mostly unselective schools—that really want you— have long been proving they're unparalleled in changing lives.

Dr. Katz gives Establishment authority to what I've been saying for decades: The worship of the Ivies is nonsense. The writers of such stuff don't know what they're talking about. Readers are bamboozled; it is analogous to the fable of the emperor having no clothes. Not a single Ivy offers the benefits these colleges do. They lack the kind of student-teacher dialogue, the close sense of community, the collaborative learning, the emphasis on values and student growth, or student involvement in his own education that these colleges do.

Of course, one size does not fit all, and everyone doesn't go to college to get an education, but these four years constitute the last developmental period of youth, and these colleges make vital contributions the Ivies don't.

Indeed, for the undergraduate, the Ivies and their clones are scams. In those universities, you will be ignored. There are no rewards for teaching, so professors, famous or not, do little or none of it. If they do, you'll only see them behind a lectern. In many of these schools you will never write a paper. Nearly half of your enormous classes will be taught by part-timers, many of whom can barely speak English. Except in science and math, almost all the courses will be easy and you'll get Bs, and even As, without doing much, if any, work. If science is your thing, find out what kind of lab help you'll get. And after graduation, you'll be deflated when the elite school's name on the diploma doesn't mean much because all it represents is that you have high academic aptitude and worked hard in high school.

Dr. Katz said the situation won't get better anytime soon. The universities are more concerned with scientific knowledge than with imparting culture; they are "uncomfortable with values"; and "they haven't traveled very far in defining a liberal education . . . not perhaps in the last hundred years." Improving undergraduate education "is simply not on their agenda." They've gone so far down the research road that "priorities have been reversed" and he questioned whether their specialist scholars, lured by promises of little or no teaching, would be much good at general education anyway.

The research universities have traditionally been hostile to undergraduates. Then when Sputnik spurred a federally funded race to catch up with the Russians, everybody became a research university.

Even the cautious U.S. Department of Education had anticipated Dr. Katz in part when it said that the fact that over 43 percent of the universities' instruction was by part-timers "threatens their value as teaching institutions."

For a half century, I've visited and written about colleges, sat in on dull Ivy classes, been a university administrator, known scads of Ivy and other professors, and been education editor of *The New York Times*. Most of that time I have been warning that the universities are gyp joints for the undergraduate. For more than three decades I have also counseled kids and parents on colleges, usually away from the Ivies, so I can say that the professors in these catalytic colleges are doing much, much more good for the nation's youth than the Ivy profs, many of whom I wouldn't hire.

Back in the mid-nineties, the provost at Lawrence University told me he'd had an epiphany when he came from Princeton University. He said, "Places like this are the cutting edge of higher education. I didn't think so when I was at a research university. We're teaching them to think for coping in a new kind of world. Now the Ivies are emulating us; at least they're giving some attention to teaching."

The provost at Hendrix College, a Rhodes Scholar, a Yale Ph.D., and now the Phi Beta Kappa Society's secretary, had something equally important to say: "Places like this are incubating the continuity of democratic values."

The little known truth is that these colleges have been on the cutting edge for decades. They were quietly proving it even in the days when prestige and Old Boy connections were the currency in a staid society. They have outperformed most of the Ivies and their clones in the percentages of graduates who become America's scientists and scholars. They have done much the same thing in producing the distinguished achievers in *Who's Who*.

That means aspirations are being raised and talents multiplied in students of a wide range of academic aptitudes, not just the A's. It also means that their seniors do better year after year on the medical college aptitude and other graduate tests than the seniors at all but four of the eleven Ivies.

Since they were outdoing the status schools even when status counted, they are the true elites in a world where status is crumbling. Today, new jobs, new careers, and new business enterprises are the rule. The demographers say that in a decade or so, people now in college will be working at jobs that do not yet exist. So competence is what counts, not connections. And these are the colleges that develop life-changing competence.

A fine example is a client who went to Eckerd College, and in her first job worked for a Harvard alumnus. Now she has Harvard and Princeton graduates working for *her* literary agency.

Today's pace of change is only the beginning. Over 95 percent of the creators of new knowledge who've ever lived—the scientists and mathematicians—are still alive today. These colleges produce the qualities needed to exploit this new knowledge: bold, imaginative thinking; being able to use what they know and to see connections; being risk-takers and pioneers.

Their effectiveness is graphically revealed in the "Ten Years Later" surveys at the end of each college profile. Students and graduates, recent and past, say they couldn't have had such transforming experiences anywhere else. They believe no other college could have helped them find themselves so happily, given them new powers and confidence, and made them better persons. Alumni talk about the wrench of leaving a family—a campus family—and they call their professors lifetime friends whose influence continues to affect their lives.

But in thirty-five years of college counseling, I've never had an Ivy client say his school had changed him or her. Their assessments tended to be different; as one client said, "It's hard to be humble at Amherst."

Vastly different was what I heard about the College of Wooster, from a sophomore, a girl who'd been voted most likely to succeed in her prep school class in Atlanta. She wrote me, "Just a year at Wooster has changed my life, and I love my teachers. None of my friends who go to Penn or Brown talk about their teachers or what their school has done for them."

A *Chronicle of Higher Education* story offered some specifics in a long story of a disillusioned University of Pennsylvania alumna. In four years, she'd had not one bit of help or advice from a teacher or staffer. She'd even had to wait in line to get just five minutes with a professor. The Ivy degree gave her no edge in the search for the first job either, as she'd believed. After a year of temporary jobs, she finally found a permanent one, as a secretary. (Everyone changes jobs in the first year or so, and after the first one, the name of the school on the diploma is meaningless; your own specific gravity is all that counts. A Princeton alum who'd been a National Merit Scholar said the market value of his degree "lasted about fifteen minutes.")

Nor does an Ivy diploma have any influence on career success, as the corporate downsizings of the early nineties proved. As is detailed in the "Required Reading" chapter, a full quarter of the Harvard class of 1958 was out of work or on welfare in 1994, and the story was the same at other Ivies. The Ivy alums didn't know how to handle nonsuccess; the graduates of these colleges would.

Many clients have sent me commencement invitations along with such notes as "Loren, Kalamazoo really did change my life!" Parents who often had gone to status schools have thanked me in glowing terms for what these colleges had done for their sons or daughters. They wrote that they wished they'd had experiences as good.

Two college presidents told me their sons got "miserable educations" at Yale University, and both used the same term. One added that his son's adviser didn't even read his senior thesis. A third president said her daughter "had a good time at Amherst, but it didn't change her any." And deans at other colleges said their sons and daughters, despite the prospect of a parent nearby, had transferred to their schools after disappointing freshman years at Ivy clones.

These colleges not only equip youths to live full lives but they work their magic on a variety of aptitudes, academic and others as important. They range from the four most intellectual colleges in the country (Marlboro College, New College, Reed College, and St. John's College) to one where a professor said, "We take in kids who didn't do very well in high school and we turn out people who compete with the Ivies." They also include colleges for the venturesome, the do-it-yourselfers, those who need structure or nurture or both, the late bloomers, the naifs, and those who need a second chance.

Every one of these catalytic places will push and stretch you beyond what you think possible, but they won't let you fall.

They attract strikingly different kinds of kids, so they do dramatically different things. Their magic is not in course content or what they do. Indeed, their programs range from the do-it-yourself challenges of Antioch College, Hampshire College, Marlboro, or New to the prescribed, no-electives of the Great Books curriculum of St. John's.

Their power lies in how they do it. The focus is on the student, not the faculty; he is heavily involved in his own education. There are no passive ears; students and faculty work so closely together, they even coauthor publications. Teaching is an act of love. There is not only a mentor relationship in class but professors become hiking companions, intramural teammates, dinner companions, and friends. Learning is collaborative rather than competitive; values are central; there is a strong sense of community. They are places of great synergy, where the whole becomes greater than the sum of the parts. Aspirations are raised, young people are empowered.

It is those qualities that develop leaders, people who can land on their feet, who are bold and imaginative, and who can see the big picture. They do it for students who are strong and intellectual and for those needing tender loving care.

The greater in quality and quantity of these experiences, the greater the effect. Major long-term research conducted by Dr. Alexander Astin of the Universiy of California at Los Angeles and by the Carnegie Foundation for the Advancement of Teaching have been busy rediscovering these truths for years, and now the National Survey of Student Engagement is doing some more.

But good things do not happen, both the Astin and the Carnegie studies found, when these things are not present, when the school is large, when assistants teach, or when it's a commuter school.

In short, the perceptive investigators show that what happens to the students in a college community is what counts, not how smart the students happen to be. In the good community they'll grow, and grades don't affect achievement in life, as you'll also see in "Required Reading."

For the colleges in this book, desire trumps SATs and GPAs. There are several reasons. Academic aptitude is only a tiny sliver of intelligence compared to emotional intelligence. IQ is not fixed at birth, but grows. People mature at different rates. They have differing abilities and qualities. Also, the computer is producing an age where graphic skills and visual and conceptual thinking become more important than verbal skills. Indeed, some of the greatest minds of the twentieth century who were dullards in school demonstrate this, as you will read in the chapter titled, "Today's Learning Disabled Will Be Tomorrow's Gifted."

In these colleges, the myth that SAT and ACT scores rank you angers even the professors who got their Ph.D.s at Ivy schools. They proudly say their students grow, that by the time they are juniors or seniors they are doing work as good or better than the Ivies they had once taught. At Hendrix, a French prof said, "Just today I told a girl, 'You couldn't possibly have done work this sophisticated six months ago.' What does that say about our SAT system?" Think about that. And she was only one in several colleges to make that point.

But the public is not aware of these truths because there's

never been any product research in higher education. Instead, myths rule and continue to jinx college choices year after year. They are the main villain in a national tragedy in which only three of ten freshmen are still on the same campuses four years later. Who knows the tragic toll that represents in broken hopes and dreams. And it's been getting worse; half a century ago the figure was four in ten.

The rule of myth is abetted by the public's thirst for rankings, such as *U.S. News and World Report*, enterprises which are inherently phony and a disservice to society. They are saying the emperor does so have clothes on.

These damaging things are compiled by statisticians who can only measure input factors, many of which are totally irrelevant to education. They know nothing about what happens to young minds and souls in the four years of college. Some anonymous Canadian has said the American way of judging the quality of a college by the grades and scores of the freshmen it selects is like judging the quality of a hospital by the health of the patients it admits. What happens during the stay is what counts.

College presidents hate and fear the rankings as an educational cancer, but they are under pressure to fudge their data to move up a few notches. Several years ago, a courageous college president, Steven Koblik of intellectual Reed College, told the rankers to go jump in a lake. They bumped Reed's ranking down several notches.

Selectivity is another phony measure. Before World War II and the GI Bill boosted the number of college-bound students (from about 10 percent to over 60 percent now) and swamped higher education's facilities, selectivity was virtually unknown. If your father's check was good, you were in. From Harvard on down, the A students, the B students, the "Gentleman Cs," and the ne'er-do-wells all sat in the same classes together. Furthermore, the education was better then. The middle group of students asked the questions that the A students were afraid or ashamed to ask and that the bottom students didn't think of.

That is still true. A mix is essential: The A students are needed, but if they're all A students, it is bad. In the words of a Wesleyan University girl who transferred to Beloit College, it was "stifling and there was no discussion at Wesleyan." At Beloit, she said, "everyone is so open; everyone talks, nobody is afraid. I find the learning is better at Beloit, even though it doesn't have the prestige. At Wesleyan the professors were distant, they'd only put a couple of negative comments on a paper and it was hard to get a conference with them. I liked the kids a lot but I thought they had tunnel vision, and there's more to life than that [study and grades]. At Beloit the professors are right there all the time. They can't do enough for you."

At intellectual St. John's College, then-Dean Eva Brann said, "We're about as selective as a pickup baseball team. All we want is people who read and can do a little mathematics." But even there, a mix is important because "some of the most useful questions are asked by the weaker students."

In the last ten years, this book and growing college-bound numbers have made four of these colleges highly selective, but numbers vary from year to year and these may be temporary spikes. The number of high school graduates has been projected to decline after 2009. Also, there are unselective twins for three of the four selective ones. For intellectual Reed there are Marlboro and New, for do-it-yourself Hampshire there is Antioch, and for outdoorsy Whitman College there are Allegheny College and Hendrix College. There is nothing like Wabash College, but even though it has become selective, its SATs and GPAs have not gone up. What kind of person you are is more important.

The contrast between these colleges and the famous universities could hardly be greater or the benefits of these colleges to the student clearer.

In the universities, the youth who needs a friend and mentor is a second-class citizen, if he is a citizen at all. He simply is cheated out of his American birthright of a good education. A lawyer friend quit Harvard after six semesters because "I was being taught by students; six of them couldn't speak English. Faculty were unavailable; they didn't have office hours, My roommate quit after one semester." A brand new Ph.D. said she left Cornell University after two years of sitting in the balcony in classes as large as 2,000, with thirty-foot visuals. "I could have gotten my degree without ever getting out of bed except to take an exam. I could have hired note-takers to do the rest."

A professor at Duke University whose daughter chose a good small college after reading an earlier edition of this book told me, "Learning is optional here, and I believe that is the case at other prestigious places. A student doesn't have to do any work to get Bs." That is also true at Harvard, Yale, and Amherst. At Harvard, an English professor reported in a faculty meeting that she could give one student "only a B+" because he had not turned in a paper that was the course's one and only requirement; there was no exam.

The phrase "Ivy League education" is an oxymoron when compared to the benefactions to mind and soul the colleges in this book bestow. Not only are they better, but they want you, and you will love them for making a new and better you. Your satisfaction will be lifelong. Guaranteed, and cosigned by an Ivy savant.

Required Reading

You're not as smart as you think you are if you believe:

1. Your college should be bigger than your high school (5,000 is the figure usually mentioned by girls, especially those from small private schools).
2. A name-brand college will give you a better education and assure your success.
3. A university will offer you more than a good small college.
4. You should go where your friends are going.
5. You don't need to examine yourself or the college.

Here, briefly, are some things you need to know about these myths that jinx thousands of college choices every year.

1. The best-size college:

Most good colleges have a population of 1,000 to 2,000 for a reason; college is a time of internal exploration and the small familial community is more conducive to such an experience. What's important is not the number of people, but the people themselves, the sense of community. The social life tends to be better at smaller colleges. Those are some of the reasons why I rarely recommended a college of 5,000 or more to a client. Good small colleges strive for all the variety they can get, while public institutions admit by formula. Most of their students are state residents less qualified than the out-of-staters, and probably less sophisticated. The large private institutions tend to be compartmentalized by specialties. You get more effective diversity in a small college for the same reason it is easier to know everyone in a small community than in a great city. As a big-college freshman complained, "I miss the diversity we had in high school." She could have made her point by saying it's a lot better to have 600 available males than 3,000 unavailable ones.

2. Which type of school gives the best education and a jump start in life:

In nearly every chapter of this book, faculty members who have taught at Ivy schools say the work of their upperclass students is every bit as good as that of those in Ivy upper classes. The fact that many of these colleges consistently outperform the Ivy types in producing high achievers and contributors speaks for itself.

A visitor to one of these colleges will hear a lot about how much students feel changed by their experiences. They also talk about how envious their friends at big universities are of the attention they get and the opportunities they have.

In March 1994, *The New York Times* reported that a quarter of Harvard's class of 1958 had lost their jobs, were looking for work, or were on welfare, just when their careers should have been cresting. A headline said, "Many in the class of '58 thought their degrees ensured career success. They were wrong." The autobiographical sketches written for the thirty-fifth reunion "did not radiate with expressions of success and optimism," said author and Yale professor Erich Segal. "Quite the contrary, they seemed like a litany of loss and disillusion." The compiler of the sketches noted that "about twenty-five percent have tumbled out." Another class member, Senator John D. Rockefeller, pointed out, "The layoffs of managers and skilled technical people at IBM, or Xerox, or AT&T do not discriminate between graduates of Harvard and some lesser school. And when the layoffs come we are not prepared for nonsuccess. We don't know how to deal with it."

In short, Harvard men failed because Harvard failed them. And Harvard was not alone. Alumni groups at other Ivy League schools, the story added, "are reporting that their members in growing numbers are suffering from the upheavals in corporate America. If there is a lesson in all this it is that a degree from a college like Harvard is no longer the lifetime guarantee of success in careers that it used to be."

Had these men gone to a different kind of college, *The Times* would have recorded a success story. They might still have been victims of the Big Bang of a new age, but their college experiences would have equipped them to land on their feet. As a recent graduate of such a college wrote me, "Antioch taught me to think. I learned how to learn. I developed a strong sense of confidence in myself. I know I could arrive anywhere in the world and not know the language, but I'd survive. In fact, I'd do more than survive; I'd immerse myself in the language and the culture and hopefully become a productive member of the community." Good as her word, she trained primary school teachers for the Peace Corps in Liberia until civil war there ended that. Then, after two months' immersion in the Sesotho language, she spent two years training teachers in a remote mountain village in Lesotho in West Africa. Now she's designing training programs for other volunteers at the Peace Corps's Washington, D.C., headquarters.

A graduate student on full fellowship, who is now listed among the significant research scientists of all time, transferred from Harvard to Princeton because the only contacts he had with his advisor were Monday notes in the mailbox. Princeton profs were happy to one-up a rival.

3. *The university as slack-filled merchandise:*

Many a former client has told me I was right, that the university cheats the undergraduate. It not only offers you less while claiming to do more, but also deprives you of your educational birthright. How? By not letting you get involved in your own education; by making you a passive ear in huge lecture classes; by consigning most of the teaching to graduate students, often foreigners who may barely speak English, and to other part-timers. You may never see a professor outside of class, you may never have a discussion in class, you may never even write a paper. That is not what education should be, nor is it preparation for a changing world. Furthermore, you may spend five years or more getting this hollow degree because you can't get into the classes you need to take in order to graduate.

The university's claim that it boasts great scholars is not just hogwash; it is false advertising. Most of them do little or no teaching, and when they do they are nothing more than performers behind a lectern in a big auditorium. Any great ideas they may have are already in the library. Involvement with good teachers is what helps young minds grow.

Outside of class, your chances of participating in some activity are slim to none unless you're one of the best. More likely you are sentenced to being a spectator. The salve has to be the Roman circus of the big football weekend.

4. *Why you shouldn't be a teenage sheep:*

Going where your friends go is a common mistake across the country. This being afraid to leave one's friends is also one of the worst blunders of adolescence. Most of them you'll never see again, some you wouldn't buy a used car from. Forget them. A whole new set of friends is waiting, and as certain as the sun rises you will have a new set in less than three weeks. Guaranteed. This herd mentality is one of the reasons why fewer than three in ten freshmen will be on the same campuses four years later. Where a person goes literally can be more important than whether he goes. (He could educate himself in the library.)

5. Why you should examine both yourself and the merchandise:

Picking a college is a crucial decision because the experience profoundly affects the quality of one's future. It can be the most exciting four years of your life. On the other hand you can plod through, largely untouched and unaffected, or drop out or fail. Such unhappy results are common. Most teenagers give more thought to learning to drive or to water ski than to picking a college.

Confront yourself honestly. Why, really, are you going? For fun or for some other reason? What are your abilities and strengths? What are your weaknesses? What do you want out of life, or in life—something tangible or intangible? Are you supremely confident or hesitantly unsure of yourself? Do you want to give or to get? Are you a self-starter or in need of nurture and structure? Are you socially self-sufficient, marching to your own drummer, or do you need warm, familial support? Do you live in the fast track? And so on.

After you have questioned yourself you can effectively choose a college, but only after you have examined it, too. And the best way is to spend a working day and a night on the campus as part of the community. Be a consumer: Go to two or three classes, ask a couple dozen students and two or three faculty members the questions important to you. Spending a night in the dorm gives you time to think over what you've been told and to ask further questions.

Ask students what their chief gripes are; whether the experience has affected them and how; whether their teachers are also their valued friends; whether they are actively involved in their own education. Ask faculty members whether they think their students are there to learn or to get grades, and what they think of them. Go to the student union and question people on the newspaper or in the student government. In short, don't go as a supplicant; be a hard-nosed, investigative reporter trying to find out if the school is good enough for you. If this one doesn't suit, don't worry; there are plenty more just as good or better that are eager to have you. Always remember that.

YOU'RE SMARTER
THAN YOU THINK YOU ARE

This whole book provides ample, comforting evidence that some colleges will indeed multiply your talents, raise your trajectories, impart confidence, make you a more effective, better person. They change the lives of A students, B students, C students, people with learning disabilities, late bloomers, the handicapped or disabled, or almost anyone with the desire to learn and to grow. In short, they make winners because they exert a special magic, intelligent caring, and tough love.

Long before Aesop wrote about the tortoise and the hare, an Old Testament writer observed, "Again I saw that under the sun the race is not to the swift . . . nor riches to the intelligent, but time and chance happen to them all." Not only are time and chance heavily weighted in favor of the tortoise, but the college experience that gets a youth involved and that works itself into his values dramatically increases the tortoise's power and speed.

Two deans at Clark made it crystal clear that they preferred "the rough student with the 500 verbal" who gets turned on by a professor, because he winds up being a doctor, a university professor, or something else he'd never in his wildest dreams imagined.

These points are typical of the evidence I have collected over the years of a truth long known: that there is no correlation between grades and achievement in life, except in mathematics, and mathematicians are born, they're not made. Indeed, the only long-term study of a very selective college's graduates—Haverford College—showed that those at the top of their classes were the ones twenty years later who were most frustrated, and who had the least satisfactory relationships with their wives and with their colleagues. (Haverford was all male during most of the study's forty-year span.)

Every year I had a few clients with learning disabilities or physical handicaps, some severe, but all succeeded. What they all had is that desire. One had a 450 verbal and terrible dyslexia. He graduated from college with a 3.5 in a tough engineering program and in 1994, when the firm was firing thousands, he was one of 2,000 graduates hired nationwide at a starting salary of $42,000.

Emerson wrote, " 'What will you have?' quoth God. 'Pay for it and take it.' " These are places eager and eminently able, if you are willing to pay for it with hard work, to empower you to take it.

WHICH COLLEGE IS MOST CHALLENGING?

Guess Again

This question pops up all the time, usually from parents. "Challenging" really is a code word for "Which is the most selective, has the brightest students?"

Higher education being a status industry, the assumption is that selectivity equals rigor. Wrong, wrong, wrong. This is one of the worst myths jinxing college choices. Eighty years of official records testify that many colleges in this book dramatically outperform their very selective peers in producing the nation's scientists, scholars, and achievers. That's what this book is all about.

HOMESCHOOLERS
ARE WELCOME HERE

Homeschooled students are a growing cohort that before long may outnumber those with learning problems. Their anxieties are different but every bit as great. Their questions are: How will the colleges view us? and are we at a disadvantage if we lack transcripts, laboratory sciences, and languages?

The answer is, the colleges that change lives are eager to have homeschoolers apply. All these colleges will view them sympathetically and very carefully; in other words, as favorably as those with high school transcripts, and in some cases more favorably. Every applicant will be judged on his or her own merits, just like all the others.

Every admissions officer I talked to was enthusiastic about his or her experience with homeschoolers. More than one was predisposed in favor of them because they said these kids had the initiative and the persistence to learn on their own, some for religious reasons, but more often because the local schools were bad.

However, homeschooled candidates do have to demonstrate three things: that they are socially ready for college life; that they have the motivation for college work; and the capability to handle the course load. Thus, they may be examined more closely than their peers with high school transcripts. The student's personal statement and essay are very important. These give the admissions people a glimpse of the individual that the objective data do not. Also, an interview is usually required of parents as well as the student. Among other things, it can help determine whether this youth is socially ready for college. Also, if a parent has compiled a transcript, it can discover what his qualifications are.

Several admissions directors told me that they've been impressed with the quality of their homeschool applicants. One said, "Ninety percent of the applicants we've had have been good. They tend to have high test scores and to be curious kids. In evaluating them, we may rely much more on such standardized tests as the SAT IIs than we normally do." That's because the SAT IIs are explicitly tests of achievement rather than aptitude.

Another said, "They tend to be people with the initiative to be self-learners, and they work well in these colleges. We like to have a portfolio of their work if there is no transcript. We don't want the GED." Some admissions officers think the GED is not a very trustworthy measure for their purposes. Still another said, "I find they are strong readers with literate minds. The lack of laboratory science is no barrier if they have the math and science concepts." Most admissions officers, he added, would probably agree.

Colleges want all the documentation possible to support the application, such as academic work done outside the family, with appropriate evaluations, or courses at a community college.

Because values are central, as they should be, at these schools, there is much discussion of them. And if you are a homeschooler for religious reasons and have any concerns about a school's position or values, call the admissions office and discuss it with them to see if it is the right fit for you. They will be happy to oblige because they also want it to be a good fit.

Today's "Learning Disabled" Will Be Tomorrow's Gifted and the SATs Obsolescence

Back in 2000, just before I started writing the first version of this revelatory chapter, a mother telephoned me with a request: "Please don't use the term 'learning disabled' to Ann when we come in for our interview."

Ann didn't even want to hear the word "disabled" mentioned. And she was not alone; some clients, often girls, even tried to deny they learned any differently than anyone else. While no one really knows, the estimates are that 12 to 20 percent of the population has some kind of learning problem. But since many adolescent males have only a cursory interest in things academic, and perform as such, the percentages don't begin to reflect the endemic maternal anxiety.

Parents and students, relax! This chapter can't turn adolescent males into scholars but it will prove the truth of its glad-tidings title. Not only can the student with a learning problem prosper in college, but by his (or her) senior year may be ahead of his problem-free peers. What's more, the achievement gap will continue to widen, even into old age. Not only have several Nobel laureates been in this category, but we wouldn't have the cell phone if its father, Craig McCaw, had not been dyslexic. He said so himself.

Neurologists explain that dyslexia and other learning problems are simply biological differences in the way the two hemispheres of the brain are connected, or "wired." In general, the left thinks in words and numbers while the right thinks visually in pictures and images in three-dimensional space. So people with learning problems tend to be visual thinkers, which is good for the new computer world, because man is the most visual of all mammals. Words came later on. Now computers are taking us back to our learning roots: pictures.

In people with verbal problems, the connections between the right and left hemispheres are different, and the different wiring tends to produce a variety of creative abilities, even as it creates problems with the spoken or written word.

Even better, the people with learning problems tend to mature more slowly, to be the late bloomers, but they also tend to be the truly gifted. Contrary to what parents usually think, late blooming is often a bonus; in nature, the most sophisticated kinds of life take the longest to mature.

Moreover, just in the decade since 1995, scientists made the revolutionary discovery that you are not born with all the gray cells you will ever have; you grow billions more. The brain, like other parts of the body, continues to grow into old age, renewing itself. And hard work stimulates it. Thus the dyslexics often outdo the quick studies, not only because they continue to grow but also because they've had to overcome difficulties. So, shame on shame; your problem may help you become famous!

The world is about to put a premium on the visual, spatial, conceptual, and creative abilities so characteristic of the dyslexics, the ADDs, and others now smugly and wrongly labeled "learning disabled." Your SAT verbal score won't cut it. It'll be obsolete.

The era now coming to an end has been that of a literate society, communicating mainly by the printed and spoken word, so those skills have been the prized ones, and the ones on which the educational system has been centered. But even in this era, as you will see later, some of the greatest scientists, political leaders, generals, artists, writers, and poets, from Leonardo da Vinci on, have been people who had great trouble with words. They were, as such people often are, visual, conceptual, and spatial thinkers.

Now the computer is changing everything. It has already replaced bank clerks. And with the advances in artificial intelligence, the computer will soon take over from the professionals in those parts of their jobs where knowledge is routine, systematized, or conventional, for example, among middle managers, attorneys, and scientists. The vast corporate downsizings of the early 1990s were a precursor of larger things to come.

But the computer's artificial intelligence hits a brick wall if the task requires imagination, creativity, intuition, the "lucky hunch," serendipity, seeing the possible connections, and taking the big leap. And this is where many dyslexics are outstanding.

We are entering a new era that has been called "the postliterate society," one in which the old adage "one picture is worth a thousand words" will be a gross understatement; one picture will be worth a million words. With the computer doing the routine and the formula work, the intelligence most in demand will be the one that can most creatively and effectively find and make use of information, not the one with the greatest store of it.

And that is one of the great strengths of these catalytic colleges, one where they easily outdo the famous ones. Students at two colleges with very different kinds of academic profiles who'd been in off-campus programs with Ivy Leaguers told me, "The Ivies might have had more information on a problem, but we could use it better."

Most of what I've said so far is the result of reading a landmark book by the dyslexic father of a dyslexic client, a former computer systems consultant, whose life is now devoted to pioneering research, writing, and lecturing in this cause, in which he is probably the world's leading expert. He is Thomas G. West, author of the scholarly, encyclopedic, and endlessly fascinating book *In the Mind's Eye* (Prometheus Books, 1997). A second book in 2004, *Thinking Like Einstein,* links visual, spatial, and conceptual thinking with the principal advances in science. The day is closer than we think, he argues, when the possibilities inherent in computer graphics "will make us think in fresh ways about human ability and intelligence."

Stressing the importance of visual rather than verbal skills, he says dyslexia is called "the MIT disease" because it is so prevalent there, that a British Nobel laureate said dyslexia enabled him to win the award, and that three-quarters of a London art school's students were dyslexic. And he points out that Einstein's creativity declined dramatically when he started using mathematics instead of his earlier visual thinking.

The first volume, which will answer just about every question on learning problems you can think of, is a great public service and one long overdue. Every family concerned about a learning problem—or even the usual problems of dealing with a teenage student—should have it in the house. To begin with, Chapters 2 and 3 will set minds at rest. And on page 172, he gives parents some good advice: relax, back off and wait a while; too much pressure is counterproductive. Also, if I were a dictator, every teacher everywhere would have to pass a test on it.

In his preface, Mr. West says this is a topic whose time has come: "As our technology, economy, and society are transformed at ever greater rates, while our institutions hold ever more tightly to outmoded ideas, perhaps it is time for some really fresh thinking. . . . The old measurement scales do not quite fit, as many have long known, in spite of what they were told. And many have suffered for no good reason as a consequence." How true!

To give much-needed comfort to parents, Mr. West goes to great pains to point out that the only pattern in learning problems, whatever names are given them, is that there is no pattern. The symptoms may overlap, get all mixed up, occur in crazy combinations, or defy diagnosis.

In both the text and appendices are lists of suspect traits a person may have that are as long as your arm, but here are some of the more common ones. Not only are they often contradictory, but nearly every parent will find their normal son exhibits four, five, or six of these traits:

- Difficulty with handwriting
- A general lack of organization
- Indifference to schedules
- Excessive daydreaming
- Difficulty with arithmetic (but not geometry, statistics, or higher mathematics)
- Difficulty with speech (delayed speech development, hesitation, or occasional stuttering)
- Ineptness or lack of tact socially, but in some cases showing exceptional powers of social perceptiveness
- Poor coordination and lack of athletic ability, but not always
- Special difficulty in memorizing assigned information by rote (but often with surprising powers of memory for selected types of information)
- Difficulty with retaining certain types of data (such as multiplication tables, an Einstein problem)
- Difficulty with learning foreign languages, especially in classroom settings (also an Einstein problem).
- Being overactive, easily distracted, inattentive, and "in their own world"

But parents should be of good cheer, he said, for many of them who've led fulfilling lives of outstanding achievements will read this list and recognize their own adolescent problems. And many of them will realize it has been a family pattern for generations.

It is small wonder that parents so often think the nonachieving teenager must have a learning problem and take (usually a him) to a psychologist, where he may be told he has ADD, when all he really is suffering from is adolescence. It is often impossible to tell the difference. But to err is human. Shortly before the 2000 version of this was written, news stories reported that up to 98,000 patients a year were the victims of medical errors. If a count could be made just of the mislabelled ADDs cases, it might dwarf that figure.

For a school to deal with students who have such a maze of traits, Mr. West said that teachers have to use multisensory learning approaches. And that in part at least is what tends to occur naturally in the colleges in this book. It occurs because learning is collaborative and in small classes, teachers tend to feel like surrogate parents in their concern for their students' welfare. A professor may give a student extra time on tests, let him tape a paper, and so on. The active ingredient is not a formal program, it is tender loving care, and it can work wonders.

However, a dyslexic who has great trouble reading obviously would have trouble at St. John's, where reading the Great Books is central, or perhaps at Marlboro, New, or Reed, where there is also a great deal of reading. A professor at Marlboro said, "People may think that because this is such a friendly, informal, familylike place (just over 300 students) that it will be just right, but it's too intense." But that might be wrong for all four places. If a student with a reading problem really wants that kind of experience badly enough, he or she should talk it over with an admissions officer without being afraid to do so.

It is very important that anyone with a learning problem should make it known when applying to any college. Trying to hide it can only create problems. Call the admissions office and discuss the matter; ask what help the college offers and how students with learning problems fare at that school. They really and truly will welcome your call. Furthermore, you are likely to get some very reassuring information. I have been recommending clients with all kinds of learning problems to most of these colleges for well over thirty years, and they've all prospered because they've had one thing in common: desire.

These colleges want to help you. Remember, as the president of Wabash emphasized to me, these colleges are not exclusive; they're inclusive, they want you. They also know that many of the world's greats and geniuses—who would have been certified as LDs—include Michael Faraday, James Clerk Maxwell, Nicola Tesla, Winston Churchill, General George S. Patton, Jr., William

Butler Yeats, Thomas Edison, Henri Poincaré, Lewis Carroll, and Albert Einstein.

THE MORALS (PLURAL)
OF THE STORY

The morals should be obvious. If you have a learning problem in today's literate society, you're likely to have the aptitudes and talents needed to prosper in tomorrow's postliterate society. And that is the one in which you will make your own career or, more likely, two or three careers.

Also, you should take inspiration from the story of a client who as a high school senior told me, "When I was in the seventh grade I could read a whole page and not understand a word of it." To make a point he applied to sixteen colleges and was accepted by fourteen. He graduated in four years with a 2.5 average, *and* he ran his own outside business all four years. All he had—but what he *did* have—was desire.

You, in the meantime, can do what others are doing: you can lick it, you can circumvent it, or you can compensate for it.

Japanese Universities
Now Change Lives Too

Japan's universities have traditionally been selective, the professors elite, and classes lecture-hall size. But now, because of a quickly declining birth rate, the competition for students is so hot that two universities have closed and a third has filed for bankruptcy.

To lure students, Japan's universities are emulating these forty colleges, becoming communities of learning with faculty-student relations that are sometimes almost familial.

They boast of their year-long seminar-size classes called *zemi*. Every professor is required to have one each year. They are part academic course, part college-level homeroom, and part counseling service. Professors become friends as well as mentors; learning is collaborative instead of competitive. The principal features are weekend off-campus trips, which are part learning, part snacking and drinking sake or beer, and, most important of all, bonding.

They become almost like families. Professors advise students on career goals and academic courses, find them scholarships, lend money to needy students, advise on romantic relationships, and even attend weddings. An economics professor, quoted in the *Chronicle of Higher Education*'s April 1, 2005 report, said one of his goals was to make his pupils better persons. An American professor said that to the Japanese students, the lasting relationships they form are what they value most; the Americans, on the other hand, want to know what the payoff is.

The *zemi* have worked so much good that several alumni have said they have been the most important experiences of their lives, and after graduation some of them continue research projects with the professors.

It is significant that when their survival was threatened, Japan's universities adopted the philosophy not of America's or Europe's elites but of the colleges in this book.

There is no chance of such a sense of community happening in American universities. The rewards of research have so corrupted the system and fixed its priorities that liberal education for the undergraduate is a sham, according to Stanley Katz, director of Princeton's Center for Arts and Cultural Policy Studies. So in this country, colleges that change lives will continue to offer the only total four-year *zemi*.

A Senior's Tips for Freshmen

After rhapsodizing in detail about how wonderful her experience at Hiram College had been, Alisha Heimbuch wanted others to profit from her experience. The secrets, she said, are involvement and hard work. Her definition of involvement goes beyond what others' might be and may help a lot of freshmen at other colleges:

I guess I will close with a few tips for prospective and new students at Hiram; it may not address the question [mine] directly, but I feel that this will be useful and give a good idea of my experience.

- Get to know everyone. Even the lady who scrubs your toilet or the guy who shelves your books will be an interesting person. This is Hiram, after all. We don't hire boring people. Beyond that, it is just common courtesy.
- Don't be fooled by the size of the library. Hiram is a member of OHIOLink, which is a consortium of practically every college and university library in Ohio. In a

matter of days, practically any book you might need will be delivered to the library with your name on it.

- Don't buy textbooks unless you have to. OHIOLink and the library carry most of them; ask upperclassmen if they took the same class last year and see if you can borrow or rent (standard=$20/book) the books, rather than buy them. The only exception really is if the books are standard reference texts in your field (*The Riverside Shakespeare, Elements of Style, Brockett's History of the Theatre,* etc.).

- Get involved in the extracurriculars. I am not a music major, but I spent four years singing with the choir (one of the best college choirs around, if I may say so), and three years playing with the string ensemble. I also took Jiu Jitsu classes taught by one of the college's security guards. He charges $20/month for up to three classes a week (you don't have to come to every class, just as many as you can make). I can now throw two-hundred-pound men on the ground, and I know fourteen ways to break someone's shoulder. For a hundred-pound weakling, this is a major accomplishment, and is indescribably empowering.

- Get to know the community. Hiram is a college; it is also a village. Get to know people. Ask the lady at the post office about her granddaughter. Compliment people on their dogs. It's just nice to do.

- Study abroad. I spent a semester in England. In retrospect, I wish I had gone somewhere more challenging—I speak the language and I had been there before, on shorter trips—but it still was one of my seminal Hiram experiences.

- If your sophomore year is not a time of great confusion, you are doing something wrong. The point of a Hiram education is to create strong, academically curious, socially aware people. You have to tear down everything you think you know in order to replace it with reality. Almost everyone I know goes through a really terrible time during their sophomore year, and I think it's because this is when that tearing down really begins. You just have to be patient, and trust that you will rebuild.

- Join the vegetarian co-op. You don't have to be a vegetarian, you just have to agree not to eat meat in the co-op itself. This is the place with the best food on campus, and also the best people. Don't worry about the time issue—it's roughly three extra hours each week for cheaper, healthier food. I was in it for all four years and still had the time to graduate magna cum laude. This is definitely a bastion of hippie liberals (unofficial Hiram slogan: "We put the 'liberal' back in 'liberal arts.' "), but it is so open and welcoming, I really believe nearly anyone could feel at home there. If you are a first semester first year, the college may tell you that you cannot join the co-op unless you are a vegetarian. Tell them you are a vegetarian.

- The school sponsors five trips to Cleveland to see theatrical productions and the Cleveland Symphony. Everyone should go. It is a great (and inexpensive) way to spend a Sunday afternoon.

- Go on a spring three-week trip to Northwoods. It is Hiram's camp in the Upper Peninsula of Michigan. Hiram students in the '70s built a big lodge and several tiny cabins. It is cold and there is no electricity or running water, but eventually, when you look out over the Pictured Rocks along Lake Superior, and you realize how very *good* it is to be alive, the lack of amenities stops mattering.

I guess that's it. Hiram is a great little school, but you have to work pretty hard and be self-motivated to get anything out of it.

Allegheny College

Meadville, Pennsylvania

Attractive Allegheny, founded in 1815, is a shining example of what the exciting colleges in this book are doing to prepare their students for a new kind of world, things that make most of the prestige institutions look stodgy. It has a long and distinguished record of producing not only future scientists and scholars, but business leaders as well.

When I first visited Allegheny in 1994, it was all revved up with a great new curriculum featuring small freshman seminars, writing across the curriculum (even in math and science), independent study, and research, all designed to make its graduates even more effective in the next century.

Now it is enhancing the connections with the world of work with more emphasis on helping students make good decisions about their college and career opportunities. It is also requiring hands-on experiences such as internships or off-campus study. All residence halls are wired for Internet access, and information technology is being used in the classroom.

Allegheny is a spacious and handsome place. It has thirty-six buildings on 72 acres, an outdoor recreational complex of 182 acres, and a 283-acre nature preserve and environmental field station. It also has an observatory, a planetarium, art galleries, radio and TV stations, and a library of 539,000 volumes and 1,200 periodicals. It is located in Meadville, Pennsylvania, midway between Pittsburgh and Cleveland, close to six lakes and several state parks for boating, swimming, biking, and skiing.

Its state-of-the-art science building is worth a story in itself, and worth a detour by any science professor involved in planning one. In 1994 I wrote that only Columbia University's graduate facility was better, but since then, Kalamazoo has largely modeled its new science building on Allegheny's and Ursinus adopted its main features in remodeling an existing one. Many colleges are proud of their new science facilities, but this one was faculty-designed—in collaboration with the architects, of course—and no expense was spared to provide the greatest possible protection from acid and other burns, with state-of-the-art hoods, shower heads readily at hand, and eye-washer attachments at sinks and water faucets. Each lab contains glassed-in, soundproof, fireproof, odorproof rooms stocked with computers, desk space, and other needs so that a student can move right from his test tube or Bunsen burner to write up his experiment.

Another bright educational idea is the unique deployment of faculty offices to provide a new way of holding office hours and encouraging collaborative learning at the same time. Along a hall is a series of little bays forming reception areas, with semi-upholstered chairs and coffee tables holding a few magazines. Two faculty offices open off each bay; students can sit and read or discuss common problems while waiting for the prof.

As Dr. Ed Walsh, a chemistry professor who headed the faculty design team, said, "The idea is to say, 'Come in,' not 'I'm busy.' We hold our office hours out there, often with two or three students with the same problem. Then they can discuss it and I'm not saying the same thing over and over again, and the teacher plays the role of moderator, letting the students discuss the problems by themselves. I can often sit there for twenty-five minutes and not say a word. This is team learning. So we call them collaborative areas because they're for collaborative learning."

Allegheny calls its new curriculum interactive because it involves tutorials and much independent study or research, perhaps with a faculty member. Even though there is a structured program of required courses, there nevertheless is a lot of freedom for those with special interests to design individual majors.

For all of this, a lot of new and young faculty, in their twenties and thirties, were hired in the early nineties. It is still a young faculty and it has helped change the complexion of the place. It has a lot of zing.

They work with a receptive group, students I found to be eager for a chance to tell others what the school had done for them, particularly some of the minority kids. As a group they are industrious and interested in their professions. Many are in their family's first generation to go to college, although this proportion has been shrinking. Nearly three-quarters receive financial aid, more than half come from out of state, 11 percent are minority or international, and nearly a fifth are following parents or relatives to Allegheny.

In shaping a new curriculum, Allegheny, like other forward-looking colleges, decided to put the emphasis on how to learn and the desire to learn, rather than on coverage of material.

Allegheny came up with solutions similar to those of other first-rate colleges. The seminar leader is the adviser for fourteen students for two years, nurturing a sense of belonging and close camaraderie. Everyone has to become informed in the sciences, the social sciences, and the humanities, and everyone has to have a major and a minor, do a senior independent research project, and defend it in an open meeting.

There is a requirement that outsmarts those who always try to make a smorgasbord of the distribution requirements by taking the snap courses. Specific sets of three courses in each division ensure that a student comes out learned in that area of study.

The emphasis on learning how to learn, on analytical thinking, and on the wholeness of knowledge creates a pervasive interdisciplinary thread. In a freshman seminar the discussion of a novel may be led by a physicist; a concentration in English will involve the study of artificial intelligence. There is also much emphasis on the moral life. Here is a place where values have long been out of the closet; students live by an honor code. And to develop analysis and good thinking, much writing is required all along, culminating in the senior project.

Results are evident. The quality of writing is much better, the quality of senior theses is "dramatically" higher, and, because they know from their freshman year that they will face this challenge, students have a stimulus to work harder and better. And some who have gotten out in the world have reported that the senior project, which made them tackle and analyze and synthesize and explain their idea, was the most valuable experience they had in college.

From the college's point of view, they've succeeded in preparing students for living and working in an economy and a world that values risk-taking, imagination, being able to see opportunities, and expressing oneself clearly.

In short, the college is changing lives. A former dean made the cogent point that an anonymous Canadian has made in different words, and that in a rational world would change the way people think about colleges: "If the measure of a great college is the transformation that occurs between matriculation and graduation, rather than the academic accomplishments of entering students, then Allegheny ranks among the finest institutions of higher education."

Allegheny's president, Richard Cook, formerly the provost at Kalamazoo, points out that Allegheny "has always had a daring spirit" as well as a commitment to the liberal arts ideal, so it's not surprising that it ranks among the top 4 percent in turning out business leaders. "In addition," he adds, "our alumni are disproportionately represented on volunteer boards, in service organizations, and in local and state government. Our educational philosophy is one of learning how to learn for a lifetime—an education for exploration and responsibility."

One mark of a good school is how much in accord the stories of the faculty are with those of the administration. Here they sing the same song. They say there is great interest in the art of teaching, that there are brown bag lunches on the subject, and week-long summer faculty workshops on teaching "beyond their disciplines." Every teacher is involved in working on curriculum matters and one important aspect is putting an emphasis on the moral (not religious) life because this is a place that believes it is central.

Most of them got their doctorates and earlier taught at Ivy League or Big Ten universities but agreed with an English professor who went to Cornell and then to Columbia when he said, "By and large, students get a better education here than at the larger schools. There the graduate assistants (who do most of the teaching) are teachers in training, and you wouldn't want a doctor in training. In the big places the quality of teaching has little to do with getting tenure; here it's heavily weighted in favor of the quality of teaching."

Many talked of the close relationships with students. A chemistry professor called them "incredibly free-wheeling." Another added by way of contrast that at Yale, although he had an important responsibility—helping political science students with their schedules—no student ever came to see him.

A psychology professor summed it up with, "This is a very committed and dedicated faculty. We offer a lot of individual attention and students do a lot better than they ever thought they could. They get a larger share of doing their own education. The students are incredibly capable and talented but often not sophisticated intellectually, so they don't realize how capable they are, and when they get turned on they don't realize how far they've come."

The students' stories and attitudes certainly made honest people of all the administrators and faculty I had talked to. I was particularly struck by how many said they had learned how to think clearly and to write well. Several said that Allegheny's financial aid offers had made it possible for them to come to college and they thought the whole experience had enlightened and broadened them. They considered their teachers concerned and helpful friends. Some wanted to make a particular point of telling the world they didn't think they could get a better education anywhere else. A girl from India said she was trying to get her friends from India to come because this was "a wonderful place and it has done so much for me."

The fellow who made the deepest impression on me was an African American who stayed behind when one group I'd been chatting with had to go to class. He very much wanted me to know that, "Allegheny made it possible for me to come to college, and it has made me a better student. In high school I had a 2.4 (low C+) average. Here I have a 3.0 (B), and I'm a junior."

Allegheny, as one administrator put it, is less "Eastern" than Wesleyan (which is west of it), less pretentious than Bucknell, which is east of it in the same state. "And," he added, "the comfort level is higher here. We bootstrap kids. This is a value-added school."

I think he pretty much hit the nail on the head. Allegheny is a very comfortable school. Kids are comfortable with each other, there's no apparent sense of one-upmanship or competition. It is a thoroughly first-rate place and the only people not likely to find it comfortable might be those who have to drive in the fast lane. But Allegheny doesn't miss them.

Ten years later, after the college's makeover, students and recent graduates could hardly be more rhapsodic. They talk about the variety of their "wonderful" experiences beyond imagining, whether on campus, in the community, in research, on internships, or in foreign lands.

They also say they've learned to think critically, write and communicate far better, and become more ethical persons who want to contribute to their communities and to the fields they enter. One of them put it this way: "What is most notable about Allegheny is that it empowers you to challenge yourself, then gives you the skills you need to empower your peers and others in the community. Allegheny made me a more ethical, involved, empowered, and well-rounded citizen of the global community."

The young faculty received special words of affection. Many called their professors "not only teachers but role models." One said, "There isn't anything they won't put aside to help you."

In watching the academic procession of faculty at graduation, one senior said she "teared up" because "so many in that group had touched my life . . . they have come to mean so much to me, and it's as difficult leaving those connections as it is leaving friends." Another one invited her adviser to her wedding.

Several who said they'd had their futures all planned found that Allegheny had opened "a whole new world" that changed their lives completely. Otherwise, said one, "I would have been caught up in an unhappy dream. . . . Allegheny has showed me that college is not always about living out your dreams; sometimes it is about finding them first."

Another graduate talked about "the plethora of opportunities that have been part of my personal development . . . Allegheny is more than just a college, it's a community where students, administrators, and professors work in concert with each other to procure excellence in all aspects of campus life."

And a sophomore added: "Allegheny has taught me to be independent, to have integrity, to be confident, and to take pride in my work. The professors are incredibly encouraging and supportive. They constantly challenge and probe my mind to go the extra distance. Allegheny College motivates me to be the best student I can be."

Clark University
Worcester, Massachusetts

orward-looking Clark has several bright new facets for the new millennium. It already had something rare anywhere, but unique in New England: a four-star academic experience in a major research university that gives a B student the chance to do undergraduate research on big league projects. And several years later, when Clark alumni wind up with Ph.D.s as tenured faculty members at top universities, the point is proven.

Such heady involvement in their own education is not limited to the science majors. Students in political science, sociology, and other disciplines have published papers as undergraduates or done such things as researching the problems of and drafting city housing policy for Worcester. And majors in philosophy and English, fields where publication is a different and tougher game, report that their profs work closely and individually with them.

The most exciting new concentration is in the developing field of bioinformation that will lead to jobs in industry or to graduate school. This new discipline involves the departments of biology, chemistry, mathematics, and computer science. And it applies mathematical and computational tools to biology, the science where knowledge is not only expanding fastest, but is too complex for traditional analysis. This new field is expected to lead to new insights and important door-opening discoveries.

To help take such things forward, a new building for the biological sciences opened in 2005 and facilities for the other sciences have been greatly expanded.

Because more students are taking more classes in the arts, and performing, as well, a center for the visual and performing arts was completed in 2002.

A brand new major is global environmental studies, which attacks not only environmental problems on a worldwide scale, but such problems as how we can achieve more economic justice and protect the environment at the same time.

In 1996, Clark became the first institution in the world to offer a Ph.D. in Holocaust history. Now the mission of its center has been broadened to include all genocides and how they can be avoided in the future.

Clark, the second oldest graduate institution in the country after Johns Hopkins, was founded in 1887 and opened its liberal arts college in 1902 with a commitment to combining research and undergraduate teaching, rather than polarizing the two, as is done elsewhere.

Experience has given Clark faculty reason to be happy with, and even to prefer, the 500/B students to the 700/As. And Clark gets a lot of them; only a third of its freshmen come from the top third of their high school classes.

Only 39 percent of its 2,900 students are from Massachusetts; 3.3 percent are African American, 4 percent are Asian American, and nearly 14 percent are foreign. By any definition—academic, economic, geographic, or ethnic—Clark gets a genuinely representative American mix of kids. And it is doing very well by them, thank you.

Its location has its pluses and minuses. Worcester is only about 40 miles from Boston, every student's Mecca, but like Columbia it's in a run-down part of the city. But that provides an opportunity for tutoring children who need it, teaching English as a second language, and various helping internships.

Dean Sharon Krefetz, a political scientist, in the course of a long interview, said, "We emphasize the autonomous-citizen problem-solver. We are concerned with social values. The citizen is a concern. If you want an educational place where students and staff are concerned with civic values, this is the place. We require a values perspective [one of the required courses]. Yes, Clark changes people. We make them more responsible and competent citizens."

Dr. Krefetz, who previously taught at Brandeis and Howard universities, said the top students are the same at all three places but she preferred the "rough" ones. "A kid who's a wonderful writer had mediocre SATs. It shows there are a lot of opportunities here for kids from different paths. Our faculty is so dedicated they work with each student whether or not they have that spark. We look for students we can inspire and reach. We feel much more gratified when rough students blossom. This is a nurturing climate; three kids who were not impressive to begin with are now on the faculties at Harvard, Wisconsin, and Notre Dame."

Although Clark has traditionally been noted for its psychology and geography departments, and the contributions of Robert Goddard, father of the space age, and other famed scientists, Dean Krefetz pointed out there are many other stars in its crown: "There are rare opportunities here for leadership and involvement in the community. Many different activities let each student find his or her niche. They foster leadership skills and a sense of responsibility, because we're not in an ivory tower but are dealing with real people with real problems."

Some students work as tutors to immigrants, teach English as a second language, or have internships in city government and whose projects turn into actual city policy. For example, "One girl researched and drafted city housing policy; another did a booklet on crime prevention that is distributed by the city. Such opportunities would be rare at a big university. Also, the city bureaucracy is not so big here as to defeat internships. And the city government leaps at our offers."

The opportunities at Clark for future political scientists, urban planners, and sociologists are probably unmatched. For more than a decade the university has been building a partnership with its community. The University Park Partnership Program has revitalized its neighborhood. It has renovated nearly 200 homes, provided 175 units of affordable housing, started programs for children, a summer camp, a boys' club, and athletic facilities. It has created a rigorous secondary school for neighborhood children in which both students and faculty are involved. Clark students not only tutor neighborhood children, they babysit so that the parents can attend school at night. The program has also built a $22 million K–12 public school. And residents of the community can attend Clark tuition-free.

Clark also has two new interdisciplinary majors; one is Environmental Science and Policy, which combines environment, technology and social science. The other is Communication and Culture, which explores how culture is both created and transmitted through communication.

Another program that Clark says is unique is the International Studies Stream in which students can meet the liberal studies requirements by taking internationally focused courses, becoming fluent in a foreign language, and studying abroad.

And if a student meets the academic standards, he can have a fifth year at Clark tuition-free and get a master's degree into the bargain.

As a good college should, Clark requires a shared intellectual experience and common intellectual achievements, not just any thirty-two courses, as Brown lets kids get away with. It is called the Program of Liberal Studies. Everyone must acquire skills in critical thinking and knowing that are essential for self-directed learning. Within a given framework, a student can select an organized program of study that will give him a broad introduction to liberal learning and prepare him for lifelong learning. Major components are:

1. Critical thinking. Each student has to pass two courses: one in verbal expression, which may be offered in any one of many departments and which emphasizes the relationship between writing and critical thinking in that discipline; the other, a formal analysis course that places special emphasis on logical and algebraic modes of thinking.
2. Perspective courses. As perspective means seeing things in their true relation or relative importance, so these courses encourage breadth. They introduce students to the different ways in which various disciplines define thinking,

learning, and knowing. This means everyone takes courses in other cultures, art, history, language, scientific study, and, last but not least, values.

These requirements apply whether one intends to major in physics or philosophy or anything in between. Furthermore, the faculty are fervent believers in these requirements; several volunteered comments on their importance. It was interesting to hear science profs boast about writing requirements. But that shouldn't be too surprising, because good writing is about 80 percent good thinking and good thinking is central to good science.

Anyone interested in becoming a geographer or cartographer—fields in which the demand in this uncertain world is both great and certain for the foreseeable future—would do well to go to Clark. Not only is its geography department justly famous, but 100 applicants apply each year for five places in its Ph.D. program, so those whose work is already known to the faculty will have a built-in edge for admission. All those accepted who don't have outside support receive remission of tuition and healthy stipends for which they work 17½ hours per week as teaching, research, or departmental assistants.

Clark is a major research university of small size, a place where a teenager can make things that he wants to happen, happen, much as he can at a small liberal arts college. He will find a faculty concerned for his welfare, a faculty of the highest competence that will set a high level of expectation and care enough to see that he works to meet it.

Dean Alan Jones, professor of chemistry and noted research scientist, said not only that Clark opens a door for the B student that is closed elsewhere in New England, but also that these kids who would be Ivy rejects get more out of college and contribute more: "The kids who get the most out of the college experience are the kids who are rougher. They meet a prof, get interested, blossom, set goals. They weren't number-one in high school but they click in this environment. Consider the case of this student:

He publishes three papers before he leaves Clark; goes to medical school. He had no idea of all this when he was sweeping floors in the school gym. Another, the son of high school teachers, was working with me in the lab and is now a prof at Stony Brook [State University of New York at Stony Brook].

"When Daddy is not a stockbroker they often don't know what the possibilities are or what they are to do. I'm more into working with kids who haven't had many opportunities—a dyslexic who came to Clark is now getting his Ph.D. in chemistry.

"The difference at Clark [from other liberal arts colleges] is the research atmosphere; we have big Federal grants that are competitive on the national scene, won in competition with MIT and Cal-Tech. People with major research reputations are at Clark and they work with undergraduates.

"This is a very liberal place. We overcome parochialism—the views they're afraid of. They have to become more open; privileged kids have to deal with others who aren't; had they gone to an Ivy school they wouldn't have had to. We open kids' minds."

Dr. Robert Ross, a sociology professor, also believes the melting-pot diversity at Clark is good for the children of the affluent, but his rationale differed. "Kids are changing. In the middle class each year there's less of a burning thirst for knowledge. There's more a sense of entitlement, and college is more of a routine than rite of passage. They're more interested in accoutrements than in process. When I went to the University of Michigan, coming to college was an adventure. Back then I could get them [the students] excited about learning. Now I have to work harder at reaching and activating than I did. These complacent, cosmopolitan children of affluent America may well benefit from going to college with kids for whom it is still an adventure."

Also, they—the complacent as well as the adventurous—do respond to the individual attention they get at Clark. One student's brother at Penn State, Dr. Ross said, "couldn't believe the attention he gets here." By any definition, he said, Clark gets a mix of students. On entrance tests they score below students at many other institutions, "but they finish above. And they're not more liberal when they graduate but more reasoned."

He was also "very pleased" with the career achievements of his majors. They've become lawyers, foundation executives, environmental-group executives, and social workers, among other things, and they've kept in touch with him.

Some took a more optimistic view of the students than the sociologist did. One of them, Dr. Cynthia Enloe, head of the government department, credited students with doing much of the groundwork that led to creation of the Women's Studies Program.

In an interview for *The Clark Progressive*, she made another cogent point: Because Clark students don't feel they're the elite for having been accepted by an Ivy school, they understand the level of work they have to do to graduate. "They don't think they can sit back and slide through life."

She probably had in mind a stinging attack in *The Chronicle of Higher Education* by a Harvard English instructor—who surely has kissed his chances at tenure good-bye—on the debasing of grades there. The instructor quoted one professor as saying she could give one student "only a B+" because he hadn't turned in the one and only paper required for her course! In another story, a Harvard student tour guide was quoted as telling a prospective student, "You'll get all As and Bs."

"This place [Clark] is so alive," Dr. Enloe was quoted as saying, "I wouldn't leave it for anything."

Students who come from all points of the compass had favorable views of the school, if in varying degrees. A freshman girl from New Orleans found this New England community compatible and very diverse, as did a student from St. Louis and another from Chicago. A couple of others thought there was so much diversity they didn't feel any great sense of community, while others disagreed.

A junior philosophy major planning to become a college professor was so enthusiastic about the help her teachers gave her with her papers that she insisted I go visit one of the teachers. I found him as interested in his students as she had claimed. He said that the kids at Clark were the equal of any others. An English professor who got his doctorate at Yale was as proud of his students' abilities and accomplishments as he was of the fact that "they call me Sarge"—in recognition, naturally, of his toughness in making them shape up their writing.

Several students said Clark had given them mind-opening experiences. A political science major said, "One thing I've learned is keeping an open mind . . . critiquing and challenging myself . . . that's when you're really alive and really learning and finally making sense of it all and being aware that a lot of different ideas I rejected when I came here can actually add to my radical ideals."

A prospective economics major said, "It's not so much the actual material you learn here but how you learn *how* to learn here, like teaching you different ways to think and to process information so whatever you go on to do later, you understand how to interpret it into your own world view."

These students also liked the fact that Dean Krefetz had just put in force a new, tougher, and more revealing rating-and-comment form for the students' evaluation of their teachers. Formerly, each department had designed its own form so it could play to its own strengths and blur any attempts at universitywide comparisons. Now all use the same form and everyone gets rated, from instructor to department head. But none of the faculty members I talked to were concerned enough about a new rating form to bring it up. The things they were eager to tell me reflected a liking for kids and a love of teaching. Furthermore, students sit in on faculty meetings; so it's something like a big family where things are laid out on the table.

Ten years later, Clark students and recent graduates are saying the same things, that Clark has changed their lives, helped them find themselves: "Clark shaped who I am today." It also opened minds, and offered opportunities they said they wouldn't have found anywhere else. They also continued to have a love affair with "amazing faculty members who caused me to understand myself, and how I might bring about positive change in the world." As another one put it, "The faculty have been great about exposing me to other options as well as encouraging me to do whatever it is I would find most rewarding, and they have challenged me to meet my full potential."

A rising junior said, "It is already an amazing experience; I've had the most helpful and rewarding relationships of my life and later on I'm sure I'll realize even more how lucky I am to attend Clark University."

Another said she'd had a "life-changing experience" in a Washington term that made her realize that her volunteer work in non-profit public service enterprises could be a career.

The benefits of diversity the faculty had talked to me about years ago were very much on the minds of both students and alums as one of the great things Clark had done for them. One girl said it "has changed my life, since I was given the opportunity to meet with people from different backgrounds I would not have been able to if I had not gone to this university. In my suite, for example, was a girl on welfare and one a millionaire and another from Puerto Rico. In high school, everyone was from the same background. There is just a diversity of interests, ideas, political views and lifestyles and hobbies, and everyone is accepted."

Another, a Republican government major who went on to earn an MBA, said being "a minority among devout Democrats I was able to expand my mind to the other side." Clark, she added, "opened my eyes to the diversity our country and the world contain and allowed me to embrace and try to understand it all."

A minority graduate said "everyone reached out to students" and that professors "had such passion for their subject and for the students that I decided to double major in art history" (with communications). "I'm glad I went to Clark, my classes, friends, teachers, and activities helped me grow into myself while respecting and accepting everything else."

An Oklahoma senior called Clark "a magical place that allows me to be myself and that has changed my life for the better. I am so excited to graduate and continue using my voice for the betterment of society." A baseball player from Connecticut said, "I have become a better student, athlete, and person since I came to Clark. I don't know if I could have had these same experiences at another school."

A 2001 graduate from Amman, Jordan, who made a point of explaining he'd not been much of a student, said that Clark was "a profound life experience for me. It was a place where I felt I could bring about change and it really left me wanting more out of life."

A member of the same class from Massachusetts said, "Faculty, administrators, and staff were the best of leaders and mentors."

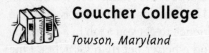

Goucher College
Towson, Maryland

Goucher has several distinctions. It was long one of the best women's colleges. It is now one of the best kept secrets of the top quality coed colleges. And it is one of the few first-rate undergraduate colleges in a major urban area—Baltimore.

Even though it lies close to the city's northern boundary, a visitor driving into the campus enters another world, a lovely tree-lined spread of 287 acres. Not far beyond it is a Mecca for boaters and fishermen, Loch Haven Reservoir.

There has been a tremendous growth also in a new focus: foreign study. Goucher, like other colleges in this book, considers it so important that it has moved to a four-term academic year of two full semesters with two three-week terms in January and May. This should permit students in any major to find at least one study-abroad program that will fit into their plans. They will find programs in every part of the world and there will be no extra cost.

Another distinction is Goucher's dramatically successful pioneering in the career development field. Since 1920 it has had one of the best, most innovative, forward-looking, and effective career-development offices in the nation, a result of its efforts to expand the job market for its women graduates. Since 1987, when it became coeducational, men also have been getting the benefit of all this expertise and wide-ranging networking that means prime job connections.

Goucher graduates' employment statistics are phenomenal. When the class of 1993 was surveyed in 1998, none of the 80 percent who responded was unemployed one year after graduation. Those who didn't have jobs were in graduate school or weren't in the job market. In the class of 1997, surveyed the same year, only 1 percent were unemployed and 72 percent of the class had responded. These are typical success stories. Any institution claiming a better record would be boasting. The moral is, if you're counting on your college experience to get you a job in a changing world, you'd be hard put to find a better bet than Goucher. One reason is that Goucher had been very adroitly and effectively using internships long before most other schools caught on. Internships cover just about every imaginable kind of job or enterprise in just about every part of the world. But that's not surprising when you consider Goucher adopted this program long ago as part of its strategy to open opportunities for women. Probably only Antioch, where every other term is an off-campus job and which started earlier, has done more in this area.

Supplementing this is a mentorship program that enables students to establish career contacts with Goucher graduates or with other friends of the college who are professionals in many fields. The mentors provide career advice and may open doors or offer jobs.

At the core of this success, naturally, is the product the Career Development Office has to offer. A Goucher graduate has had a

NORTHEAST: GOUCHER COLLEGE ◆ 53

good liberal education as any institution in the nation can offer, and in the important ways, better than any prestigious university. What are some of these ways? Richness of experience from being an active participant in independent study or student-faculty research projects, seminars, and tutorials; from enjoying close relationships with scholar-teachers; and from being a contributing member of a community of learning, not just a passive ear earning course credits. All these things add up to the crucial twenty-first-century ability to go ahead on one's own. The Goucher graduate has met the highest standards, and has been the beneficiary of a superb faculty whose members love teaching and who take genuine interest in the individual student.

Goucher deserves, as do many other colleges in this book, much more attention from parents and their college-bound teenagers. For those who think they want to go to a college in a city, Goucher is an ideal school. By 2004, the percentage of men in this former women's college had reached the critical mass of 40 percent. The population has increased to 1,400, with an eventual goal of 1,500. Only a third of them come from Maryland, the rest from the mid-Atlantic, other parts of the country, and many foreign countries. Over 15 percent are minorities.

Like the other colleges in this book, Goucher is inclusive; they take about 80 percent of their applicants. So, if you want the challenge of doing your best in a first-rate community of learning in a lovely setting, you will like Goucher.

Goucher gives merit grants to nearly half the freshmen ranging from $300 to full tuition. And slightly over half get financial aid packages of loan, grant, and campus job. So it could be cheaper to attend Goucher than a public institution with a much lower sticker price. Goucher no longer requires an interview. Instead it is one of the colleges that carefully reads all the material in your application. Except in unusual cases, the interview doesn't tell anything more than the written material, so do a careful job telling your story accurately and fully. And if the admissions officer sees motivation and promise, he or she is going to say yes.

Goucher's campus is taking on a new look with a focal point called the Athenaem, a complex including a new library, an auditorium, an open-air plaza, seminar rooms, information technology resources, and a café. There, speakers, actors, and musicians can perform or express themselves.

Several new theme residences are to follow the wellness and healthy-living complex, where suites open into common rooms. In one, residents agree not to smoke, drink alcohol, or use illicit drugs, and there are a variety of health-related programs. All the new residences are designed to get students to come together to eat or discuss events of the day or what went on in class.

As is the case in several other colleges in this group, there is a strong commitment to volunteerism. For several years, students in the writing program, for example, have been working with underprivileged kids, many of whom have been helped from elementary school through high school. There is also a partnership in science with an inner-city high school.

At Goucher everyone lives by the Honor Code. They also work hard. The students I talked to seemed to bear out the faculty descriptions of them as hardworking and interested in intellectual pursuits. The many merit awards are bringing in more and more serious students of high academic ability, which ensures a mix of abilities, something needed for good discussion classes.

Every freshman takes a seminar called Frontiers, an interdisciplinary exploration of a current topic, chosen by the instructor. Each class of a dozen or fewer is taught by professors from several disciplines, and the object is to integrate the various aspects of a liberal arts education.

A theater major thought there wasn't enough vocational emphasis. Another transfer said Rollins College in Florida was "frivolous" but Goucher was "fine." Everyone else I talked with during my visit, whether history, dance, theater, philosophy, teacher education majors, or athletes, said it was a choice they would repeat if they had to do it over again.

A few years ago, economics and related areas would have been the most popular majors. Now the humanities have taken over. More than one-third have gravitated to English, art, art history, communication, dance, dance therapy, languages, music, philosophy, and theater. Economics is now in the second tier, along with education, historic preservation, international relations, management, political science, and sociology. A quarter are in math and sciences, including computer science. And the math at Goucher, incidentally, is a hands-on affair focusing on real-world applications wherever possible and integrating it with computer science. Goucher was one of the first to introduce computer courses as well as to require computer literacy.

Beyond the freshmen seminars, students have to fill specific distribution requirements so that no one can leave Goucher as a specialized ignoramus. Goucher is also deeply concerned about preparing its graduates for the twenty-first century, and one of its efforts is a new major, the Cognitive Studies Program, which explores how people learn. In one of its courses, students are investigating with the aid of a mathematician, a computer scientist, a psychologist, and a philosopher, the possibilities of artificial intelligence.

Goucher has an array of support services that good students often find as useful as do those with problems or disabilities. One is a voluntary writing program to help students improve their skills to meet the writing proficiency requirement, or to do better in other courses. More than one-third of the student body makes use of the Academic Center for Excellence (ACE); a lot of the bright students discover in college that they don't know how to study effectively. The ACE not only helps those with learning problems but also conducts sessions on test-taking techniques, test anxiety, and time management, and it is used by the B students as much as by anyone else.

Three years ago, the college had another bright idea, one that is reminiscent of the way Emory and Henry in Virginia helps those in dire straits. It spotted the toughest courses and assigned to them supplemental instructors who work with students in study groups. And it has been shown that students learn better and more effectively that way than by working on their own. It is another example of collaborative learning that helps make these colleges so effective.

As a result of this program, no student flunked chemistry the first semester of 1993, and poor grades in biology were reduced by two-thirds.

Freshmen get an introduction-to-college course, Transitions, that meets throughout the first semester to enlighten them on things like time management, the college's expectations of them, rules, their own responsibilities, social problems, study-abroad opportunities, career options, the Career Development Office, and graduation requirements. This has reduced bad grades by one-half.

These efforts not only improve the college's retention but also the student's own self-image and satisfaction. If a student doesn't realize his potential he will tend to externalize his frustrations and blame them on the institution. The imaginative approach that has long helped women realize their potential and has opened doors to them in a frosty world is now also getting the men up to speed.

A typical Goucher student, one professor said, is worldly and traveled, but as a high schooler was not committed or achieving enough for the Ivy schools. But they come here, he said, "and they get turned on." Another said his own son had been a B student in high school, came to Goucher, sampled a wide variety of courses, got excited about philosophy, and is now going to graduate school after getting top grades and scores in the 700s on the Graduate Record Exam (comparable to like scores on the SATs).

"This college," said a political science professor, "fits kids with basic skills. It is a nurturing environment. It is competitive but not a paper mill. They are transformed at the end of four years; the developmental curve is very high because the teachers here love their subject matter and what they are doing."

At Goucher, teachers said, students develop the capacity to read critically and to think critically, both crucial skills. They also said the level of expectation is high and that "the flow of good, noted speakers we have is important." One professor who had taught at Brown said there is no comparison between Goucher and Brown when it comes to close student-faculty relationships. "This," he added, "is everything I thought it was supposed to be."

Ten years later, Goucher students feel the same way they did, they're glad they came and call the experience the best years of their lives.

A junior said, "I have truly enjoyed my three years at Goucher. The college offers many different types of opportunities that cater to each individual, whether it be classes, study abroad programs, or social events, there are many ways to be involved and to make a difference in the Goucher community. Our small, tight-knit classes have allowed me to formulate relationships with my professors and have enhanced my educational experience.

"The campus is beautiful, the people are friendly, and it is just a wonderful place to be if you are looking for a small, close community and an overall happy atmosphere. Then Goucher is a perfect choice."

A sophomore girl said, "When I was applying to colleges, I had never heard of Goucher, nor had my high school counselor. My dad forced me to pick two colleges from Pope's book to apply to since most of the kids in my high school apply to all the same schools. Goucher was one he specifically wanted me to look at. After about two weeks of protest I finally gave in and visited Goucher. It appealed to me most because it was a small liberal arts college that had a strong biology department. Also, it was located near a big city, but was still an actual campus. Pope mentioned that Goucher was perfect for students with a B average, and that a lot of the students were awarded merit scholarships, which was what I would need if I attended a private, out-of-state college.

"After receiving acceptance and visiting again, I knew that Goucher was the right place for me. Coming from a very competitive high school three times the size of Goucher, I was very happy with the community-like feeling on campus, how easy it is to get involved, the small class sizes, and the personal attention students get. If it had not been for Pope's book, I never would have heard of Goucher and missed out on the best years of my life so far."

A freshman who had heard the "sales spiels" of over twenty colleges, starting her freshman year in high school, said she was lucky to be at Goucher. She considered liberal arts colleges "a dime a dozen on the East Coast" and had not even wanted to consider it, but her mother suggested she read *Colleges That Change Lives*. After her second visit to Goucher she "fell in love" with it. She said there were no labels or stereotypes, but rather a sense of community where everyone is accepted and it's not necessary to "hang out with the frat boys or theater crows." Goucher encourages students to expand their horizons, she added, and interact with other students, and "no one is rude or disrespectful to students who don't fit into their stereotype; everyone gets along." After talking to other friends at private universities I realize how lucky I am to attend Goucher."

A Massachusetts freshman who came to Goucher under pressure from her parents said, "I didn't know it would change my life until I realized Goucher is more my home than where I lived the first eighteen years of my life." She said she had made lifetime friends, was on a field hockey team "I was born to be on," and was able to pursue several intellectual interests as well, and in a life-changing community.

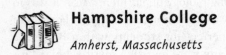

Hampshire College
Amherst, Massachusetts

No college has ever been born of such distinguished parentage to such high expectations, so maligned in its adolescence, and matured to fulfill its promise so brilliantly as Hampshire.

Dazzling might be a more accurate word. In only thirty-five years, two graduates have won MacArthur Foundation "genius awards," as has the college itself, one has had a Pulitzer prize, film industry alumni have had fifteen Academy-Award nominations and three Oscars, as well as Emmy and Peabody awards; one in five has a terminal degree, several are publishing scholars, and several have won fiction writing awards. The famed Tuskegee Syphilis Study of 1997 was headed by an alumna M.D. And just in the last ten years, Hampshire seniors have won sixteen Fulbright Fellowships, three Truman Fellowships, two National Security Education Program grants, and nine other fellowships.

As Education Editor of *The New York Times* during the college-going panic of the late '50s, I did my part to extol the virtues and promise of the imaginative New College plan created by neighboring Amherst, Mount Holyoke, Smith, and the University of Massachusetts. At a time when getting into college, especially a good college, was the American family's high-voltage anxiety, this New College proposal was one that could live on tuition alone and thus could be replicated. It seemed a magic solution.

When it finally came into being as Hampshire College in 1970 in a former apple orchard on the southern edge of Amherst, it had what was hailed as a dream faculty, and its central idea was—and is—total immersion of the student in a broad liberal education that he himself would largely design.

With its four founding institutions it became part of a new Five College Consortium allowing students at one school to take classes at any of the other four. Some courses—dance, theater, Asian studies, and astronomy—were cooperative ventures, and a bus system linked the campuses. But Hampshire would be unique: Grades were replaced by written faculty evaluations; there were no academic departments; no freshmen, sophomores, juniors, or seniors; no fraternities or sororities; and no intercollegiate athletics (although the school now has intercollegiate soccer and basketball).

Within a framework intended to prevent his coming out a narrow dilettante—as one can at Amherst, Brown, and others—every student, with faculty advice, was his own intellectual architect and builder. He had to provide the ideas.

Hampshire suddenly was one of the most sought-after schools in the country and it attracted throngs of independent, energetic, and imaginative people. It also lured youths who chose not to notice the responsibilities required by this intoxicating freedom. Most teenagers have a planning span of eight to ten hours and to them it looked like the primrose path or the yellow-brick road.

When the dilettantes found it took more work, structure, and planning than they had bargained for, dropout rates and parental disaffection grew. Also, the academic freedom was often seen as frivolity, especially when a news story in 1984 described an upper-level thesis titled, "A Career in the Field of Flying Disc Entertainment and Education" (Frisbees). What wasn't publicized a few years later was that the thesis author had become a product-development and marketing consultant for two firms. Hampshire was getting a bad rap, and it lasted for several years.

Happily, those days are long past. Hampshire's 1,400 students—from nearly every state and a dozen foreign countries—are there because the admissions staff does its best to make sure Hampshire is the right place for them.

Today no college has students whose intellectual thyroids are more active or whose minds are more passionately engaged. A few equal it, but most don't come close, including Hampshire's Ivy neighbors. Students are not only happy, they feel free to declare that their peers in the other colleges are missing something important.

The effect persists. Although it's only been awarding diplomas since 1975, more than half the graduates have advanced degrees. Remarkably, Hampshire ranks sixteenth among all the institutions in the country in the percentage of future psychology Ph.D.s.

Its record in the film industry is simply astounding. It has outperformed even the major schools, such as UCLA and NYU, in turning out writing, producing, and directing stars.

Best known is Ken Burns, creator of *The Civil War, Baseball, Frank Lloyd Wright,* and other documentaries. Others include Paul Margolis, who wrote the TV series *MacGyver,* John Falsey, whose *St. Elsewhere, Northern Exposure,* and *I'll Fly Away* set new standards in TV programming, and Jeff Maguire, whose screenplay, *In the Line of Fire,* was nominated for an Academy Award. More are on the way.

There are two reasons why Hampshire graduates achieve so much. One is the kind of person the college attracts. The other is what the college does for them by equipping them to become their own wide-ranging explorers and connection-seers. As one Hampshire student said of a Five College seminar on another campus, "Some of the others had more information on a topic, but I can take information and turn it around, use it better."

In another decade, Hampshire alumni will probably be leading the pack as cutting-edge innovators in many fields and in developing new technologies with potential business applications in the new world of global entrepreneurship. The man who has more patents than any living American, Jerome Lemelson, has given the college $3.2 million to develop courses and programs designed to stimulate innovation and entrepreneurship.

Some now under way—in artificial intelligence, digital imaging in film, river ecology, animal behavior, innovation in farming, and aquaculture—are already affecting the learning process. A physics professor involved in the farm course said, "The Lemelson Program has broken down the walls between the liberal arts education and the search for solutions to real-world problems, so that what we're doing is no longer just a theoretical exercise." Several student inventions have come out of the Lemelson program.

The experience of three decades persuaded the administration to change its plan in 2004 to require first-year students to have some breadth of exposure so they could make better long-range program decisions the second year. They must now take one-semester courses in each of the five interdisciplinary schools that replace traditional departments. They are: Humanities and

Cultural Studies, Social Science, Natural Science, Cognitive Science, and Interdisciplinary Arts. They must also choose three other courses from the offerings of all of the five colleges.

For Division II, which he starts thinking about in his second year, he selects two professors to serve on his concentration committee and discusses with them how he might best address his interests and goals. He drafts a concentration statement describing his learning plans for the next two or three semesters. It must meet the professors' concern for intellectual rigor and breadth.

And by its nature it is a broad gauge. Such topics as Education and Social Mobility, or The Influence of Schooling on Moral Development, like the erosion topic, become wide ranges of inquiry and are far more flexible and demanding than the confines of a simple history, sociology, or geology major.

This richness is largely responsible for the intellectual excitement. Everyone is embarked on a learning adventure that may take them to places they never dreamed of. It's not surprising that a prime conversational topic is "What are you doing?" or that the Hampshire students tell a visitor that on the Five College buses they are the only ones talking about their work.

As a student works his way along his Division II project, the teachers provide criticism, advice, and evaluation. The examination is no written test. It is a serious and lengthy evaluation of a portfolio of papers he has produced in his coursework or for his research project, or an evaluation of an internship or some artistic products. An additional component has been added to the Division II requirements; namely, some exposure to and understanding of issues involving Third World and minority cultures.

There is nary a grade on his Hampshire transcript because a student learns much more from thoughtful written critiques of his work, of his strengths, and in suggestions for improvement than from an A, a B, or a C. This system has proved a boon in the real world. Such detailed pictures of the students give them a distinct advantage when they apply for jobs or for admission to graduate school. However, they do get grades for courses taken at one of the four other schools in the Five College Consortium, and these will appear on their transcripts.

Values are important at Hampshire. The experience is intended to foster a concern for others as well as to develop individual talents, so before moving on to Division III, a student must perform some service to the college or to the community. It may be anything from participating in the college governance to working with disabled citizens.

The final year, Division III, is largely spent on a major independent-study project under the guidance of two Hampshire faculty members and a professor from a neighboring college or a professional working in that field. Usually, the project explores in depth a specific aspect of the Division II project.

Two other advanced activities are required. At least one must be an advanced-level course or a teaching activity, such as helping a faculty member with an introductory course, or serving as a second reader on a Division I exam committee.

As at many other colleges, there is a January term which allows for any one of a multitude of adventures, from foreign study to trying an otherwise unavailable course at another college.

A computer science professor who went to Oberlin College as an undergraduate summed it up this way: "This is the only place for those who can see an educational opportunity and pursue it. I have two second-year-student coauthors doing research on a graduate level, and another doing publishable research. Some are even working on artificial intelligence (a graduate level area). Hampshire is the only place where this could happen. Hampshire is a unique opportunity for people with drive. Encouragement does it; it helps pull him up to the level where he can do it. Somewhere else he'd be spinning his wheels."

A theater professor added that she has students directing plays after the first semester, they are so eager to get busy and reinvent the wheel, another way of saying they're caught up in the enterprise.

Others said anyone who comes to Hampshire "has to care

about the world of ideas because here they have to be engaged. And they are passionately engaged. They work on weekends; when they get going on a project, their stopping point is when the job is done."

They also offered these opinions about their students:

- They are concerned with ethics, actively involved in social service, and tolerant.
- Hampshire students have built-in crap detectors, much initiative and flexibility, they invent new careers, and the graduate schools want more of them.

These professors had all gone to traditional, prestigious colleges but all thought that Hampshire prepared young people better. Its students develop good study habits and good instincts for what's important. They know how to write a good job report, and they have developed a broad view. They've also been forced to think. Some courses, for example, require students to write one-page summaries of what they've done and how they arrived at a problem's solution.

Another teacher attested to the computer science professor's claim that encouragement was the secret. She said, "There's something that happens and you see it happen before your eyes. Kids get transformed. I'm supervising a Division III project of a student who's always tried very hard and always before this when she'd bring in her papers I'd say 'you're not analytical enough' and her eyes would almost fill with tears and she'd say, 'but I tried so hard.' And we'd explain, and finally, this year, she got it and she's going to do a great job, and she said to me, 'I love it so much I can't bear to graduate now that I've discovered what it's about.' And that's really a pretty exciting thing.

"What do you need to do to get it? It's tolerance for uncertainty; everything isn't cut and dried."

Students I spoke with had two recurring themes. One was the kind of person who should come to Hampshire. He should be interested, motivated, and feel strongly about doing independent work, and "be a little bit of a self-starter—you'll learn how to be a self-starter." He also has to have a reason for coming; he may not know what it is, but it isn't just going to college. He should be able to tolerate uncertainty and know the value of it, and be able to imagine.

The other theme was even more frequently expressed, and that was how much diversity there is. A New York City boy from a high school class of 850 that embraced 75 to 80 ethnic groups said he found much more diversity at Hampshire. "They were all middle class. Here there are all sorts of people; for example, I met my first gay [person] here. But the real reason is that here you get identified by the work you do; the question is; 'What are you doing?'"

In addition, they had a lot to say about being deeply interested in their work, and being convinced of the superior quality of the classes at Hampshire. One girl added, "I took a class at Amherst and thought it was terrible."

The sense of community also came through strongly and consistently. "Here," as one student said, "everybody's together. You know all the profs. It's small and intimate and everybody's so friendly."

As at so many of the other schools in this book, Hampshire students said their experience deeply affected their values. One girl expressed a common feeling when she said, "Moral judgments are definitely affected. People are so much more moral and nonjudgmental here. You learn how to listen."

Hampshire is in a class by itself for those who have the drive to profit from it.

Ten years later, Hampshire asked graduates to assess what this college with student-designed programs and no grades had done for them. The result was rave reviews saying there was no college like it. No Ivy university would dare ask to be graded one to ten on the questions Hampshire asked, nor would most selective colleges. Here they are:

- I developed meaningful and lasting relationships with my professors.
- Helped me exceed my own expectations.
- Is like a graduate school for undergraduates.
- I produced more in-depth and original work than I would have elsewhere.
- Provided me with valuable life skills.
- Prepared me for a job in my field.
- Evaluations were more meaningful to me than grades.

Most gave tens or nines to all but two of them. Those getting the rare low grades were the life skills and preparation for a job in one's field. But a few defined skills very narrowly or had changed fields. Most comments, however, were that Hampshire prepared them for "anything."

Asked to compare the value of a Hampshire education with a traditional one, many expressed some variant of "Hampshire requires each student to discover his or her own voice," and, "while sometimes extremely demanding, the reward of self-discipline and then creating unique and highly tuned works is that a student builds skills, self-confidence, and a highly marketable resume."

As a result, several pointed out, Hampshire graduates not only get the jobs but get into the best graduate programs. And they prosper because they've already been doing graduate school work. "It's a cinch," was one response.

As for jobs, many comments were summarized in this one: "The Hampshire experience is, in a strange way, exactly how the world works, and kids, and often parents, have a hard time wrapping their minds around this."

Evaluations got a lot of credit for their success in getting into top graduate schools or in job competition. An alumna who had served three years on a law school admissions committee said applications from "Hampshire and its cousins" that use evaluations, (Reed, New College, Evergreen, Marlboro, St. Johns, and Antioch) "were more carefully considered than standard schools which could easily be fitted into a meaningless matrix of grades and LSAT scores." Others said evaluations were what got them into Ivy graduate programs or got them jobs. "A good evaluation," wrote one, "is like a recommendation." Others said evaluations "usually are a significant benefit."

They hold grades in contempt. In their view, grades are antithetical to realizing one's potential, to doing one's best work. One alumna had a revealing story. She got an A+ on a paper at another of the five colleges. "However, even before I got the grade I had ideas about how I could revise it and make it better. The teacher told me not to bother, I'd already gotten the A+. I realized how limiting grades could be, since I had done as well as possible according to this teacher's standards, I didn't need to push myself further. Since I have started teaching college classes, I have had the opportunity to grade papers or to withhold grades and write an evaluation. Students whose papers are not graded grow as writers more than those whose papers are graded."

An alumna who is a teaching assistant at UCLA, said the 400 students in her class were "obsessed with grades" but not with learning.

Some of the other comments were:

"How can you beat five colleges for the price of one? You really can inhabit the world of Smith, Amherst, UMass, and Mt. Holyoke, and it's amazing to give yourself the extended experience that those four other schools provide. It makes a small school much larger."

A graduate student at Harvard said, "I transferred to Hampshire from NYU because I was frustrated with the education I was getting at NYU. I was learning facts but I wasn't learning how to think. It felt a great deal like high school: Memorize the answers, pass the tests. Hampshire was the polar opposite. Not only was I learning how to think, I was taught the value of the process of learning and to think about accomplishments in terms of my own progress and not as an assessment of how much better or worse I was doing relative to my classmates. It removes the silliness of competing with others and enables you to focus on what it is you are in school to do—learn."

"You don't get letter grades in the real world, you get communication, and evaluations are communications of your progress, like my regular meeting with my boss."

An alumna said Hampshire had prepared her well for the tough, case-based curriculum of veterinary school, and that evaluations had been very important to her.

Another graduate student said, "The lack of grades is key to the success of Hampshire, because learning at Hampshire is about pushing oneself rather than simply competing with others. Without grades, there is no limit placed on the learning experience and the product it generates."

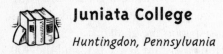

Juniata College

Huntingdon, Pennsylvania

For as long as I've been interested in colleges, Juniata in rural central Pennsylvania has shown up in the top ranks of the National Resources Council's surveys of which colleges produce the nation's scholars and scientists. A day's visit showed why. This school is not on every suburban high school senior's lips, but it deserves to be. It has a powerful sense of mission. It has a powerhouse faculty trained at the top universities. And it has eager young customers who become high achievers.

Testimony to this is the impressive record of its alumni in science, teaching, business, communications, and government. One, Dr. William Phillips, was corecipient of the 1997 Nobel Prize for physics. Five alumni are members of the National Academy of Science, several are professors or deans at top research universities and medical clinics. They include top news executives, MTV cinematography award winners, the developer of Teflon, and Dr. William von Liebig, the inventor of the Dacron tubing used in blood vessel and heart replacement. Juniata's new science center is named for him.

That combination produces dramatic results, especially in science, Juniata's strong suit. Ninety percent of its applicants to medical, dental, veterinary, and optometry schools are accepted. For medical school alone it is a grand slam 100 percent. Furthermore, science professors emphasized, unlike many schools, they don't weed out anybody, even someone who requires nurturing. More than half the science students get involved in undergraduate research; some years all do.

Juniata has received grants of $1.7 million from the National Science Foundation to further strengthen their science programs and to work with high schools. Faculty have received research grants of $1 million. The college also got a Merck innovation award. A chemistry prof pointed out, "We have outstanding lab equipment. We throw away equipment other colleges would be glad to have."

With a $900,000 Howard Hughes grant, Juniata is doing something unique. It has a combined chemistry and biology lab which integrates the study of both disciplines, teaching students cutting-edge research techniques in molecular biology.

The William J. von Liebig Science Center is an imposing $20 million structure in which 10 percent of the space is to be devoted to student research.

Juniata also has what few colleges have, a 365-acre field station on a lake, an area that includes its complete watershed. Four new buildings provide classrooms, labs, and two residence halls. The college says this field station "will transform how environmental education is taught."

Construction was also under way in 2004 for a comprehensive center for the performing arts. In 2003, a center for entrepreneurial leadership was completed.

Though many of the faculty have research grants, the school's attitude is that scholarship is not something apart from teaching, but a way of modeling.

In the crowded school-teaching market, 90 percent of Juniata's graduates get secure jobs immediately after graduation. Of its 1997 class responding to surveys, 98 percent were employed, in graduate school, or in other planned postgraduate activities within six months of getting their diplomas.

Worth special note are two facts: One is that Juniata has an outstanding record of inspiring women to become scientists and doctors—60 percent of the freshman chemistry class usually is women. Another is that nearly half (47 percent) of their enthusiastic alumni contribute financially. Few colleges can make such a claim.

A dean said, "This is a value-added place. We serve students from rural communities. We provide upward mobility. There is a heavy emphasis on faculty-student contact. There is a strong sense of community, with no fraternities or sororities. The sense of community is enhanced by Mountain Day, when the school closes down on some unannounced day and everyone goes to a nearby state park and plays for a day. And at Christmas, Madrigal Dinner, faculty and administrators wait on the students."

Juniata is a place where women not only get as much attention in the classroom as men, but is also a place where they have many role models among the faculty. Indeed, there could hardly be a better place for women to develop. There are six women professors in biology, chemistry, and mathematics, as well as women on the Allied Health Committee, which makes graduate and medical school recommendations. Biologist Debra Kirchhof-Glazier, who heads the committee, said, "Our classes are female friendly. Women tend to respond to relationships, so I know every name in my classes, and all the students know each other, even in big classes. We put name tags in a basket and mix them up. Each student picks one, then locates that person and becomes acquainted. In our classes the women are definitely vocal, and I pick on women to be sure they speak up. We had one shy woman run a large class on eating disorders, and another on how to study."

A remarkable 80 percent of the student body participates in intramurals and their intercollegiate teams are all bona fide students. The men's volleyball team in 1994 was the Division III champion, and the women's team has been in the playoffs the last nineteen years.

All admitted students get merit scholarships ranging from $4,000 to $12,000 a year, and high-achieving students can compete for scholarships that pay full tuition as well as room and board.

Most of Juniata's 1,400 students come from Pennsylvania, but thirty-seven states and twenty-eight foreign countries are providing an increasing share. About 78 percent of the applicants are accepted; it is inclusive, as it has to be to be in this book. The middle 50 percent of acceptees have total SAT scores in the 1,050–1,250 range, and most were in the top half of their high school classes, but many of those were rural schools.

Whatever their backgrounds when they come, students soon acquire worldly perspectives. There are always some foreign faculty members and exchange students on campus. Everyone is encouraged to study abroad for at least one semester in their major area during junior year. They can choose from an array of programs, which include direct exchanges of both students and faculty with universities in France, Germany, Japan, and Mexico.

Whether direct exchange or not, every foreign term involves total immersion. The Juniata student becomes a member of the host university's student body and community. A junior may go as a business major but he or she comes back knowing some of the host country's culture. In contrast to most other universities' foreign-study programs, which provide separate enclaves for the U.S. students apart from the host country's, Juniata's foreign programs are much more international. Thus the experience is more intense and the feedback and the rewards are greater.

Students are free to design their own majors with the advice of two faculty members, but their study must include the core curriculum providing the framework of a liberal education. It has cross-cultural requirements. One, for example, is called Heart of India, team-taught by an Indian professor and a student with the help of Juniata profs of chemistry, geology, religion, and history, all of whom have been to India. Another, less elaborate, is The Greek Mind.

There is a great emphasis on experiential learning and nearly every student serves an internship in one of many businesses, research institutions, universities, or others arranged by the college.

As at many other good colleges, seniors must prepare a research project over two semesters, develop it, and present it in a colloquium of students and faculty. They also must take a course called Values Study, which is just what the name says, and which is team-taught by faculty members from several different disciplines.

On just about every campus I visited, faculty members were happy with and proud of their students. Here I got the feeling that by the time they were seniors Juniata students must be ten feet tall. The terms most used to describe them were "honest," "highly motivated," "hard working," "professionally or vocationally oriented," and "having a strong desire to serve." Many of them arrive unsophisticated but bright and eager. Their good qualities are what sell most faculty on coming to Juniata.

Other faculty went further. One who had taught at those places said the kids at the top were just as bright as those at Middlebury or Haverford. Another, a science prof, said, "Our kids are performing at a higher level in grad and medical schools than they did in college. They often find they've done some of the work here. We take the average kid and open doors for him."

To underscore her points she told these two stories:

"One of our seniors who was rejected by the medical schools he applied to in 1986 went to grad school at the University of California at Davis and has been hired by Harvard as associate professor in charge of the cardiology lab at Brigham and Women's Hospital.

"Last year at Harvard medical school, a Yale graduate asked two of ours where they'd gone to college. When they told him, he said, 'Juniata, where's that?' But on the first exam, both our graduates got As and the Yale man got a C. Showing him their papers, they said, "This is where." A chemistry professor could hardly wait to add that in 1993 the world-famous Mayo Clinic in Rochester, Minnesota, accepted six applicants nationwide for its grad school clinic and two of them were from Juniata.

All these things don't happen just because teachers are interested in the students and the students' work. As at other colleges in this book, Juniata's faculty is committed to improving its teaching methods. They confer with each other, comparing notes on what works; they have a team of faculty that will consult with any teacher who wishes help, and they sit in on each other's classes. They call "fantastic" both the interest in teaching that has been aroused and the fact that many profs have revised their teaching methods to make them more effective.

As one might expect, the students would write enthusiastic letters of recommendation for their profs anytime. The volleyball players were naturally proud of their success but wouldn't want to be anyplace else anyway. Science students were even prouder than the athletes, sure that they could lick twice their weight in Ivy Leaguers, an attitude that was pervasive in the science buildings. It was not just the students who were infected; one secretary told me: "We're good!"

The English, business, and other majors sang the same song. One called the learning environment "fantastic" and the faculty challenging and full of parental concern for their progress. It was clear the teachers were friends and mentors as well. And to a favorite question about being able to have dinner or spend a night at a faculty member's home five years from now, several said the problem would be in deciding which one to choose. A couple of housewives taking courses part-time were as enthusiastic as the kids.

One little group of upper-class students felt so strongly about the quality of their experiences that they asked me, "What's the difference between this school and Amherst?"

My answer was that Amherst has more very bright, more sophisticated, and more well-to-do freshmen than Juniata, but by the time they're seniors the situation has been reversed. The Juniata seniors' talents have been doubled and sharpened, and they have been better equipped to cope, to adapt, and to take risks— things that they will have to do in this new world. And women could not have more encouragement or better role models than at Juniata. Amherst, on the other hand, has turned out pretty much the same kind of person it took in; there, getting in was the great achievement in life. Juniata students seemed to like my answer.

What kind of person would be happy at Juniata? Most teenagers would unless they need the big city, want to be in the fast lane, or aren't interested in learning. If they want to be able to feel that they belong and that people are eager to help them, they will be happy here. Thirty years ago most of the students were first-generation college and from mid-Pennsylvania. That is no longer true and there is more diversity—a third of the freshmen are from out of state—and there's a good contingent of international students. Also, the college's heavy emphasis on foreign study as well as foreign-student and -faculty exchanges has helped change things.

And anyone interested in the health professions could hardly find a surer entrée into a graduate program or medical or veterinary school. Not only is Juniata's record phenomenal, but it has been achieved with students who did not come to college with impressive test scores.

A teenage girl, especially one who may lack confidence, should know that no place will make a greater effort to see that she feels at least as important as any male, and that she flowers.

Things like these are some of the reasons Juniata's alumni are so eager to help and to contribute financially. "Alumni fly in from Oregon to do volunteer jobs," said a professor. "It's absolutely fantastic!" Satisfied customers are the proof of the pudding; there should be more places like this and more people should know about them.

．　．　．

Ten years later, students and alumni still think no other college could have the same impact or change their lives as much. They talk about their "amazing" experiences, the closeness, and the help and encouragement of their professors. And several of them attribute their success to the intellectual challenges Juniata made them meet.

The most eloquent, however, was a 1992 graduate who was the first in his family "to achieve a college education." He is now a physician as well as a playwright who produces plays that address issues raised during his life as a doctor.

He said he came to Juniata when he was seventeen and his family was "devastated emotionally and financially" by the death of his father at age forty. He chose Juniata because it was close to home and because it had an excellent medical school acceptance rate.

"What I had not expected," he said, "was the degree to which Juniata would change my life and enable me to make use of my grief; skills which have served me well as an obstetrician/gynecologist dealing with many triumphs and tragedies every day were taught to me more intensely at Juniata than any other aspect of my medical education or training. Because of my experience in theater at Juniata, I was better able to understand myself, my family, and my future patients. I became a double major in theater and premedicine after my freshman year. I was accepted into medical school immediately after graduation, an opportunity virtually impossible at any other institution. Today I continue to write and produce plays. I also helped establish a national nonprofit called Her Heart's Wish, that grants the wishes of women who are dying. I have no doubt in my mind that Juniata College forever changed my life and transformed me from a grieving adolescent into a medical doctor who has never forgotten the lessons learned in Huntingdon, Pennsylvania. I remain forever grateful to the mentoring and challenges that Juniata presented to me. I feel almost blessed to have found such an extraordinary place."

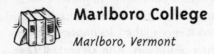

Marlboro College
Marlboro, Vermont

Ten years ago I wrote: "Marlboro College, nestled in one of Vermont's scenic hills near Brattleboro, has fewer than 300 students. They design their own programs—a poor idea for most collegians—but if I had $100 million I'd give a third of it to endow this school. There's no other college experience like it. The rest would go to Antioch and Hampshire, where students also design their own programs. Reed and St. John's, where they don't, would be included if they were as needy."

Today I would change two things. There are 330 students, and I'd give half the $100 million each to Marlboro and Antioch. Hampshire's fiscal health is better now.

Each of these five schools has an ethos of commitment to learning and performance. They turn out the essential leaven of democracy: bold, clear thinkers; people of vision and character. You will find the Marlboro adventure far more intense and intellectually demanding than Harvard, any other Ivy or Ivy clone. There simply is no comparison.

Nearly 70 percent of them go on to graduate school, and to the top ones. Nearly 60 percent contribute financially, which puts them near the top of the heap, even though Marlboro alumni tend to be in non-profit fields.

One of the fruits of the GI Bill, Marlboro was founded by returning veterans in 1946. Walter Hendricks, who had been teaching GIs in France, gave his old hill farm to realize his vision of a college where education would take place "mind to mind." He had the help of Robert Frost, Dorothy Canfield Fisher, Ambassador Ellsworth Bunker, and the famed scientist, educator, and regent of the Smithsonian Institution, Dr. Caryl P. Haskins.

What tiny Marlboro has given to society in its short life is simply astounding for a college so little known and so little sought after. It shows what kind of young people it draws and what it does for them.

In just five decades Marlboro has produced an impressive array of alumni that includes editors at *The New York Times* and *The Wall Street Journal,* a newspaper publisher, college and university professors, bankers, CEOs in business, doctors, lawyers, research scientists, artists, and poets.

Even more dramatic are the figures on Marlboro's exalted rank in the production of future scientists and scholars. Only three schools—California Institute of Technology, University of Chicago, and Reed—turn out higher percentages of future Ph.D.s in the life sciences. Only ten do better in theology and religious studies. Just seventeen top it in math and computer sciences.

And as it should be, it's a good mind in a sound body. Its cross-country ski teams were second in NCAA Division II in New England in 1985 and third in 1986, pretty good for a student body a fraction of the size of its competitors. It also has teams in volleyball, tennis, basketball, ultimate frisbee, and touch football.

The founders provided for a self-governing community modeled on the New England town meeting, with everyone on a first-name basis and, as at St. John's, with no faculty ranks. The basic tenet is that academic learning is inseparable from the community in which it occurs. Students, faculty, staff, and administration all are equal voting members. The town meeting can even vote down faculty decisions on academic policy, but the faculty can override by a two-thirds majority.

At first glance, Marlboro looks like a homey, old-shoe, nurturing place in the country for someone who needs help, the plain white frame buildings are so informal and the people so friendly. Indeed, in their first life, some of the buildings were barns and a farmhouse. But that impression is deceiving. Marlboro's academic program is rigorous, and someone who is dysfunctional is likely to be hurt. Physically disabled people would not find the slopes easy to negotiate. This is a place for self-reliant person who are interested in ideas and the life of the mind. Students here tend to be a year or so older than other college students, and that makes a significant difference in the level of maturity.

Important new things have been achieved in the last ten years. A capital campaign raised $20 million, a $400,000 grant from the Freedom Foundation funds an expanded Asian studies program that brings experts to the campus and sends students and faculty on research trips to Vietnam and China.

A $1 million gift to the DNA lab offers science students new research opportunities; there is a new performing arts center; the size of the library has been doubled; and there is a new suite-style dormitory. A new weekly "dedicated hour" brings each professor's advisees together for problem-solving, socializing, and maybe a sundae.

Financial aid has been beefed up as well. In addition to its commitment to help every student who qualifies for financial aid "to assemble the resources necessary to attend," it offers merit-based scholarships of up to $10,000.

As for admissions requirements, if you really want to go to Marlboro and can show the admissions committee in an interview that you belong there, you're in. You will be asked if you really understand the writing requirement and the Plan of Concentration, and you'll be told that the demands are tough.

Two-thirds of the applicants are accepted, about one-third are in the top third of their high school classes, and their SAT scores average around 1,100.

For graduation there are only two requirements beyond the usual one of earning 120 credits with Cs or better, plus a sort of family obligation to the place. The first is that every freshman has to pass muster with a twenty-page work of clear writing by the end of the year. Because good writing is mainly good thinking, this is quite demanding. Otherwise, he can have the comparative luxury of taking a variety of liberal arts courses for the first two years. These provide for breadth and for introductory courses to one's areas of interest.

The second requirement is a Plan of Concentration designed

by the student and one or two faculty advisers that fully occupies the junior and senior years and involves putting together a whole thesis. It is a focused course of study, but the range and the variety have no limits. Marlboro may have only forty-two faculty members and its physical plant may lack the expensive new science buildings that many other colleges have, but that faculty and the outside resources available can satisfy any intellectual bent. The fact that 70 percent go to graduate and professional schools in a multitude of different fields says so.

A Plan may be cross-disciplinary and it often changes, deepens, and broadens as the learning progresses, raising new questions and the need to explore new areas. A concentration in World Studies, for example, requires two terms in two different cultures.

As for the common obligation, one day a semester, everybody pitches in to work on some of the things that need fixing or cleaning up. Indeed, some of the buildings were built by students, staff, and faculty.

Instead of going to a class three hours a week, a junior or senior will meet one hour a week with one of his or her tutors, to report on what has been done, to plan, or to discuss. For example, someone doing a project on environmental science and environmental policy and ecology may be having tutorials with a biology, a political science, an economics, and perhaps a sociology professor. Otherwise the student is very much left to his own devices and self-discipline.

As one girl said, "there is no place to hide." Everything is riding on what she is doing on her own—and on her own initiative. It is a far heavier responsibility and a good deal more work than the conventional way. It takes someone able to go ahead on her own to handle this kind of freedom. It is the reliance on student initiative that separates Marlboro education from one-on-one elsewhere.

The Plan is a heady adventure, one that attracts transfer students to Marlboro, and it is what alumni talk about as their most exciting and stimulating experience. Juniors and seniors were telling me the same kinds of things Reed students did about how rewarding it was to work on their projects or foreign experiences on their World Studies internships.

Whatever his or her particular Plan, all Marlboro graduates have proved to themselves that they can define a problem, set clear limits on an area of inquiry, analyze that object of study, evaluate the result, and report thoughtfully on the outcome of a worthy project.

One of the great things about the Plan is that it puts teachers and students on the same side of the fence. The final evaluation of every student's Plan—which includes a three-hour oral exam—is conducted by an outside examiner, an expert in the particular field who may be from Amherst, Columbia, Harvard, Williams, or elsewhere, along with Marlboro faculty members. So the student's teachers are being evaluated too.

The outside examiners often give better grades than do the Marlboro faculty. A Cornell professor said the one he examined compared very favorably to Cornell's top honors students in English. An MIT professor went further. He said a senior physics major's knowledge of relativity was "greater than that of all but the rarest MIT graduate." Marlboro's physics lab may not be as showy as some at other schools, but in the summer of one student's junior year it got her an internship at the Argonne National Laboratory working on the Hera Electron-Proton Particle Accelerator. A Yale divinity-school evaluator called another student's work "quite extraordinary."

The attitudes of students here echoed those at a few other places in this book. I have talked to no group of young people more thoroughly sold on what they are doing. Marlboro is a do-it-yourself kind of place, said one, "and if you want something to happen, you've got to make it happen yourself." That's a virtue, he added, because the world is full of people waiting for someone to tell them what to do. Another felt that Marlboro's little democracy gave her a sense of personal power and independence, and "I'm no longer satisfied to leave decisions that affect me up to someone else."

Nor is there anywhere else a more palpable sense of trust and of being engaged in a common enterprise, if one of infinite variety, than at Marlboro. The library is open twenty-four hours a day and operates on the honor system; nobody is monitoring the borrowed books. The student leaves a dated, signed card in a checkout box by the door. The computer center is also open around the clock.

Not once during my visit did anyone make that frequent small-college gripe that everyone knows your business. That certainly is the case, but here it tends to make people think of the consequences of any action or churlish attitude that is going to be known to the whole community.

The loyalty to the college seemed incredible, and I was told that was true even of those who'd left without graduating. Everyone I talked to spoke with evident interest in their projects and their plans for now and for after graduation.

They also seemed more mature than most, which is not surprising, because the average age here is a little higher than at most other colleges. These are people interested in ideas, so while they may come expecting to study religion or theater or whatever, they may wind up going to graduate school in philosophy or Russian studies, or even graduate schools of business. The experience has helped them find themselves.

Students also become self-sufficient socially. Marlboro is not even a hamlet. What after the Revolutionary War was a town of 3,000 now has a very good inn, a post office, and about thirty houses scattered about; Brattleboro is ten miles away. So a Saturday evening's entertainment may evolve from someone's bringing music to the student center for an impromptu party with dancing. The college also has a full schedule of imported concerts and lectures by noted people. In the summer it is the scene of the Marlboro Music Festival.

It is not just a conceit that causes Marlboro to use many pages in its catalog to describe individual faculty members as people with many interests in addition to their scholarly ones. One, for example, went to Cornell, got doctorates in divinity and in literature, started Outward Bound programs at Skidmore College and at the State University of New York at Potsdam, had his own wilderness programs, was also a university professor in New Zealand, and is at Marlboro because he loves the outdoors and the kind of place Marlboro is. He is, in short, one lively person, and typical in his enthusiasms and his love of what the college is doing.

Marlboro is an egalitarian place where respect is shown. There is more intimacy in the best sense and more interaction than at other colleges, thanks especially to the two years of one-on-one tutorials. Students are heavily involved in their own education, which is a collaborative effort of student and mentor, with the mentor risking some judgment too. For all the demands, it is a place of relaxed camaraderie. During a midafternoon visit, I watched the president and a faculty member in a pickup basketball game with students, and the whole place made me think of an extended family hanging out in shirtsleeves.

Who should come here? First off, one has to be self-sufficient socially because this campus is at the end of the road. It is rural, pastoral, and hilly. Next, one must like people and be prepared to be a working part of a small self-governing community.

But above all, a Marlboro student should be a person who isn't going to be scared off by what one professor said: "The more you demand the more you're going to draw. We expect a lot of our seniors. People who come here should be interested in ideas, the life of the mind. That's central here. And they must be self-reliant."

That number, like the number attracted to Reed or Antioch, or St. John's or Hampshire, is small, but they constitute a Gideon's army. Gideon, in one of Israel's crises, culled an army of a few hundred from a host of thousands and defeated the Mideanite oppressors. The analogy is apt.

Ten years later, a 2001 graduate, Edward Augustyn, has provided the best, most vivid account of a college experience I've ever known. It will help you decide whether to take this adventure, and it would be wrong to try to summarize it. Here it is:

"It's hard to explain how Marlboro College has influenced who I am today. The reason I say this is that I attended Marlboro at the tender age of thirty-two after I danced professionally for ten years. Prior to my career as a dancer, I attended an honors program at a large urban Catholic university in Chicago which paled in comparison to the quality, richness, and, above all, the intensity of my Marlboro experience.

"I imagine that I had the necessary characteristics that it takes to succeed at Marlboro before attending there. As a classical dancer, I was highly disciplined and successful in one venue. Added to this I always had an intellectual bent, read voraciously, and was highly independent. Marlboro has a high dropout rate for the caliber of its student body as well as the quality of the program. You get a sense of why this is, as the academic pressure is intense and the independent nature of the program adds to the level of responsibility a student has for him- or herself.

"I chose Marlboro over seven other highly rated and better-known liberal arts colleges. I didn't consider the college seriously until I visited. Although the program sounded intriguing, I thought it was too small and too rural. It was the last school on my list but I didn't want any opportunity to slip by so I made the commitment to interview on campus.

"I have to say that I was blown away by the beauty that surrounds the school. The winding country road that leads to the top of the hill crosses small farms and ponds. You can hear the sounds of rivers and streams and see the green mountain valley from the top of the hill. I told myself that I would not let the postcard setting sway me.

"I visited Lynette Rummel's class. She's one of the professors of political science who supervised a tutorial founded by six young women preparing to go to Muslim countries for their World Studies internships. The class was examining Islamic women's issues.

"It was late afternoon and from the window of one of the rooms in Dalrymple Hall you could see the entire valley and the emerging leaves. The students seemed a bit sleepy. One of the young women laid her head on the desk. After Lynette introduced me, discussion began. I don't remember the details of the class but the energy remains with me to this day. Dialogue was like crossfire. You could literally see the trail of an idea as it went from student to teacher and then bounced back between students. The young woman who I thought slept through class lifted her head repeatedly to interject. I must admit that I was highly intimidated by the level and commitment of these people. At age thirty-two I had never been part of nor had I seen such a heated exchange of ideas in class—especially from twenty-year-olds. There was no lag in energy for the entire time of the class. From those few moments on I knew that this place was special and all I talked about when I returned home was Marlboro. Marlboro was glued to my tongue and I knew that this place would make me work harder than any other place I visited or could imagine attending.

"As a general observation, I thought the students were rather unkempt and lacked in general hygiene. I vowed that I would not dispense with hair gel or deodorant once I became a Marlboro student. What I didn't realize was that this was often a survival tactic rather than blatant nonconformity.

"Within three weeks I had pulled an all nighter, slept in the library, and practically stopped combing my hair. And I only had three classes my first semester. Things got worse by semester's end.

"Marlboro has a twenty-page writing portfolio requirement that you must pass within two semesters if you are to continue at the college. It is a blind-review process, which means that your writing instructors are not allowed to judge their own students' work.

"In preparing for this requirement, I did not change clothes for five days in a row, slept on a couch in the science lab, and I had no idea what I smelled like. At 7:00 a.m. we formed a queue outside Dalrymple Hall to turn in our portfolios. I wasn't the only disheveled freak turning my work in at the last minute. Forty percent of the class did not pass the first round. I was one of the lucky ones, but I barely made the grade. This was a significant lesson to me—that this place was serious about student achievement.

"I survived the ordeal. I realized how lucky I was to have teachers that took my writing seriously. They scrutinized absolutely everything and to great detail. Needless to say, I grew by leaps and bounds.

"I expanded into familiar territory but in unfamiliar ways. I focused in ethnographic studies and researched the burgeoning identities of young dancers through tutorials and field site research. My main Plan sponsor, Carol Hendrickson, guided me through this process. She earned her doctorate at the University of Chicago, wrote two books, and served as an expert witness for Guatemalan legal issues. I followed the progress of teen dancers at a high quality school in nearby Brattleboro as they came to the realization that they were being rejected by competitive conservatory-college dance programs. I also interviewed retiring dancers in the second half of the essay to see how their identities as dancers remain with them after they have left the field. She guided me through the writing of a 110-page paper that she suggested I try to publish.

"Plan writing was an intensely personal pursuit as I tried to make sense of my own transitioning identity as a dancer. In the second part of my Plan, I wrote an essay with the guidance of writing professor Gloria Biamonte, about the one point in my career where I truly felt that I had become an artist.

"For the third part of my Plan, I worked with dance professor Dana Holby on a community choreographic project using dancers from Brattleboro, where I was teaching open classes, as well as some of my classmates. It was a tribute to my grandmother who passed away while I was in school.

"When examining these accomplishments, Marlboro gave me the time, the place, and the financial backing to explore ideas and develop leadership qualities while earning my degree. I had to organize my curriculum and the methods by which I would accomplish these goals. My Plan teachers gave me the guidance to fulfill them.

"Dana gave me the opportunity to teach ballet as my work-study position while I was a student and my town connections also strengthened my teaching skills and community-mobilization efforts. I was able to holistically integrate the community of Marlboro and the Brattleboro dance community, and find ways to incorporate these areas into my studies.

"I must say, however, that perfectionism, particularly with writing, caused me to graduate three weeks late. Regrettably, I had to tell my mother that I would not be graduating with my class. She did not understand why. When I finished my booklike thesis and the two-plus hour oral exams in early June, I sent her a copy. She couldn't believe that I wrote so much and so beautifully. She had a sense that Marlboro was no ordinary college. There is so much about the school that I can only glean the surface of what I experienced. But I am definitely a success story and Marlboro was instrumental in helping me expand my own ideas of how I could contribute to society in life after dance.

"I went on to graduate school to pursue an MFA in dance and I am now teaching full-time at a large university. I have taught two theory courses and I have tried to engage the students in a manner that profoundly affected me. Some students appreciated it. Many others think I push them far too hard. They are not used to someone like me.

"Next year I will be teaching as an assistant professor in dance at a small, private and prestigious college in Pennsylvania. They were very familiar with Marlboro College and, in some ways, I think they realized that I would bring the kind of quality that I received in my education to their institution. They are absolutely right."

McDaniel College
Westminster, Maryland

McDaniel, an exceptional college that has been multiplying talents and changing lives for almost a century and a half is, only thirty-one miles from Baltimore, but it was Western Maryland until a name change ended the confusion in 2002. The new name honors William Roberts McDaniel, who over a period of sixty-five years, was a student, professor, administrator, and trustee.

McDaniel was founded in 1867 as a "creative and innovative liberal arts college." In those days the word "radical" would have been more accurate since it was the first coeducational school south of the Mason-Dixon line, and one of the few anywhere open to all, regardless of sex, color, race, religion, or ethnic origin.

Since then it has been creative and innovative enough to become one of the top fifty seedbeds of America's scientists. But before that, its seniors scored higher on the Medical College Aptitude Test than those at four of the Ivy universities.

And in the thirties its football team, coached by botany professor Dick Harlow, displayed creativity, innovation, and other qualities sufficient to beat a lot of the big boys, including the University of Maryland and Boston College. (McDaniel competes in the Division III Centennial Conference, often called "The Ivy League of small colleges.") Professor Harlow himself was distinguished enough to be hired later by Harvard as zoology museum curator and football coach.

The attractive 160-acre campus, just fifty-six miles from Washington, sits atop a prominence overlooking the little town of Westminster, and from the rear lounge area of its stunning new library is one of the loveliest views on any campus, across a central Maryland farm and woodland vista to the Catoctin Mountains, site of the presidential retreat of Camp David. In a half hour, students can be in that area for hiking, picnicking, swimming, or canoeing.

Of the campus's forty buildings that give it a familiar, good college look, the library is the crown jewel, with its stunning architecture and the tranquil charm of its interior spaces. Homey little wedge-shaped enclaves of stacks and reading nooks done in polished dark wood and soft pastel carpeting fan out from an atriumlike staircase. It would be hard to find a more satisfying spot to spend an afternoon or evening. The library's 200,000 volumes are online, which also means the resources of other university and college libraries are available to students and faculty. A major project of restoration and remodeling of six classroom buildings was completed in 1999 with the opening of the new Science Center, the better to continue to develop the college's future scientists whose scores on the Medical College Admission Test put most of the famous schools to shame.

Ninety percent of the faculty of ninety hold the most advanced degrees in their fields; the student-faculty ratio is 12–1 and there are no teaching assistants, but statistics don't reveal either the quality of the teaching or the sense of family enterprise they bring to development of their young friends.

From 1993 to 2004, the college grew from 1,200 to 1,600 students, who come from twenty-three states and nineteen foreign countries. About 60 percent are from Maryland, a percentage that has been steadily dropping as the able Vice President for Admissions and Financial Aid Martha O'Connell spreads the word farther afield. Eighty percent of the students get some form of financial aid: scholarships, grants, loans, or work-study jobs on campus. About 60 percent get need-based awards ranging from $200 to full tuition.

An average of 1,600 part-time graduate students take courses on or off campus in any one semester, most of them in the college's internationally recognized program for training teachers for the deaf. These courses are also open to undergraduates.

This is another college that can boast of taking B and C students and making them success stories. The median SAT scores for freshmen are about 561 verbal and 560 math, which means there are as many scores below these figures as above. And 80 percent of all who apply are accepted.

Here students are involved in the governance of the college as well as in their own education. They hold full voting membership on most policy-making committees, right along with the professors and administrators. There are also three student visitors to the Board of Trustees, and two student representatives on most Trustee committees.

As at many other schools, there is a mix of rural, small town, urban, and cosmopolitan backgrounds, and a student can find his or her own group or a cross section of people to talk to. Fewer than 20 percent of the students belong to fraternities or sororities, which they may join in their sophomore year. Although members have the option of living together in a section of a residence hall designated by the college, the Greek system isn't divisive nor does it dominate the social scene.

Mainly, this is a community of nice, earnest, unassuming, quietly self-assured teenagers who realize they are getting a first-rate education and who regard their teachers as their friends and mentors. As one senior testified, "I took the Graduate Record Exam (chemistry) in December and I knew every question; that's how well prepared I was."

Deans, faculty members, and students agreed with him on the feeling of family, but they all emphasized that it was a family in which expectations were high, the standards firm, and the grading tough. Perhaps one reason for its gold standard in grading is the way the requirement for competence in that crucial area—writing—is enforced. The instructor doesn't do his own grading. Everyone has to pass a composition course by writing an essay on a topic chosen by the instructor, but the essay is then graded by two other professors, allowing for no favoritism.

This kind of atmosphere may be one of the reasons faculty members in political science, economics, chemistry, and English all boasted that their kids get into the best graduate and professional schools because they're "so outstanding." A Stanford professor asked the English prof to send him more graduate students; a political science prof who had taught at Georgetown thinks her students at McDaniel are just as able; and an economics prof said that at Harvard Business School two of his students got higher grades than some Ivy classmates.

Technology has ended lectures and note-taking, at least in biology classes. Professor Esther Iglich said she wanted a class of participants in discussion, not a bunch of stenographers. So she puts her lecture notes on the Web in advance, so students can go over them beforehand. Then they can ask questions and have discussions in class.

The teachers' pride in their students is reciprocated. A senior history major, who had been accepted by Penn State, paid her deposit, and had been assigned a dorm room, decided to make a second visit to McDaniel. A full day there made her realize she'd be in much smaller classes and that she'd been able to talk to her professors and not be just a number.

Four years later, she feels she has several advantages in the competition to get into one of the best Ph.D. programs: Her profs know her well and, as a result, will be able to give persuasive recommendations, and she feels better prepared than if she'd gone to Penn State. "We write a lot and we do oral presentations [not possible with large classes.] Do I know how to solve a problem? Oh yes! The profs try to show that a problem can be solved in more than one way, and that you may not have the whole truth, or that other views may be true. We learned to collaborate. I wouldn't change and my friends wouldn't either." She will tout McDaniel to her own children.

Others echoed what she had to say about learning how to solve problems and added that the four years there had affected their values and had made them more open and aware.

One senior said, "Some of my classes have been so small that the prof said we could take the final exam any day of the week that suited us. There's a lot of trust here."

Another added, "It's very homey here. There's a lot of interplay among freshmen and upperclassmen and it's very valuable. It has helped me grow."

Three chemistry majors all said they had their names on research papers; a sophomore already had her name on three. As one of them said, "There is more opportunity here; we can do research." To have been coauthors of published papers while undergraduates will not only help them get into the best doctoral programs, but will be stars in their crowns later on when they start job hunting.

A communication/writing major who had been sold on the college because "everyone was so nice" has had three internships—at a radio station, at a TV station, and writing a funding proposal for a low-cost housing project—all of which will stand her in good stead when she applies to graduate school.

What they and others were saying was clear: Faculty members were eager to help students to go as much in depth or as far as they wanted; they set no limits. Several students made a particular point of saying that the readiness of faculty members to take time out to talk to them or show them around when they had visited was what really won them over.

As those students have testified, McDaniel is a friendly, democratic place where there truly is a sense of family.

Ten years later, alumni brag about how much McDaniel has done for them, even when as students they resisted. The student testimonials seem even more enthusiastic than on my visits a decade ago. Particularly striking was how many students called McDaniel "my home away from home," in just those words. They often mentioned that faculty members would give out their home phone numbers, or that they felt grateful for profs' advice and guidance in finding themselves. Frequently they said their teachers had become their friends and would invite them home for dinner.

A 1987 graduate, now a top executive in a management consulting firm who has directed major projects in a score of countries, had been one of the objectors. As a sophomore he resisted both doing a study term abroad and taking Spanish. Professor Tom Deveny persuaded him he could have a term in Valencia, Spain at less cost than staying on campus and that he could also graduate on time. "Whatever you do," he added, "stick with a language. Language will be your ticket later in life." Dr. Deveny was right on both counts. The term in Valencia helped him become proficient in Spanish, which gave him a door-opening job. And that started an adventurous career "revolving around facilitating dialogue and problem-solving between people and groups of differing organizations and cultures, including diversity training for rocket scientists." And twenty years later he couldn't thank Dr. Deveny enough.

An alumna in medical school said she was using two of the same textbooks she'd had at McDaniel, and that "I explained a lot of immunology to some of my classmates and I'm the chief dissector in our anatomy group. It is a little scary to cover so much material so fast, although multiple choice is a lot easier than one of Dr. Paquin's essay tests. I'm glad I showed up for classes, studied all the time, and did all those annoying problem sets, projects, papers, etc. You prepared me just as well as my peers who came from Harvard, Cornell, NYU, Columbia, etc."

Two 2003 graduates, Melissa Pingley and John Olsh, said they are "personally advising Alan Greenspan," chairman of the Federal Reserve Board, "Holly on his use of Taylor's rule, and yours truly on his jazz collection." John's first interview question was, "What are the Fed's primary goals and how do they go about achieving them?" He also had to tell how the Fed would increase the money supply. "Upon answering, and thanking McIntyre for teaching Money and Banking, I was then told by the interviewer, 'I think you're the first recent grad who has ever answered that correctly.'" They had not asked Holly the same question. "So now," John added, "the Fed is quite aware of McDaniel's excellence!"

One reason McDaniel produces risk-takers is that it also has taken risks and turned out success stories of its own. In 1999, Marty O'Connell, then dean of admissions, gave a second chance to a rejected applicant whose first choice was the then Western Maryland. She now has a master's in social work from Columbia University. In a thank-you letter to Dean O'Connell she wrote, "The letter of denial was quite distressing but I decided that my determination was far superior to my ability to accept the denial. After reconsidering, you decided to take a chance and accepted me conditionally. I made a promise to myself to demonstrate to you, to Western Maryland [now McDaniel] College, and to myself that I was able to succeed and to be a reminder that chances are worth taking. My determination guided me to pursue my passion for helping others. I graduated cum laude. Beyond my academic achievements, I believe it was the four years I spent, both in and out of the classroom at Western Maryland, that allowed me to learn so many lessons which included the insights to learn about myself and others. Thank you for taking a risk and giving me the chance to make it. I am forever grateful for the chance that you took, and I hope that if posed with another situation similar to mine that you use my story as an example of what can happen when you take the chance."

That is only one of the many ways in which McDaniel produces the risk-takers a democracy needs.

A junior raised on a farm who'd been a ribbon-winning equestrienne was sure she'd been born to be a veterinarian, was the star of the biology department, and had won a research grant, but poetry kept intruding; so did singing. But now, thanks to teachers who helped her find out what it was she really loved, she's an English major, and full of gratitude to McDaniel. A business/economics major spoke for her and many others, saying "McDaniel allows me the undeniable comfort and opportunity to explore all possible ventures."

A rising junior said, "I've only been at McDaniel two years and it's already changed my life. It hasn't changed my views but only strengthened my beliefs in myself. It's corny, but here you are truly someone that matters. We see our president and wave, we smile when we pass each other on the sidewalk en route to class, and I really truly feel like we care about others. I have an amazingly wonderful family in Salisbury but this is still undoubtedly my home."

A social work major said that when a prof heard her complain she hadn't had a home-cooked meal in a month, he invited her home for dinner for a week.

A transfer from a university of 25,000 students said that at McDaniel "everyone was eager to assist me with any of my needs" and it had become her "home away from home." She felt so grateful that she became a tour guide. "I don't try to sell them on the school merely because I like it," she said, "but I highlight all the positive things McDaniel has to offer and that I have benefited from. I know that I am greatly helping, and giving back to the McDaniel community."

A senior said the people, both students and professors, were "the main thing" that was so wonderful and was what had changed her. "I've had a lot of mind-expanding conversations both in and out of class. I meet up with people at parties [and] we're just as apt to open some strange philosophical topic as who's dating whom and other such gossip." (Perhaps that's why she has changed from becoming a music teacher to becoming a writer.)

Another ad for McDaniel that money couldn't buy came from two chemistry majors who had become engaged at McDaniel and went to Yale for Ph.D.s in chemistry. Both had been accepted at several selective colleges but said their experiences and their education had been unparalleled. The young lady said that as a freshman she couldn't have conceived of going to a place like Yale. "I think the most important thing I learned at McDaniel is that I am capable of so much more than I ever thought I was. That is something you cannot learn just anywhere. The students and teachers helped me discover who I really could become."

Once at Yale, she and her fiancé both discovered they were

much better prepared than their classmates. At McDaniel, her fiancé said, "The course work is very comprehensive; rather than teaching about their own area of expertise, professors truly work on expanding their knowledge and ours. It definitely made taking the GRE in chemistry a much easier task." They said that working collaboratively rather than competitively had also been a boon. They had been research collaborators with real professors and already had published papers, whereas the others "had only helped green graduate students, and then only around the edges."

 Ursinus College
Collegeville, Pennsylvania

Ten years ago I wrote that "About thirty miles northwest of Philadelphia is a new star of the first magnitude in the small galaxy of colleges that change lives. It is 130-year-old Ursinus, named for a sixteenth-century German scholar. It is a friendly and unpretentious place of just the right size—1,500 students—on a scenic campus of 160 acres."

A decade later, that star is getting brighter every year, thanks to a visionary president with a strong sense of mission and a committed faculty of scholars who love to work with students.

Today it is the only college in the Middle Atlantic states in a group of twenty nationwide to be cited for exemplary educational practices by an offshoot of the National Survey of Student Engagement. It also has become one of fifty liberal arts colleges whose seniors can apply for Watson Fellowships for a year of creative research. And it is one of the 8 percent of colleges good enough to have a chapter of the prestigious honor society, Phi Beta Kappa.

Many other good things have happened since my visit there in the late nineties. An elaborate $25 million performing arts center opened in 2005 to accommodate the lively and growing interest in theater. Not many colleges can say that four of their drama productions a year are student produced.

The faculty has been increased by 20 percent, which makes possible new majors in dance, theater, art, American studies, and neuroscience, as well as minors in environmental studies and Japanese. Students can also initiate their own majors.

Undergraduate research has always been important at Ursinus and now nearly a fourth of the rising seniors get $2,500 stipends to work directly with faculty members every summer. This again is something not many colleges can say. In addition, grants from the National Science Foundation to get more women and minorities into scientific careers, and from the Howard Hughes Medical Institute help make undergraduate research so widespread that every major in some disciplines is involved.

Now, students not only are encouraged to take foreign study terms, but they have such varied internships as working in the House of Commons and at *Tatler* magazine in London, in the advanced biology lab at Tubingen University in Germany, in a drug rehab institute, and at a bilingual private school in Madrid.

A new housing plan encourages freshmen in the required Common Intellectual Experience (CIE) classes to continue their discussions of the big questions of life by grouping them in living clusters by class groupings.

At Ursinus there are more computers than students. Every student is issued a laptop, and there are over 200 desktop computers and workstations on campus.

Until twenty years ago, reflecting the German religious roots of the area, Ursinus had kept its light under a bushel; recruiting, for example, was a no-no. Now it is casting its net more widely and has students from nearly every state and twenty foreign countries. The minority population is nearly 10 percent and growing. They have their own activity house, which they named Unity, where they put on programs both for the whole school and for the townspeople. Here, everyone belongs.

Ursinus's academic emphasis also changed, from a career-oriented to a pure liberal arts school as the result of the synergy of a faculty and a new president, both making commitments to the liberal arts ideal. The president, John Strassburger, a former Knox dean, and the faculty set out to make Ursinus a life-changing community of learning. And they have succeeded.

The college accepts about three-quarters of its applicants, whose median SAT scores are in the 1,100–1,300 range, and nearly half of whom were in the top tenth of their high school classes. Ninety-two percent of its 139 faculty members have Ph.D.s or terminal degrees. The student-faculty ratio is 12–1, often a bragging statistic elsewhere but an understatement here. It fails to reflect how much the teachers are involved in their students' lives.

This is a place where professors talk proudly about how dramatically their students grow in skills and in self-confidence in four years, how their aspirations rise, and how their perspectives broaden. The startling fact that three-fourths of Ursinus's seniors will be in graduate or professional schools within five years is ample proof. The students for their part see themselves in such a different and brighter light than when they arrived on campus that everyone I asked the question of said they would want their children to come here to have the same kind of experience.

Its center line is a core curriculum, which means everyone has a shared liberal arts foundation, one in which there is much discussion of values. Just as important, every student is actively involved in his or her own education. He or she has to have a capstone experience, such as a senior thesis, and also works on some other independent project.

Almost everyone goes beyond the requirements and does some independent research as well. Many of them present their papers at professional meetings or collaborate with faculty members and become coauthors as undergraduates. The college provides access to a wealth of internships. Nearly half study abroad, and the percentage is growing.

Writing across the curriculum, even in biology and mathematics, is one of the hallmarks of good colleges. Ursinus, however, carries it to a higher level. Every senior has to pass a course in which he writes as a professional in his field would write. "This," said a biology prof, "is the transformation from an amateur to a professional."

The professors are mentors rather than lecturers. Dr. Victor Tortorelli, a Pied Piper who is also chairman of the chemistry department, takes great pride in the fact that the newly remodeled science building, with its state-of-the-art designs pioneered by Allegheny and Kalamazoo, promotes collaborative learning. Here, professors and students do their research not in separate labs and offices, but side by side. They are fellow workers. Such closeness may boost a student's confidence that he too can do what his teacher is doing, and that's what often happens.

As another professor said, "Students come to us as passive recipients and leave as active learners. We transform them!" One of the newer faculty members added, "I've been here four years, so I've seen my first class through, and the change in them is striking."

"How do we transform them?" asked economics professor and faculty coach Dr. Heather O'Neill. "We have high expectations. As seniors, they do as good work as Ivy students."

The students agree. Nearly everyone I talked to said his or her life had been changed, whether by seeing new worlds opened, by having their horizons broadened, or by becoming more tolerant. But more important, nearly everyone spoke of having a solid new confidence in their ability to do things they never before would have thought possible, or even thought of. And it seemed clear that these were not the kind of teenagers who had come to college full of self-assurance.

When I read to a group of junior and senior girls the testimony of a Hiram junior that "many catalytical things have happened to me. These are incredible people, they love to teach; they are always making cross connections from one area or discipline to another, always pushing me to do better . . .," they said that was just what was happening to them. Because the school had opened new worlds to them, everyone in the group was working on a different major than the one she had planned to pursue as a freshman. Many had had no idea when they arrived that they'd be so heavily engaged in their own educations or that they'd have to work so hard. Nor did they have any idea they'd find the work so satisfying or feel so good about themselves.

One of the facts of life that even some of the campus leaders had learned the hard way was that getting involved was the key to the happy experience. Time after time, both black and white students would say something like, "I wasn't happy at first, but then I got involved." The involvement can be almost any kind of activity: an internship, a foreign study term, working on a project with a professor, or starting a new club or team. Whatever it is, students say their instructors are always supportive. And such support often continues for years after graduation.

The interest and pride faculty members take in their students just spills out. A conversation with a group of them turns into a bragging session similar to a group of proud parents, who are so eager to tell what their young charges are doing. Here are a few of the things they wanted the world to know:

- Almost everybody does independent research. In psychology, it's 100 percent.
- We send students to professional conferences to show their work and they come back with ribbons.
- It's a rare biology major who graduates without doing independent research, although we don't require it.
- Our literary magazine illustrates one of our differences. At one college in our conference their glossy job is put out by professionals and carries stuff few students read. Ours is written and produced by students, and students read it. Reading something a fellow student has written is more likely to stimulate an uncertain teenager to think,

"I can do as well as that," than is the polished work of a professional.

- The students are putting on a show of their art work in the Berman Museum this afternoon. You should go see it; it's a good show and it's all theirs.

This kind of atmosphere changes the lives of professors as well as those of students. They get a new value system seeing their young friends doing the sophisticated kind of work they couldn't have done the year, or even semester, before. It becomes their achievement as well, so they keep pushing and suggesting. It is axiomatic that in a caring community, where standards and expectations are high, students will rise to meet them. That is one of the things that makes a distinctive college, where the result is greater than the sum of the parts.

While some new Ph.D.s know that teaching is their real love, it is common at colleges such as Ursinus to hear professors say they'd arrived intending to go on to research universities, but then something happened. They find they're in a kind of academic world that they didn't know existed, a warm and supportive community they'd not known as university graduate students and teaching assistants. They also discover that seeing their students blossom under their care changes their outlooks and their values.

Some see the light for other reasons. One of these was a classics professor who credited the school's increasing diversity for his epiphany. "Here's how it has transformed me: For the first time ever, in my 101 Western Civ class, I have about an even number of black students and white students, and for me that's kind of scary; it makes me aware of my need to teach them the failings of the Western intellectual tradition, how colonialism and oppression can be presented or explained by the Western way of thought. And the other night I went to the Martin Luther King vigil at Unity House. I went there mainly because I was hoping some of my students would be there. I wanted them to know that

I was trying to reach out. I never would have done that a few years ago when we had only a very few minority students."

The attitude of the minority students is reciprocal, so much so in fact that it can make things difficult for an activist. The co-founder of the black awareness organization that operates Unity House was an emphatic young lady, a sophomore planning to become a doctor. She thought her African-American sisters and brothers were "apathetic." She said, "They don't feel like there's a problem. I do." Asked if it wasn't true that everybody got along very well at Ursinus, her activist frustration showed: "That's the point. People are not uncomfortable, but there's a line."

But then she herself started talking much like the others: "The school does listen to students," and in fact its "very personal" atmosphere influenced her decision to come here. Then she went on to concede that she'd pick Ursinus if she had to do it all over again, and that she would "definitely" recommend it to her children.

This girl had come from a small, predominantly black high school. However, the multicultural adviser explained, that was not a big factor in her attitude. She said that coming to a predominantly white college is a culture shock for African-American students, whether they'd gone to mostly white or mostly black high schools. For the first time, she said, they found themselves living with white students around the clock, rather than dealing with them only five or six hours a day at a commuter high school.

An African-American chemistry major, a senior who'd gone to a predominantly white Philadelphia high school and who had already been accepted in a Ph.D. program at Purdue, said, "Ursinus opened my mind." Otherwise, she meant, she wouldn't be going to graduate school, in chemistry or anything else.

Others that I spoke with said Ursinus had made them look at themselves and had opened new areas of interest that had caused them to change majors. Every one said he or she would send their kids to Ursinus. They said such things as: "Faculty relations are excellent!" "Most definitely changed me!" "Definitely want my kids to come here!" "Exposed me to how others think, broadened my horizons, made me see all the options out there." "Ursinus is different and better."

In short, they were saying the same things that students all over the campus were saying. Typical was that of a senior girl who was headed for a Ph.D. program in art history. She said, "I wasn't happy at first, but I realized I had to get involved. I had been concentrating on my studies. I became a house coordinator, I interned in the multicultural house, and I went to Spain as a junior. That term changed my view of myself and it changed my major from international relations to art history. At a big school, I wouldn't have gotten the attention that changed me. All my teachers have been very supportive. I now have the confidence to say I'm qualified to be the leader or get the internship, or to present myself well."

At Ursinus, every prospect pleases the student who wants to do something to improve him- or herself. Summer research programs are plentiful and grants are there for the taking with a good proposal. Internships abound, and a student interested in his subject may work with a professor on a project and wind up seeing his name on a paper or book as coauthor while he or she is still an undergraduate.

A couple of students also had urged me to see the student art show, so I went. The exhibits filled most of the gallery's first floor, one very large and three smaller exhibit rooms. While quite a few of the works were very good, what was impressive was their great number. There simply couldn't be enough art majors in a school of 1,200 to produce that many exhibits. A lot of non-art majors were being exposed to art courses and showing their work. The place was full of interested teachers as well as students, seeing what others had done, enjoying the refreshments, and balloting for the best in the various categories.

Academics and athletics are brought together at Ursinus thanks to the idea of a retired athletic director who had been an academic dean. He had faculty members be coaches-of-the-week for the home games. They would design plays that the coach would use during the game, give pep talks, and be on the sidelines during the game, looking official. The first year, Ursinus won its first league championship, probably with the help of two good pep talks. Since then Ursinus has about broken even between coaches-of-the-week games at home and the away games.

Before the Muhlenberg game the first year, a political science professor wore a tie with the opponent's colors. At the climactic moment, he cut it off, shouting, "We cannot settle for a tie!"

For the final, and decisive, home game, an English professor paraphrased what he called the greatest pep talk in history, Shakespeare's St. Crispin Day speech of *Henry V* before the battle of Agincourt. For the Ursinus team, it was the same kind of event. Here's his version:

> *This day will be called Ursinus Day.*
> *Every year on this day you will strip off*
> *your shirt and show your scars, and say,*
> *"These wounds I got on Ursinus Day."*
> *You will grow old and forgetful, but*
> *even when your hair is all gray*
> *You will not forget the names of this day:*
> *Gilbers the coach, Rhodenbaugh, Barrera,*
> *Orlando, Oliver, Faso and Floyd,*
> *Hagenberg, Parks, and all the rest—*
> *You will teach your sons these names*
> *And every day on Ursinus Day*
> *You will raise a toast and say,*
> *"We few, we happy few, we band of brothers."*
> *And whoever hears you will be jealous*
> *And hold their own lives a little cheaper*
> *Because they were not happy here today*
> *They were not here on Ursinus Day.*

Ursinus won, 14–0.

Ursinus is an exceptional place, a community of learning, a family where the young have their aspirations raised, their minds stretched, their powers increased, and their lives changed.

Professional football teams may sometimes look to prayer to win games, but Ursinus, as befits a first class liberal arts college, has found that its more intellectual, albeit more secular, approach is very effective. In two seasons, the home game win/lose record was 10–5, while the away game record was 5–9.

At Ursinus, teaching is not only an act of love, it is a kind of surrogate parenthood that continues long after the college years. As good parents they challenge, encourage and develop good and confident thinkers who will cope in a new world.

Ten years later, Ursinus gets the same rave reviews from its students that it got ten years ago. To make the point, here is what a junior from New Jersey had to say, and a rising senior from Pennsylvania.

"Ursinus has given me the opportunity to pursue my academic and extracurricular interests. I came to UC premed, expecting to be challenged, but I had no idea how much I would work. To be premed here, you have to really want to have it, because it takes a lot of time and effort. It's an exercise in multitasking. The teachers really want you to succeed. At UC you're a whole person, not just a number. They encourage you to pursue your interests. With teachers from different disciplines teaching CIE, I had the chance to take a professor I normally wouldn't have. She was one of the best teachers I've ever had, and I consider her my friend.

"Although I spend a lot of time doing schoolwork, I do have a social life. Ursinus has a club for every interest, and it's really easy to get involved. There is something to do most nights of the week, whether you drink or not. I don't want to leave Ursinus for breaks; it's become my home."

"I just cannot say enough about Ursinus. From the moment I

stepped onto the campus, I have felt at home. As a nerve-ridden senior in high school, Ursinus made me feel that my accomplishments in high school were worthwhile and that I was well prepared to face the challenges that college would bring. From my interview and tour here that day, until the present, I have felt that I can contribute to Ursinus's campus, and that my contributions are unique and my existence here means something.

"At Ursinus I have known the struggles of changing a major as well as redetermining a future career path. Throughout my insecurities and struggles, Ursinus has supported me academically, socially, and otherwise. The close-knit community has fostered my relationships with faculty members turned mentors. I have been able to build relationships with career-services faculty who have helped me remap my future plans, deans who have supported me as a resident assistant and student, and even the president of the college.

"How many college students can say that they have had numerous conversations with the president of the college? And [that] he knows them by first name? Not many I'm sure, but at Ursinus, holding conversations with the president, the dean, or a highly esteemed faculty member is part of every day. We are lucky here, as students, as faculty, as a family, working together to support one another day in and day out."

SOUTH

Agnes Scott College

Decatur, Georgia

Agnes Scott is one of the best colleges around. It is a women's college that has all the advantages of a coed one, and, the women there say, a lot more besides.

First, there are thousands of attentive young men at seven heavily male institutions nearby, eager for dates. One junior said every girl can have a good social life if she wants it.

Second, in the classroom it is women who lead the discussions. No one has to defer to some tedious male rambling on.

The young women here say we have the best of both worlds. What's more, they graduate with a confidence and power to manage their own lives that few colleges bestow. The proof is that hardly more than a dozen of all the colleges and universities can match Agnes Scott's track record in producing future scientists, scholars, and other kinds of achievers.

In the new millennium, this 115-year-old college is near its expansion goal of 1,200, but even with 200 more students it will be getting more selective as the number of college-goers continues to grow. But it hopes to remain inclusive. A dozen new faculty members have been added, making the student-faculty ratio 9–1.

And 100 percent of the tenured faculty have Ph.D.s or terminal degrees.

The campus has several new and expanded facilities. The largest is the dramatic new $35 million science building, and every student, regardless of major, is encouraged to do research with a faculty member. There is also a new campus center for student gatherings that has a computer lab as well as such usual things as café, bookstore, and post office. The library has been doubled in size and the observatory has been expanded to include a planetarium. Agnes Scott is the only private college in the state to offer a degree in astrophysics.

Three-fourths of the applicants are accepted. A little over half are from the top tenth of their high school classes and the middle range of SAT scores is 1,100–1,290.

It is a diverse student body. Nearly 20 percent are African American, and it is one community; at lunchtime in the cafeteria it's a salt and pepper scene; I don't remember seeing all black or all white tables. Furthermore, students told me, it is one family. The black students put on a Christmas production that includes white students. There is no need, one girl said, to go to predominantly black Spelman College. "I know who I am here."

Most students come from the South or Southwest, about 9 percent are international, 5 percent are Asians, and 3 percent are Hispanic. A visitor, however, wouldn't think of this as a Southern school. Instead, the words most likely to spring to mind would be cosmopolitan, warm, and diverse.

Financial aid is another area where Agnes Scott shines. Nearly two-thirds of the students get need-based aid, and because it is well endowed, it is one of the few schools that meets 100 percent of every applicant's need. The average aid package [in 2005] was $21,500. In addition there were nearly 40 merit scholarships that averaged $9,000.

Downtown Atlanta is a convenient, ten-minute subway ride away, and it is a major metropolitan center with rich cultural, financial, and scientific resources. That's not strong enough; they're tremendous. They include the famous art museum designed by the English architect John Portman. All major corporations have Atlanta offices. The Atlanta Federal Reserve Bank offers both wonderful internships and future job opportunities.

Biology students are especially lucky, since the nation's Centers for Disease Control offers unmatched opportunities for internships with scientists working on the nation's major health problems. The biology faculty has students taking advantage of this great opportunity every semester. A biology professor said, "Over half of the biology students are doing research, and the Centers for Disease Control is our Federal Reserve."

The first knot of students I encountered on campus set the tone for my visit. They were a half dozen African Americans chatting outside a building between classes. And even though it was just before finals their mood was relaxed and happy. Two seniors all set for graduate school had special reason to be, but the sophomores and juniors who were still far from jobs or graduate school were just as confident. "The personal relationships here are great," said one, mirroring what a professor said later in the day: "We are ambitious for our students. We take a lot of risks for them." That was typical. Students and teachers were both saying "I love you."

The incentive for a shy or uncertain girl to be herself and to do things starts in the classroom. If she would like to make a point, she doesn't have to "defer to some guy." Furthermore, the classes are very small—seminar size—and they tend to be discussion, and she can lead the discussion.

But when males are wanted, there are plenty calling for dates from Emory, Georgia Tech, Georgia State, and half a dozen others in the city. To a vigorous nodding of heads and assenting words, a junior said: "Put this in your book: Agnes Scott is a great choice for a woman who wants to have a social life because it is in Atlanta, and there are so many boys. There's a balance between academic and social life. Any girl who complains she's not having a good social life is not making it happen, because she can totally take that in her own hands."

With equal force, she said, "It's so wonderful, going to class and not worrying about what you're saying or what you're wearing. In a coed school I've never heard a girl leading a discussion, never!" She also had visited all the selective New England women's colleges before choosing Agnes Scott.

Her enthusiasm reflected a pride that reminded me of the way the men at Wabash, the nonpareil men's college in Indiana, talk about their school. Furthermore, it was often the chance, unplanned visit that had altered their views of what they wanted in a college and sold them on Agnes Scott. Five of the girls I talked to had come to Atlanta intending to apply to Emory, but fell in love with this campus where, unlike Emory, everyone was warm and friendly and where the sense of community, missing at Emory, was palpable.

Several girls were eager to testify that it was neither Southern nor typically women's. The first, from Jacksonville, Florida, who had applied to fifteen schools, including Emory, said: "At the other schools I found the girls flaky and aloof. Not so here. This is a totally different set of girls. You have real conversations, and people are a lot more open-minded here. There are more diverse backgrounds here. I applied to Ivy schools but I thought the opportunities were better here. You get more help here. There are excellent internships and foreign study programs. It is more participatory here."

A friend added: "Tell girls that here, girls are not like my image of a girl's school. I became more open. It's not stuffy here, as it is at Emory."

The next one said, "Agnes Scott definitely affects values. After I came here I was appalled and wondered how I ever could have been so closed-minded. How could I live eighteen years and not see other points of view? Here you have to argue the other side; you have to be open and evaluate the other side so you can argue persuasively. You find there's no black and white—the whole world's gray."

Most eloquent was a junior, a hard-sell advocate for women's colleges. "It's so intellectually alive here! It's not like high school where we were fighting over boys. We have Atlanta with all its attractions and Emory and Georgia Tech. It's a great choice for girls who want a social life! Women's colleges have so much to offer it's not even funny. I think women can get a better education there. Coed colleges can't educate women in the environment they need the way women's colleges can. They can thrive better in a women's college environment."

Like some of the others who had shopped the women's colleges, she didn't find any like Agnes Scott. "At Smith the professors were trying to draw out these women and none of them would talk, and I know these women were intelligent. Then I came to Agnes Scott and everyone was talking. I even came to a biology class and everyone was talking. The women at Agnes Scott seemed so much more intellectually alive than the women at Smith.

"I was just so amazed by that. Also, everybody smiled at me and smiled at each other and they smiled at my parents and I was so embarrassed to have my parents along. So I found that this intellectual community was also very friendly. "I'm totally for women's colleges and I'm going to force my daughters to go to women's colleges!"

After saying, "I don't want to follow that act," a girl from Virginia for whom Agnes Scott had not been her first choice, said she was happy she'd landed there because, "it is not stuffy but happy, and there's no reason why you shouldn't do your best; the professors want to help you." To this another noted that even though it's next to a big city there is such a sense of community that "I have professors call if I miss a class. They will not let you fail here!"

Another who'd been a shopper said she'd found no school as alive or the students as involved. She agreed that on no other campus were the kids so warm or open, but Agnes Scott had special advantages. The Honor System was very important to her, and besides, "What more can you ask than Atlanta, or the Kaufman program for Women Entrepreneurs?"

A girl who had been nodding at all this wanted to be sure I appreciated the Agnes Scott difference: "My boyfriend is at Harvard and he was telling me how happy he was that he even had a chance to talk to one of his profs." She was in a different world, one where professors share students' hopes and inspire new ones. They also start them on the way to realizing them. For example: "The economics department tells freshmen that [the] field needs women and is rich with promise. So a professor said, "We have nine majors in graduate school from a college of 800 [in 1998]. Why so many? Because we're able to talk to them early. We have five interns in the Federal Reserve Bank in Atlanta, and a music major is one of them. Here, women become leaders." Here are some of the reasons:

- An Atlanta Semester program that its director says is the only one of its kind is designed to start women on the road to leadership roles in business and in society. It combines internships in city-betterment activities with academic work.
- Women here have the feeling that they have the power to choose the option they want for their lives. They are told, "You are the author of that story." And they are achievers.
- We talk about values a lot; we come out of a faith tradition. We try to get students to think beyond themselves, to be of service to the community.
- The Honor System is the cornerstone of life at Agnes Scott." The Honor System is run by students; exams are not proctored, and it just goes without saying that each one will live up to the compact with conscience that everyone put their names to as freshmen. The document is framed and hangs in a broad stair landing, along with those of three other classes. Like Martin Luther's ninety-five theses of conscience tacked to a church door, it is a public statement reflecting the high expectations of each member of this family.

- Collaborative learning is encouraged with two centers: one for writing and speaking and the other for math support and learning. Both have student tutors, which benefits everybody, because there's no better way to learn something than to teach it.

The curriculum has requirements that ensure exposure to the elements of a liberal education, but there is much flexibility. Everyone must take freshman composition and be exposed to the sciences, humanities, and language. A year-long "global experience" in the sophomore year expands horizons and enforces at least a rudimentary working knowledge of the language of the country they'll be studying and visiting that year.

When they come back, there are internships and research opportunities to fit every interest, as well as independent study projects that are expected in most departments. After hours, they can use the school's expanded physical activities building that was state-of-the-art in the late nineties. Or they may try out for one of the seven intercollegiate teams: basketball, cross-country, soccer, swimming, softball, tennis, and volleyball.

The college has something more important than a formal program for those with learning disabilities. The faculty provides a full measure of tender loving care, and anyone with a learning problem can take risks and get full support. Students with learning problems are welcomed, and they prosper. Agnes Scott is a hospitable place for them. For those with physical disabilities, the college has gone to great lengths to make its facilities accessible and to make life there pleasant and convenient.

For many years, decades in fact, I had known from all the published indicators of quality that Agnes Scott had few peers in developing women who helped make this a better society, but only seeing this community in action can impart the full force of its happy élan and its sense of mission.

· · ·

Ten years later, seniors and both recent and older alumna are grateful to Agnes Scott for having "helped me find my voice" by going to a women's college. One went beyond that to praise the "fun and active" social life, much better than she'd had in high school, thanks in her case to Georgia Tech.

A 2004 graduate spoke for many when she said, "I have become much more aware of the changes I can make in my life and others, and the importance of women in higher positions in the workforce and politics. Through the challenges at ASC in and out of the classroom, I want to go into higher-education administration. I want to touch the lives of many others."

Several talked of the support they got in becoming self-confident enough to become the persons they had wanted to be, or to accomplish anything they set out to do. A 1977 graduate said her experience had taught her how to think, analyze, and draw her own conclusions, adding, "This has helped me in all areas of my life and my career, from raising a family and contributing in my community to providing leadership in my company."

A junior called the support of the Agnes Scott community "amazing" because it gave her the confidence to study in another country. "If I could succeed here I could do the same thing anywhere. I now realize my friends and colleagues here are more than just people to have fun with, they are a vital support group. Not one of us could make it alone, and that is what has changed my life."

Many of them had warm words for their "great" professors who had pushed them but cared for them and helped them discover themselves. One sophomore added, "The professors have transformed me into a confident student with a thirst for knowledge. They not only encourage you to learn the material, they also help you own that knowledge. The diversity at Agnes Scott is also amazing; it has helped me open my eyes and broaden my perspective, and it has an amazingly beautiful campus."

The mother of a seventeen-year-old starting her college search said she hoped her daughter would have an experience "as rich in learning and friendships and growth as mine was." She said, as did others, that Agnes Scott had stretched her, opened her eyes to the world at large, and that the professors were "wonderful and accessible."

A 1989 alumna said the faculty "are truly there for the students, not just their own research goals as I experienced in graduate school." She credited the "special attention" she got from other teachers for starting her on the course to graduate work in Information Systems and a successful career in the computer industry. After her fifteen-year reunion she said she was "constantly amazed at the accomplishments of my classmates. All are truly amazing women committed to a life of continual learning." And ASC, "seems to be unique in the bonds it creates among its alumnae."

A freshman from a low-income family, and the first in her family to go to college, said she needed a school "that would be supportive while pushing me to achieve. I have found that at Agnes Scott. I am involved in many campus activities despite the heavy course workload and I have already found leadership positions in my first year. I feel I have made a difference on campus. Agnes Scott has influenced me to be a stronger individual and to dedicate myself to the causes that matter in my life."

 # Birmingham-Southern College
Birmingham, Alabama

Birmingham-Southern College has had a remarkable rebirth in the last few decades, from a struggling college to an educational treasure that changes young lives for the better. It is a learning community that challenges and broadens its students and imbues its graduates with confidence, values, and a need to serve. In return, its devoted graduates think there's no college like it, and they have good reason to think so.

Emerson said an institution is the lengthened shadow of one

man. In this case, "shadow" is the wrong word; it should be something bright, like "glow," and the man is Neal Berte, whose sense of mission and whose vision literally remade the college in his twenty-eight-year tenure. He retired in 2004, and Daniel Pollick, the able president of Lebanon Valley College in Pennsylvania, was picked as one who would carry on the mission.

The city in which the college is located has had an equally dramatic renaissance, metamorphosing from "the Pittsburgh of the South" to being named by the U.S. Conference of Mayors "the most livable city in the country."

Among the many new buildings on this now-beautiful campus is an extensive $25 million state-of-the-art science center. Among other things, it will enhance teacher-student collaboration, interdisciplinary connections, and undergraduate research. The old science building has been extensively renovated to accommodate the Division of Humanities.

To give the men what the women already had, a residence hall has been converted into attractive three- and four-bedroom suites.

Other additions are a large fitness-and-recreation complex with a pool and other facilities to meet any need, and a comprehensive student center that includes a theater, a ballroom, a computer lab, and various lounges in addition to the usual bookstore, mail room, and food court.

Sixty-three percent of BSC seniors go on to graduate school, and it is number one in Alabama in the number of students accepted into medical, dental, and law schools. BSC also has notable academic laurels in sports. It is an NCAA Division 1 school where 81 percent of its athletes graduate, and more than 60 percent have B averages.

One of the outstanding things about the college is its social concerns, which put those of most colleges to shame. The aim of a required core course is to produce citizens who will be the leaders working for the public good, whether locally or nationally. It is an interdisciplinary course in which a literature professor might give the literary background to issues in the news, a political scientist might discuss elite behavior, a mathematician might comment on decision making, or a black judge might give a section on civil rights. In addition, every student has a term of hands-on experience in some local organization. This was one of President Berte's ideas for which the Luce Foundation awarded the college a $175,000 chunk of seed money in the nineties.

Outside of class, over 70 percent of the students are involved in one of the college's several community services in Birmingham or in any number of places abroad. The service experiences generate such comments as "I learned I could make a difference," or, "it forces open the doors of the world so that you can no longer ignore what's going on out there as someone else's problem." A 2004 graduate said, "the Service Learning Department opened my mind and more importantly my heart . . ."

The college's Foundations plan for general education has expanded the liberal arts idea to give students the skills they'll need in a new technological society. It stresses cross-disciplinary study and the connections of theory and application. Learning is collaborative, not competitive; students work in teams on a problem. They also live by an honor code, although with collaborative learning there is hardly need for one.

Learning also has a mind-blowing dimension in foreign study terms that both students and alums cite as high points of their college experience.

The Academic Resource Center has become much more than a place to help with writing or study skills. It provides training, tutoring, and help in a wide range of things: critical thinking, technology, foreign languages, data analysis, and library research; in fact, almost any problem a student or a staff member might have.

The college also can boast it is one of only six liberal arts colleges with a Phi Beta Kappa chapter and internationally accredited undergraduate and graduate business programs.

It is a warm and friendly place with a strong sense of community and one of increasing diversity. Ten percent of the students are African Americans, 3 percent are Asians, and 2 percent are international students. Everyone is helpful, starting with the post office. An alumna said that as a freshman she had lamented one day not getting any personal mail. Next day she found a hand-written note in her box saying, "In case you did not get any mail today, here is a note. Love, the BSC post office." She added: "That's when I knew I'd chosen the right college."

An African-American freshman who said her mother had made her attend this college of 1,800 mostly middle-class, middle-of-the-road, and motivated white teenagers said she'd been converted by the way both students and faculty reached out to make her feel she belonged. Now, she said, "I really like it." No longer did she want to hide safely away in the huge University of Alabama.

Her affection for her school was echoed by students from Croatia, Korea, China, and many towns big and small in this country. And the college's high retention figures are eloquent confirmation: 92 percent of the freshmen return for the sophomore year, and three-quarters of an entering class graduated in four years, percentages that put it in the top 10 percent of private colleges and far above any public institutions except the University of Virginia and Berkeley.

Most of the students come from the south, 60 percent from Alabama alone, but the admissions staff has been actively recruiting in other parts of the country, particularly in the Midwest and Southwest.

Birmingham-Southern accepts nearly three-fourths of its applicants, and for nearly half of them, the school is their first choice, which tends to mean that morale is high; students don't feel they're rejects or that theirs is a fallback choice.

The mean SAT scores are in the low 500s verbal for both men and women and in the middle 500s for math for men. Twenty-three percent score over 600 on the verbal and 34 percent score over 600 on the math. Nearly 40 percent were in the top tenth of their high school classes.

What all this means—and people take colleges' SAT averages and class ranks far too seriously—is that anyone with a B record in a solid program, and a lot of those with lesser records, will be welcome, but they had better be serious about planning to work, and have some evidence to back it up. As the director of financial aid said, "We're looking for potential for success, and we want to make it possible to come here."

The faculty, many of whom have taught at major universities, say that relations with students are close and that they get a lot of pleasure "when you see a kid from a small town in Alabama open up." They also say that students are willing to share their personal problems with their teachers. All this helps explain why they say Birmingham-Southern has an impact on its students. A lot of faculty members believe it enough to send their own children here.

A history professor said so many alumni are eager to find spots for interns, to help in the job hunt for graduates, or to otherwise help their alma mater that "we can't find work for all of them." A sociologist who had taught at the University of Georgia said, "Alumni treasure their experience here, and for the right reasons—not football weekends—but for academic as well as personal growth. That certainly was not the case at Georgia."

A political science prof who had taught at the University of Florida put his finger on a central difference between Birmingham-Southern and the university when he said, "There is a great difference in teaching at public and private schools. There you identify the school with football and partying; academics are secondary. Students go to class almost as observers. You can do that in a class of 200; you can't here." His burgeoning Latin-American Studies program sends 100 students to Latin-American countries every year; it sponsored a faculty colloquium on the North American Free Trade Agreement, and it awards travel grants to the best proposals for foreign study projects.

A music professor said, "Most of the professors from other schools I know are jealous of our students; they win most of the scholarships in competitions." He then produced a list of nearly fifty who had major scholarships or fellowships in this country and abroad, who held important jobs, had roles on Broadway, or were members of major opera companies.

Nearly every conversation I had with students elicited some

comment about what a close-knit community it was. A sopho-more girl struck a common chord when she said, "When I visited here I was really impressed. The students here are really accept-ing. They tell you the same things the admissions people do."

A couple of fellows on athletic scholarships were as emphatic as a religion and philosophy major had been that this college had made them question and think through their attitudes and values. As one of them said, "I think this school builds character. Stu-dents live by the honor code. We are challenged to think so that we don't just accept."

Some who had been accepted at Vanderbilt, Duke, Rice, Emory, and elsewhere, and the Croatian girl who had considered a score of other schools, all said the high standards, the sense of family, and the close relationships of students and teachers had won them over.

What all of this says is that Birmingham-Southern is a high-quality, caring place where a person from any part of the country would not only be comfortable but would grow intellectually, morally, and personally. That is not to say that the activist who marches to his own drummer at a place like Antioch should come here expecting to turn it upside down. Nor will the big-football-weekend addict be fulfilled. But the community here will accept and tolerate both. And if they stay long enough it will do them a lot of good.

Ten years later, BSC students and alum could hardly be more en-thusiastic about their alma mater, or more grateful. It is an ongo-ing love affair, as their superlatives reveal. Here are some of them:

- After two years at a big name university, I realized what a wonderful education I was getting at BSC, how much more challenging, and how devoted the professors were to their students. The college's emphasis on service was infectious. Then at law school a professor told me he was so impressed with the BSC students he'd had, he wanted his own daughter to go there.

- My experience at Southern revolutionized my view of myself and the world around me. I am a better neighbor, employee, citizen, and friend because of BSC.

- I only recall my time there with wonderful tenderness. It changed my life forever.

- By graduation time I knew I had to be involved in community action instead of moving to Florida and singing jazz.

- At BSC everyone encourages you to dream so big, and then tries to find ways to make sure those dreams become a reality.

- I was a National Merit Finalist. There are few things in life I'm as grateful for as my experience at BSC. I miss it terribly. The English faculty contains some of the smartest, coolest, most wonderful professors to ever exist. Not only were they amazing instructors, they also became my friends.

- I can't imagine where I'd be right now if I hadn't been guided by my professors. Somehow they could see that my future involved not science, but music and the arts when I was determined not to.

Centre College
Danville, Kentucky

If one were to put activist Antioch at one end of the spectrum of high-quality colleges, and life-of-the-mind St. John's with its Great Books and no-electives curriculum at the other, Centre would probably find its name appropriate to its position.

Centre students are bright, wholesome, polite, friendly and

personable, eager to do well, and serious about what life holds for them. Intellectually curious, they take many courses outside of their majors, but they are neither future philosophers or college professors nor Antiochian risk-takers or revolutionaries. For the most part, they might be called the intelligent, responsible (and very engaging) center.

But by 2005 it was a sophisticated Centre with a new global view. Eighty percent of the student body had had at least one term overseas and the college was "guaranteeing" it at no extra cost, as well as an internship, and graduation in four years, or another year tuition free.

Faculty say "the kids come back transformed." So do the kids. They call the foreign study terms the best experiences of their lives. This is one of many reasons alumni giving has been more than 66 percent in most of the last twenty years. It is number one in the nation.

It would be hard to have malcontents in a community so familial that it makes students "sad" to think of leaving and alums "grieve" that they can't come back.

It would be hard to incite rebellion in such a familial community. They never had it so good. A caring faculty does so much hand-holding, students feel (as they do at Antioch) that they own the place. Class sizes average a clubby and conversational sixteen; each faculty member teaches seven courses and has a heavy responsibility for his advisees as well.

If a student misses two classes in a row, the instructor will call to see if anything's wrong and alert his adviser. Professor Milton Reigelman said, "We're so small, a problem can't fall between the chairs." (After much faculty agonizing the college recently decided to increase the enrollment from its traditional 900 to 1,070).

Walking around its beautiful campus, whose majestic trees look like they have been there since the college was founded in 1819, one would imagine a community twice that size. At one end of its architectural spectrum are historic landmark gems from the

1800s. At the other, more modern, end is a lovely structure that Centre claims is the finest arts center in the nation for a college its size; indeed, a university would be proud to have it. It was designed by The Taliesin Associated Architects, the firm of Frank Lloyd Wright's students.

This impressive center gives the historic and charming town of Danville considerable cultural bragging rights. Each year some of the most acclaimed dancers, singers, orchestras, popular musicians, soloists, choral groups, and half a dozen of the best Broadway musicals perform in it. They have included Rudolf Nureyev, Mikhail Baryshnikov, the Bolshoi Ballet, Ella Fitzgerald, Ray Charles, the Philadelphia Orchestra, the Beach Boys, Art Garfunkel, Roberta Flack, The Four Tops, and many others.

Centre can also claim distinction in the high number of the faculty's and administration's children who choose Centre, despite the liability of having a parent around. And some come back—often against parental advice—after having tried a distant or more famous place.

Centre's seniors, if they have good records, can be sure of getting into the best graduate or professional schools. Some years 100 percent of their medical school applicants have been accepted. That also goes for getting jobs. Even during the recession of the early nineties, 96 percent of its graduates had jobs or were in graduate or professional schools within six months.

Another plus for Centre is that the number of freshmen majoring in science has climbed to 50 percent, thanks to a state-of-the-art science building. That percentage includes a growing number of women, which indicates a climate that draws women into careers where they've often been shunned or were afraid to enter.

Centre's enviable retention record also testifies to its quality and character. Even though, unlike the Ivies, hordes of high school seniors aren't pushing and shoving to get in, 90 percent of its freshmen return for the sophomore year and more than 75 percent graduate in four years. And Centre accepts 75 percent of its applicants.

Half of the acceptees were in the top 10 percent of their high school classes, and that figure includes all kinds and sizes of high schools. The middle 50 percent of the class has SAT scores ranging from 560 to 680 verbal and 530 to 650 math, and ACT scores ranging from 25 to 30. This means the other 50 percent had scores above or below those ranges.

Financially, the school is a bargain, costing several thousand dollars less than quality colleges in the North. Over 60 percent of the students receive need-based aid, and the average aid package for 2005 was about $17,000. If the scholarships awarded on merit are added, the percentage receiving aid rises to 90 percent.

Its faculty—as can be said of the other colleges in this book—is earnestly committed to and excels at the art of teaching. It is obvious that they like the kids they're teaching and enjoy working with them. Moreover, not only is there an unusual sense of community and mutual regard among the faculty, but between the faculty and the administration as well, which is a rarity. Profs who've been at the most famous universities said they've never experienced the kind of collegiality they enjoy at Centre.

No university faculty compares with Centre's in the impact it has on the growth of young minds and personalities. Ninety-seven percent of Centre's teachers hold Ph.D.s or terminal degrees earned at the best institutions, and they are active scholars. They not only publish, they draw students into their research as coauthors and often take them to professional meetings.

Centre holds another mark of distinction as the place that runs the Governor's Scholars Program. This is a state-financed program in which gifted Kentucky high school students are brought to the campus for special summer courses.

The faculty, in its diversity of origin, is more representative of the United States than is the student body, which is two-thirds Kentuckians, although thirty-three states and twelve foreign countries are represented. The college is embarked on a recruiting campaign to increase the percentage of students from other parts of the country, as well as its 8 percent minority students.

The faculty, one professor said, is also more liberal than the students, whom a sociology prof described as "the corporate class of Kentucky." He called the college "the ruling-class college of Kentucky. We have no competition [from state colleges]. For a Kentucky teenager the choice is a prestige college or Centre. And if they pick a prestige college they often come back here after a year or two.

"The dominant culture" at Centre, he said, "is working together to do what is expected. It is not an intellectual student body. We in sociology draw our majors from the oddballs; the students are 60 percent Greek [fraternity and sorority members]." He was one of those who was struck by the faculty attitudes: "The faculty politics here are the best I know of, [in terms of] the collegiality," and he'd been at Swarthmore and at Yale.

Like others, he remarked that change is in the air, and is changing the students. Besides increasing the size of the student body and seeking greater diversity, its program improves on the traditional core curriculum idea of a shared intellectual experience. It is designed to develop in students the ability to imagine and create, to think and reason analytically, to solve problems, to integrate and synthesize complex information, to use language clearly and persuasively, and to make responsible choices. To achieve these goals, students are exposed to aesthetic, scientific, technological courses and perhaps one in math; three in social sciences, one cross-cultural, two in fundamental questions; one in Integrative Studies. There are also foreign-language and English-composition competency requirements, and there is much emphasis on writing throughout the four years.

The Fundamental Questions courses are interdisciplinary and team-taught. One course, for example, Civil Rights in America, involves political science, history, economics, and theology, and might be taught by profs from two or even three of those disciplines. A course titled Business, Society, and Ethics uses case studies to examine the scores of values and competing concerns, in addition to profits, in the modern corporation, such as environmental issues, employee rights, employer responsibilities, consumer protection, working conditions, and so on.

Another force for change is foreign studies. Several professors said this was making a great contribution and that students returned with a broader vision in addition to a new sophistication.

A breezy, live-wire emeritus economics professor, an Oklahoman, and a Harvard Ph.D., who previously taught at Harvard and at Middlebury, had, as might be expected, a much different slant than the sociologist. He preferred the Centre students to those he'd had elsewhere. And he thought change had already taken place in student attitudes and outlooks. He said, "I'm an entrepreneur and the kids from this background are winners; they're gonna hustle more than the Ivies. I'd bet on one of these before I'd bet on one of the Ivies. The profs here are more liberal than they, and the Integrative Studies Program has had an effect on them. I know personally I've had an impact."

An economist who had taught at Duke, considered Duke's and Centre's students "comparable, very similar in quality, and very motivated to learn; [with a] zest for knowledge." He was impressed that a large number want to go on to graduate school, and he thought Centre had a real impact on its students, especially in learning how to learn.

A classics prof who had taught at the universities of North Carolina, Florida, and Texas agreed, but said Centre's students don't represent the extremes at the big institutions. "These are really outstanding students; they are outgoing, polite, and not very adventurous. The school has an impact; particularly now that we have a foreign program, the kids come back wonderfully changed. Also, the undergraduate research in which students coauthor papers and get to go to professional meetings is a wonderful thing."

A philosophy prof, a former Jesuit priest who had taught at Notre Dame as well as at Texas, drew a double parallel: Centre's and Notre Dame's students are not only similar in ability but in sophistication; neither group is urban or streetwise. He also noted a major change in the student body; students are less interested in fraternities and sororities, and the tempo of scholarly activity has greatly increased.

"The faculty is much more representative of the United States than it was, and the level of decency and collegiality is extraordinary, not only among the faculty, but between the faculty and the administration as well," he declared. "Our students are wholesome and intelligent; what we are pushing for now is diversity. This is a wonderfully nurturing place with a lot of writing."

The students reciprocate. Every one I talked to would make the same choice over again, even a senior history major from Richmond, Virginia, headed for graduate school, who said at first he wasn't "gung-ho" about it because Danville didn't offer such metropolitan divertissements as opera or ballet. He had tried Washington and Lee University, "despised it," then East Tennessee State: same verdict. He came to Centre "by accident" and stayed. Centre, he said, "is vastly superior to W&L educationally; it reinforces your values and helps you think things through and arrive at good and valid conclusions." Another said, "It has opened my eyes and is changing my way of thinking and is teaching me to trust my own judgment."

A senior from New Orleans added that the atmosphere was warm and friendly, but that the social scene was changing because of "administrative interference" in students' social events.

Every student I talked to said that while the majority were in fraternities and sororities, that wasn't essential to a good social life or to being a big woman or man on campus. There was total agreement also that anyone who came back to visit after five years would have dinner or spend the night at any one of several faculty member's homes. In my random sampling not one said he or she would make another choice or fail to tout Centre to their own kids.

A young woman disputed faculty descriptions of Centre students as not being venturesome. She pointed out that in off-campus programs in which she'd been involved with students from prestigious institutions, she had always been impressed by Centre students' comparative intellectual curiosity and venturesomeness because they took so many courses outside of their majors. In fact she considered Centre unique for this reason, and she wondered if the Ivy-type students weren't scaredy-cats protecting their grade point averages because their eyes were on law, medicine, or business school.

The level of satisfaction among the students, faculty, and administrators is high at Centre. They like their lovely surroundings, their teachers, their colleagues, and the civility of their community. And as this young woman implied, they are happy that the new Centre is helping them become something better and beyond "the corporate class of Kentucky" to pioneers in a new world.

Ten years later, Centre seniors and alums are even more enthusiastic, if that's possible. They think Centre is without peer, that they couldn't have had the same opportunities, or challenges, elsewhere, and they want their children to have the same. They talk about how much the professors still mean to them, how "intense and challenging" Centre had been. Two who had been top high school students had been shocked to get their papers back with Bs and Cs instead of As. They told how it has made them more critical and analytical thinkers and better persons. Most of them talked about how happy they'd been in their foreign-study terms and how their eyes had been opened to a whole new world and broadened their outlook.

A 1994 grad attributed her success in helping bring a Ukrainian company into the market economy to her professors' always teaching her "to go for it."

A 2001 graduate said, "Centre gave me so many opportunities; the relationships are nothing short of extended family. It was such an important and defining moment in my life, and parts of me want to return so bad it hurts."

A senior called the faculty "second to none," saying that because they challenged him to think, his political and religious views are much different. However, they did not impose their views, but had him support his. "I've spent four years in the most intense, fulfilling environment possible." Furthermore, during an internship at the U.S. Department of Labor, his work was as good or better than that of Ivy Leaguers because some of his memos went straight to the secretary.

Pretty much the same story was told by an alum working on his Ph.D. who said he had an advantage over university graduates because of Centre's "exceptionally rigorous" training.

Some other typical comments were:

- Centre demands you remain focused on the life ahead.
- Talking about tough topics with peers or profs was as normal as goofing around.
- You could never slack off because each person motivated the others.
- My term at Strasbourg was the happiest four months of my life.
- I want my children to have the same experience.
- I didn't learn to love learning until my profs at Centre opened up the world intellectually and showed me how to learn. I'm a teaching assistant at Miami University with classes of 200 and no contact with the students.

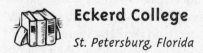

Eckerd College

St. Petersburg, Florida

When Eckerd was only thirty-five years old, I wrote that it was one of the country's most attractive academic bargains and a hot growth stock. Ten years later, it is outstanding. It seems to have about twice as many buildings on the 270-acre campus. All in native flora, except for big shade trees, it is a verdant thumb on the coastline of Boca Ciega, with the Sunshine Skyway Bridge in the distance.

The new buildings include a multimillion-dollar state-of-the-art library twice the size of the old one, and it boasts a coffee bar and reading lounge. There are new air-conditioned residential clusters on the waterfront, a new visual and performing arts center, new classrooms for its 1,600 students, and two natural pond areas that are homes to a greater variety of wading birds than on any other campus.

A smart innovation provides a lot of free bikes. A student can pick up a "yellow bike" wherever he finds one, ride it to his destination and leave it for someone else. For socializing, the Triton Pub has a large-screen TV, pool tables, a state-of-the-art sound system, a grill open all day, and a Thursday night music program.

More important, it has won two major academic honors. It has been awarded a chapter of Phi Beta Kappa, the scholastic honor society to which only 8 percent of the country's colleges and universities belong. It also is one of the top fifty colleges in producing future Ph.D.s, the nation's scientists and scholars.

Proof of its allure is its great and growing diversity. Massachusetts, New York, and Illinois are second, third, and fourth sources of students after Florida. Indeed, there are so many students from the Northeast that this college in the land of year-round baseball has a lacrosse team. The students come from forty-five other states and sixty-seven foreign countries.

In the field of marine science, Eckerd is in a class by itself by virtue of its magnificent, and unique state-of-the-art marine laboratory. No Ivy or any other school has anything to match it. The structure is set back from the water to preserve the shore line, but a dock with a large underwater tube reaches out into the Gulf of Mexico and sea water circulates through a large tank, where sea animals are in their native habitat so students can observe and work with them as they live. As a faculty member said, "It is a unique way to teach our courses."

Eckerd is too young to show a record of alumni achievement such as percentages in *Who's Who,* Pulitzer-Prize winners, corporate executives, creators of new enterprises, or major benefactors, but the effects of a good college experience are clear.

My client sample naturally is limited, but in more than thirty-five years in which two or three or more clients a year have gone there, none has ever expressed any dissatisfaction. The college's own survey of graduates over a fifteen-year span offers a more definitive and glowing response. One alumna, now a very successful literary agent, wrote to me fifteen years after graduation: "Going to Eckerd was a delightful experience, one, needless to say, I will never forget, and I feel confident that my education was as good as can be found anywhere in this country . . . (and I shouldn't put it in the past tense. Eckerd taught me, among other things, that education never stops)." She is married to a Princeton alumnus.

The academic dean, Lloyd Chapin, goes one better; he says Eckerd's students get a better education than at the Ivies. Why? "Because students here are involved in their own education; because faculty members work at improving their teaching; they are actively engaged in comparing techniques.

"Our Academy of Senior Professionals program in which distinguished retirees provide a different point of view in the freshman Western Heritage or in the senior Judeo-Christian Perspectives classes are unique in the way they work. The retirees live on campus and occasionally act as counselors or career advisers or on personal problems.

"The faculty here are as good as at the Ivies. They not only publish but their principal interest is teaching.

"Here there is a sense of community."

He makes the often unappreciated point that the faculty at any good college is every bit as well qualified as any Ivy staff; after all, they all got their doctorates at the same elite graduate schools.

"The Eckerd faculty publishes." He pointed to a long row of recent books. "They haven't published as much as the Ivy faculties but they are working on the cutting edges. They are as good as faculty members anywhere, and I staked my own kid's welfare on the belief they are. My daughter had a better experience here than my older children did at Colgate or Emory. Furthermore, the Eckerd faculty does more for its students than do the Ivies' faculties. There is a great deal of involvement; we have faculty retreats on taking each student seriously, and as an individual.

"Elsewhere, faculty members tend to regard their classrooms as their castles, but here we have teachers' forums in which groups of twenty will share teaching techniques and discuss things that will or that won't work. Over half the faculty is involved in these forums. There's a lot going on in this area.

"Our faculty members' tenure depends on teaching. They can't get tenure unless they're good teachers. That's why our students do course evaluations every year. And the stiff graders don't suffer. Students regard the profs who set very high standards and grade hard as 'compassionate hard-asses.'

"Also, mentoring [personal and academic advising] is taken seriously here. We try to evaluate it; the students fill out questionnaires at the end of each term evaluating both teachers and mentors. The results tend to be bipolar; both the brickbats and the bouquets are very positive."

Eckerd's freshmen and faculty get a head start on getting acquainted with a multipurpose month-long autumn term before school starts. Freshmen can study any one of a dozen or more topics: Behavioral Bases of Stress, Coastal Oceanography, American Politics, Religion and Public Policy, or Sociology of Sex Roles. The teacher for each group of twenty becomes the academic and personal mentor for each of them for the year, and each group stays together as a Western Heritage class. Autumn term is thus an orientation with no upperclass students around and promotes bonding among the freshmen and with their mentors. They also get a course credit, and placement testing is done.

At the end of the year, each freshman chooses a second mentor in his intended major or field of concentration and both stay with him from then on. He thus has a second opinion for general help and for making his big decisions, such as if he wants to design his own major.

Eckerd is on a 4-1-4 schedule [January term in the middle of the year], so everyone uses the winter term for a change of pace: a term at another college, international-study tours, a project on campus, or something very different, like studying poverty in Appalachia, pottery in New England, or languages in upstate New York.

The Academy of Senior Professionals—300 of them—gives Eckerd freshman and senior classes a unique zip. It is a group of people, some retired, who've had distinguished careers in a broad range of fields and who act as sort of an adjunct faculty. They may act as resource persons in the classroom, counsel students on academic or career matters, or give talks or conduct colloquia. Some live in college housing on campus and some nearby.

The Western Heritage and Judeo-Christian Perspectives classes they help teach are both value-oriented, and the mature viewpoints of retired corporate executives, generals, professors, writers, and others bring a different and usually nonacademic viewpoint to class discussions, besides offering a counterpoint to the authority of the professor. For example, a sociology prof who is a pacifist has as his professional a retired major general. There is a mutual respect but the class is a lively one.

In a writing class, the Pulitzer Prize–winning author James Michener critiqued students' efforts and had a reputation for always finding something good to say about every paper, no matter how bad. Michener also left the college $1 million.

Dean Chapin says, "I like these students best, compared to Emory and Colgate. In basic intellectual quality they're as good, and they're more enthusiastic and less cynical. Emory is cold and competitive, with much social ambition and grade grubbing. Here there's a sense of community and a lot of student involvement."

Prof. John Reynolds, chairman of Marine Sciences, raves: "The students here are superb. Eckerd attracts kids who want to give something back to the community. They are superb human beings who will also contribute.

"What we accomplish: We give them the tools. We are blessed with capable, fine teachers who confront values and make linkages across seemingly unrelated disciplines. Our research crosses boundaries, our environmental program is interdisciplinary. We are concerned with ethics and issues; I have to think about how I feel about mammals and articulate that. The autumn-term class involves not only learning about mammals, but also such questions as, do we manage or mismanage them? What are our values in this matter and how do we face them?"

Eckerd has an honors program providing two years of independent study and research for students of outstanding ability, and for those who might someday be college faculty members a two-year Apprentice Scholar Program, financed by the Ford Foundation, develops the skills and habits of professional scholars.

In this, my third visit to Eckerd, all the students I questioned expressed some form of satisfaction with what the community was doing for them. I was also impressed, as I had been on previous visits, that the minority students seemed particularly integrated into the mix. A dark-skinned senior from Curaçao said he felt such a warm sense of family he didn't particularly want to go home, and that the school had broadened his horizons and taught him time management.

More than one student felt that the absence of fraternities and sororities contributed to the sense of community. A literature and religion major, also a senior, said that if it had not been for the mentor program and a caring faculty, when he got into drugs and alcohol in his freshman year, "I wouldn't be here." But now he thinks he'll go to a seminary, work in the Peace Corps, or do some kind of ministry.

They, like others, said Eckerd had challenged their points of view and their value systems and had affected the development of the latter. Two premed seniors said the Western Heritage class had had an impact "from day one." One of them added, "Eckerd taught me how to balance my life; I find I can do so much."

These comments are in line with what seniors have been saying for many years in the school's own survey of graduates. More than 90 percent have said their values have been affected, as have their abilities to think critically, to work independently, and to define and solve problems, their enjoyment of learning, their understanding of self, satisfaction of life, competence as a person, ability to get along with others, and openness to new ideas. Few thought it had affected their religious beliefs, although 70 percent said it had influenced their understanding of the Judeo-Christian tradition.

Ninety-six percent said Eckerd was a good choice and nearly two-thirds even approved of the food, a standard source of complaint on many campuses.

But more immediate is the comparative testimony of a former client who came to me after a year at the University of Pittsburgh, and who then chose Bryn Mawr over Eckerd, and after a semester there finished at Eckerd. She had this to say about Bryn Mawr, which is as Ivy as a women's college can get: "I think Bryn Mawr is an excellent school, and it is unique . . . one fits in very well, or one does not fit in at all. One of the things I could not get used to was the aloofness with which most of the students treated each other. I thought that at a women's college everyone would feel more comfortable and open with each other because we were 'all girls,' but I found just the opposite to be true. It seemed there was a lot of competition and a lot of stress. I also couldn't get used to all the political correctness that was going on.

"My problems with finding out about my French requirement in the beginning of the semester made me feel like I was back in a big university, caught up in red tape. . . . I was also surprised at how little contact the students had with the professors outside of class, and how formal the relationships between the students and the professors were."

After she'd been at Eckerd a while, she wrote me: "I love Eckerd. I love my classes. I love the weather, and I've met three girls in my dorm who are the first good friends I've made since high school. I play soccer every Friday, I have a blues show every week on the Eckerd radio station. I'm auditing an extra literature class, and I've signed up to be on the staff of Eckerd's literary magazine. I also took beginning sailing lessons, and I can sign out for a two-person sailboat at any time on the waterfront. The warm, sunny weather down here is wonderful, and all the people are very friendly. I started feeling comfortable here right away . . . and the school is big enough so that new people don't stick out."

Ten years later, Eckerd gets loving, rave evaluations from both students and alums. It also has some dramatic stories of average or less-than-average prospects becoming graduate students, Ph.D.s, and doctors. The adult education program also has its stories of lives being changed. These things could only happen in communities like the ones in this book.

Euphoric is the only word that describes the way students and recent graduates talk about their experiences. Here are some of them:

- The most challenging and rewarding time of my life.
- It gave me an advantage in graduate school. It was the most amazing four years of my life; I was devastated to leave.
- I left a far better human being.
- The profs don't just teach, they motivate; they mold us into better students and better people.
- A dynamic batch of profs, and they all care, and take special steps to see that you get the most out of Eckerd.
- Friendliness permeates the campus, students look out for each other.
- The dean of students was at my side in the hospital at 2 a.m. It made me feel there was always someone there to support me.
- Everyone is supportive, understanding, passionate. After six years, Eckerd continues to change my life.
- I was not prepared for the academic rigor, but because of the faculty I succeeded.
- Eckerd taught me more independence and more about myself that I could have dreamed.

- I had amazing relationships with the profs; the sense of community helps students jump in and get involved.
- You can grow anywhere, but here the profs know your name and ask about you and are genuinely interested in the answer. Every prof I had remembered my name all four years and were friends and mentors, and their doors were always open for an afternoon chat.
- Eckerd has ripped me apart, built me up, torn me down, and I continue to emerge as a new person every day, every week. I put myself back together, Eckerd helps.
- I was able to have the most wonderful experience of being able to learn as much outside the classroom from my professors as I did inside the classroom.
- Eckerd was a once-in-a-lifetime experience that has forever changed my life and I am thankful and proud to have been a part of such a wonderful community.

These and others talked about how many opportunities they'd had—one played in the Tampa Symphony—how their various foreign-study terms had widened their horizons, how they had discovered themselves, and how they had learned how to really think, among other things. One said she wanted to become a teacher to give others the kind of experience she'd had.

A physics professor's favorite success story has made him an opponent of any SAT cutoff score for admission. The hero, now a physician in Maryland, arrived at Eckerd with a total SAT score below 800, and "a very inconsistent high school record," largely because of a "chaotic" family life. But he wanted to be a doctor. His first essay was ten pages, all in one paragraph. But "he never had to be told anything twice, and he was a sponge for information." He made an A in Calculus I and graduated as a physics major, got a Ph.D., worked in the field for a couple of years, decided to enter medical school and got his M.D. in 1998.

The professor adds, "Richard Strilka's case shows clearly that SAT scores and even high school records don't always predict a student's potential."

The close teacher-student relations at Eckerd can work wonders. A marine science professor sent Jenna Lodico, a C student in her science courses, on an oceanographic research cruise for a month the summer after her junior year. "She did a wonderful senior thesis for me, on the cutting edge of science. She presented it at the American Geophysical Union conference and so impressed the scientists that several wanted her to go to their graduate schools. By working very closely with her on a one-to-one basis, we at Eckerd College changed her life. After graduation she wrote me in a thank-you card, 'I never imagined I'd be going to graduate school.'"

The director of service ministry said, "I've had many, many students say a particular service experience has been deeply meaningful and life-changing for them." A senior, Jill Braly, spent a spring break working for a Florida migrant-workers coalition and in the tomato fields as well. "When I returned to Eckerd," she said, "I knew I would never be the same. My eyes have been opened in a way that textbooks and professors could never have done. I felt an undeniable urge to serve others. I could make a difference. I am sure I will continue to feel a sense of civic responsibility and desire to serve my community."

Another, Jerald Hess, spent several weeks living in a primitive camp in the Myanmar jungle teaching English to refugees from the civil war there. That made him decide to go into international law so he can assist refugees.

An emeritus history professor says Eckerd's program for adults works wonders, especially for married women at a loss as to what to do with their lives. His favorite story is of a woman with two small children, who graduated with high honors, but was rejected by the University of Florida Law School, which averaged in a disastrous junior-college record of fifteen years earlier. They said she "had not demonstrated her ability to do college work." She applied to the university's graduate program in history, took museum courses, became a power in the art-museum world, has her own consulting business, and teaches two graduate courses in museum studies at the university.

Emory & Henry College

Emory, Virginia

On a beautiful campus of lovely buildings and stately trees in the colorful hills of southwest Virginia, Emory & Henry does a far better job of developing contributors to society than Virginia's three most prestigious and selective institutions.

Emory & Henry is an extended family that uncovers unrealized talents, instills values, and develops the desire and the ability to serve. It is a national asset. It has aspects of the parable of the talents since the well-known three turn out pretty much what they take in, whereas Emory & Henry doubles talents.

Emory & Henry is on the edge of a tiny village near the small town of Abingdon, which is famous as the home of the Barter Theatre. It is a caring, nurturing community, a place where everyone smiles and speaks to you, that has a strong sense of family. It also is most unusual, and may be unique in the way it works closely with parents to guide kids before they need help.

Nearly half of the students come from a radius of 100 miles and some are the first generation to go to college. Nearly 70 percent come from Virginia and the rest from twenty-five states and from foreign countries. The college has been casting its net more widely as it has become better known.

The personable Dr. Thomas R. Morris, a widely quoted expert on the Constitution and on Virginia politics, who left the chairmanship of the University of Richmond's political science department to come to Emory & Henry, is the rare college president with a sense of mission.

He is rare in another way that reflects the kind of person he is; he is deeply concerned for the well-being of his community. He lived the first full week of his presidency—bag and baggage—in a freshman dorm because he'd heard there'd been a lot of complaints about a lack of hot water and nobody had paid any attention to them. Now there's plenty of hot water, and he became an instant hero. Of course, as a survivor of Virginia Military Institute's notoriously rough first—Rat—year, he was tough enough to stand a freshman dorm for a week.

Since then, dorm life has been greatly improved. Major renovations have given the dorms new furnishings and décor, as well as new, more comfortable furniture. There's even a new fitness center in one of the men's new residences.

Some members of the Board of Trustees worried that, because he has written several books and is frequently interviewed by television and newspaper reporters, he might not be sufficiently interested in the school's athletic program; and students worried they might be getting a stuffy pedant. But about five feet of one wall of his office is alive with a blood-red-and-white portrayal of the Washington Redskins' football great, that 180-pound David, Larry Brown, slashing his way through the Goliaths of the New York Giants' defensive line. And at lunch half a dozen students chorused of their new president, "He hasn't missed a game!"

He still hasn't missed a game ten years later. Even though his kind of job requires a lot of fund-raising travel, he plans his trips around E&H's football schedule.

Emory & Henry lost President Morris in January 2006 when Governor-elect Tim Kaine named him Virginia's secretary of education. The board of trustees started a national search for a worthy successor.

The beauty of the campus undoubtedly played a part in the original decisions, but kids are here because they want to be here; they love it; they take a warm pride in it and their regular-guy president, and they want to learn. I didn't meet anyone who wished he'd gotten into some other school, which is unusual, because at nearly every college, except maybe Harvard, there is a sullen cohort of rejected suitors of another institution.

It is also a rare educational bargain, boasting not only a talented as well as caring faculty, but a solid core curriculum—the sine qua non of a shared intellectual experience—that provides a liberal education on which students can build in graduate school and in later life. Everyone takes a Western Traditions sequence, a Great Books course, a religion course, one Value Inquiry, and a Global Study sequence. And everyone is also required to develop his or her writing skills.

E&H is also a financial bargain; 90 percent of the students get financial aid, and in 2004 the college got its largest bequest ever, a $10 million gift, for more scholarships, from the daughter of an alumnus.

The college's sense of family extends to the parents as well. They are asked to send letters telling the dean of students what they think are the needs of their sons or daughters for prospering there. One mother wrote that she wanted her son to wear a jacket and tie to dinner, a request that somehow fell between the cracks. But they often alert the dean to needs that the college might otherwise be unaware of, such as learning problems, physical or personal matters, and so on.

There have been some dramatic cases of growth as a result. Dr. Ron Diss says, "All the learning-disabled students succeed when they want to." When challenged he re-emphasized the word "all."

My own experiences support his claim. In more than a thirty-five-year span, every single client I've had who worked to overcome his or her disability succeeded in college, some with dean's-list records; and some went on to professional or graduate school.

When a parent's letter says a student has or may have an attention-span deficit, some form of dyslexia, or some other problem, Dr. Diss alerts the faculty adviser. He then follows up weekly with faculty members.

Dr. Diss gets grade reports of every student and calls in for conferences those who get a D or an F. He also gives tests where necessary or provides study-skill sessions, remedial work, or tutoring.

"Everything is cross-referenced," said Dr. Diss. "We know who the at-risk students are, and they get the help they need when it is needed." As a result, the percentage of Ds and Fs, and, hence, dropouts, is now very low.

The college emphasizes discussion classes and writing for two reasons: One is to involve students in their own education; the other is that much more teacher preparation is involved in a discussion than in a lecture class because the instructor must have a question to cover every point he wants to make. At the same time, more is demanded of the student; he not only has to have read the material to be discussed, but he must have thought about it, because he must be able to talk about it in an insightful way.

The dean sits in on classes because he is looking for empathy with students and for good teaching. Tenure depends on both; being an active researcher isn't enough to keep a faculty job here.

Several faculty members testified that what the college is doing to develop abilities and talents in students produces results. One of them, a teacher with empathy enough to win teaching awards, professor of history John Roper, said E&H students, even those who come less well prepared than others, do well in graduate school. "The kids here are better than they think they are. They are eager; they are genuine. They never worry about asking the naïve question. The white students are not as racist as kids elsewhere. Many of these kids live in the same houses their grandfathers did. They have a country shrewdness; if the train's leaving, they've got to catch it. They're not as well prepared as some, but that troubles me little. We're an add-on school.

"I've enjoyed teaching these kids more than any others I've ever taught [at the University of South Carolina and the University of North Carolina]."

Not only do they do well in graduate school, he added, but the General George Marshall Library in Lexington will take any E&H student as an intern because the scholarly work of their predecessors has been so good.

Dr. George Treadwell agreed that many of them aren't well prepared when they come, but that when they're seniors they go on to the better graduate and medical schools, "and they write well."

He added that the college has a definite influence on the

youths' development, not only because of the value-oriented courses they must take but also because there's "a great deal of personal contact with faculty members. In fact, fairly often, faculty members will come here for less money simply because of the E&H philosophy."

Emory & Henry's professors are outstanding. In 2003, one of its faculty, Dr. Teresa Keller, won the Virginia professor of the year award. That was the fifth time in fifteen years that E&H had won the prize, more often than any other institution in the state.

Dr. Ed Damer, author of a best-selling philosophy textbook, *Attacking Faulty Reasoning,* said, "This is a challenging place; it excites me, and I've been teaching here for thirty-five years. These students are here because they want to be here, because they're interested in learning."

In conversations with a couple dozen different students, not one said he or she would go someplace else if they had to do it all over again. All of them spoke warmly of their relationships with their teachers and with their fellow students. And the answers to one of my standard questions—"If you came back here five years after graduation, would you have good enough friends on the faculty that you'd have dinner or spend the night at the faculty member's home?"—were either "Yes," "Certainly," or "You bet."

Surprisingly, no one had a gripe about a prof who was a clunk. More than one spoke with pride about their undefeated football team in which the star halfback could practice only three days a week because of labs, and the best lineman's class schedule was so full he could practice only one day. The students' pride in the team's achievement and in the rightly ordered priorities of players, coach, and college was at least equaled by Dr. Morris's when he proudly described the players' commitments and their accomplishments.

Anybody's reaction to those students would be, "What a nice, genuine, open bunch of kids: honest, unassuming, warm, and emanating a quiet self-confidence."

What former students think of their alma mater is one of the true tests: How do its graduates believe fifteen, twenty, and thirty years later that this experience has affected the quality of their lives?

On the theory that a person puts his money where his heart is, few colleges, Ivy or other, can match the esteem in which E&H is held by its graduates. For fifteen years, E&H has ranked among the top 1 percent of the more than 2,000 four-year institutions in the percentage of alumni making financial gifts.

E&H is a friendly, homey kind of place that is likely to give you strengths you didn't know you had if you've felt put off by the competition for grades in high school. If you're interested in learning, know that E&H looks closely at GPAs and courses taken, while accepting a wide range of SAT scores.

And if you think you might need help—and more people do than admit it—this is a place where caring people will help you over the hump.

Finally, the fact that faculty members say the students are here to learn says something very important about the nature of a place, and it's not too often I get that kind of response.

Ten years later, what students say is heart-warming testimony to how much this college is doing to develop the kind of minds and hearts that make the world a better place.

The dominant themes are that Emory is "family" or "home"; awareness that they've become better, more critically thinking persons; and that they want to "make meaningful change in this world that needs critical and compassionate individuals."

Several seniors said they didn't think they would have had such wonderful opportunities anywhere else to participate in so many sports or activities, to have such leadership roles, and to be able to feel a sense of importance. Some said Emory was the reason they were getting into graduate schools. And some said they're going to cry when they leave. Here are some of the typical ones:

A senior girl headed for law school said, "Emory & Henry does more than influence you, it gets into your blood. I felt immediately at home with all the smiling faces of people willing to help me with anything. The opportunities we are given allow us to be ourselves and to grow and learn in ways that would not be possible anywhere else. Don't let the surrounding cow pastures fool you, there are always plenty of things to do and to get into the Emory community. We all join together in work and play in order to create a group that is truly family." She added that she wouldn't have gotten the same personal attention anywhere else, and without it, wouldn't be going to "such a prestigious law school."

A junior said he'd been "a poor student in high school" and expected to be the same in college until "a professor told me, 'Will, you're as smart as anyone in my class, and you can make an A.' With new confidence I worked hard and made the highest grade in the class, and I've been on the dean's list every semester since. This professor's casual but genuine remarks may have really changed the course of my educational career and my life—for the better."

Another said he was "just passing through life," but Emory & Henry "has instilled a drive to succeed like I've never felt before. Because of this, I've gained opportunities that I would not have had at another college, such as conducting research at other universities with people at the top of their fields. Because of the small, close-knit community that Emory maintains, I've been able to grow as an individual in all respects."

A sophomore said his involvement in service programs made him realize that public service instead of a photography or photojournalism, was his calling, so he changed his major to a triple one of political science, public policy, and community service. "There is something here for everyone," he added, "It feels just like home. I have been given a chance to become comfortable with the person I am today."

A senior said the close relationships with faculty members "and their great concern for my success" have motivated him to go on for his Ph.D. so he can become a professor too.

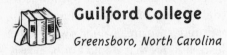

Guilford College

Greensboro, North Carolina

One would never guess that the country's hottest producer of oil geologists is a Quaker college of 1,400 students founded in 1837 in Greensboro, North Carolina, that accepts 75 percent of its applicants. It is.

Six of its geology majors have key positions in the four major oil companies. Three Guilford graduates—two of them women—head the oil explorations in Southeast Asia for Amoco, Chevron, and Texaco. The one at Chevron, the youngest ever to hold such a job, hit oil on her first two drillings. Another woman heads Amoco's explorations research. A male alum is an advanced exploration geologist for Texaco, and the sixth graduate is exploration geologist for Exxon in Calgary, Canada. In addition, Texaco chose two Guilford graduates for their Frontier Division, which makes global decisions for the company. Several other Guilford alumni are in staff positions with major or independent oil companies, or are doing consulting.

Guilford has several other claims to fame; it has led all institutions in the state in winning prestigious Danforth Fellowships. And it produces such achievers from a stock of teenagers with SAT verbal scores in the 500 range and high school records that put just a little more than a third of them in the top decile of their classes.

Guilford has a major observatory on top of the Frank Family Science Center and is one of sixteen colleges and universities picked by the National Aeronautics and Space Administration to participate in a joint venture of special programs at flight and space centers and research laboratories to prepare NASA leaders of the future.

For the South it is a liberal institution. Being Quaker, it truly is a friendly place. The individual, values, and social concerns are the important things. There is an honor code, but an atmosphere of trust has been created that makes it unnecessary, in the view of a math professor whose family has gone to Guilford for five generations. "In twenty years," he said, "we've had six cheating cases. The atmosphere is noncompetitive; it's 'I'm competing against myself.' We encourage collaborative work, but of course each student draws his own conclusions and makes his own arguments."

In the intense competition for African-American students, Guilford has done well; 7 percent of the student body are African Americans, and they graduate at the same rates as whites—more than 70 percent. Significant is the way my question was answered: "While I haven't bothered to look, blacks do as well as whites and graduate at the same rate." Even when I first visited more than fifteen years ago, Guilford stood out as one integrated community, in dramatic contrast with many other places. On a more recent visit, when I was hearing from a black secretary only good things about Guilford students, I asked her if she'd send her own child here. She said, "My daughter's a sophomore here."

President Donald W. McNemar, who taught international relations at Dartmouth and came to Guilford after serving as headmaster of Phillips Academy in Andover, Massachusetts, said, "We combine the liberal arts and preparation for a career on a value-based education. These unique programs prepare students to be leaders in a rapidly changing world. Guilford graduates leave with values, skills, and commitments which enable them to make a difference."

Guilford's wooded 340-acre campus in a northwestern suburb is a lovely place in which to have the experience the school offers. Many campuses are attractive, but this one has a special charm, and Quakers, like New Englanders, keep everything picked up, painted up, and fixed up. No visitor has ever said that a Guilford building—or even a dorm—looked anything but fresh as a daisy.

Especially charming is Guilford's Carnegie Library, which houses 250,000 volumes, and fiber-optic linkages to other libraries make it the equal of that in a major university. The original 1908 building has been renovated and greatly enlarged with a two-story, atriumlike addition that provides 400 inviting places to study, and a seven-room art gallery. It has both cozy carrels and a light and airy openness that is both alluring and good for grade point averages. Among its special and endowed collections is a comprehensive Friends Historical Collection of rare books and periodicals and 600 volumes of Carolina Quaker records dating from 1680.

It is one of the few colleges in the South that has intercollegiate teams in lacrosse as well as in the more usual ones of baseball, basketball, football, golf, and tennis, in which it is formidable.

Although Guilford's fame in geology is a great coup, and there is much student research here, chemistry professor Dr. David MacInnes and his students are also doing leading-edge research in metal-free batteries (important to pacemakers and to all kinds of portable gadgets). One professor did a major piece of the research that made a plastic battery possible. Math and physics students publish in undergraduate journals.

Involvement is required in other fields as well. Everyone goes through a core curriculum planned to ensure a liberal education. Most classes involve discussion and have eighteen or fewer students, which means there's no place to hide. Majors in sociology, government, and religious studies must do internships. Government students may spend a term working in Congress with a North Carolina representative. Sports medicine majors must get experience in two jobs.

Over a third of the students take a foreign-study program in China, Mexico, Central America, Italy, Ghana, England, France, Germany, or Japan. They go with a professor in groups of twenty to twenty-five.

There is a special sense of family here as palpable as at Earlham, a Quaker college in Indiana. As is Quaker custom, students and teachers are on a first-name basis. Dr. Elwood Parker, the mathematician of long family ties, said, "As a fund-raiser, the first question I invariably get from an alumnus is about some faculty member, how he is; that reflects a kind of relationship that is

more powerful here than at any other place. We're all in this together. There is a lot of team teaching."

Dr. Parker taught one class without a textbook, which was a
challenge to his philosopher teammate. In departmental meetings, faculty members not only discuss how they're teaching and
trade tips, but also ask about how particular students are doing.

In an introductory geology class I visited, a dozen students
working in teams of two or three were poring over great sheets of
a gigantic three-dimensional jigsaw puzzle simulating a section of
the earth twenty-six miles by sixteen miles and five miles deep
called the Quaker Quadrangle, its geology invented twenty-five
years ago by Dr. Cyril Harvey. He, incidentally, had been a whiz
kid who went to the University of Chicago after the tenth grade.
Dissatisfied with existing manuals, he decided to write his own
lab program. His idea was to design a tool he could use not only
to simulate geology, but also to give the experience of scientific research and discovery with three-dimensional thinking. The students were arguing points about its history or whether it was a
logical place to expect to find oil. Such facts as rock configura-
tions and drilling costs at a given spot were all stored in a computer, and as students checked things out, they were solving their
problems by using the information in a textbook. "As they solve,"
Dr. Harvey explained, " they make their own discoveries, the principles in the book become real, and it's a personal experience, an
emotional kick—in fact it's almost magical the way they're thinking for themselves."

It must be; one of the Texaco exploration directors hadn't intended to be a geology major until he got hooked on the Quaker
Quad. It may also be one reason why the first three holes proposed
by Guilford graduates were discoveries. One of those who hit said
that this was the most important course she ever took, even counting those in graduate school, that prepared her for her job.

Two other anecdotes are apropos. A senior geology and English major told me she'd been a C+ student in high school but
that now, Dr. Harvey was recommending her for graduate school.

"You realize your potential here," she said. "Ninety-eight percent of the profs are caring. I think we're spoiled." She was trying to get her sister, who was not having a good experience at Brown, to transfer.

Amoco's exploration head, as a brand-new Ph.D. from the University of North Carolina, at first failed to get the job after an interview. She went back to Guilford, not to UNC, to get advice, because "you told me I was good." Dr. Harvey told her Amoco had made a mistake and to go back. She bought another airplane ticket, told the bosses they'd made a mistake, and they hired her.

Dr. Harvey has since retired, but two true believers in his approach and his philosophy, Drs. Dave Dobson and Marlene McCauley, are carrying on his work, using the Quaker Quad and turning out first-rate geologists.

The rest of the Guilford's faculty also thinks their students are good. They think they benefit from comparisons with those at some of the other places where they've taught, including Emory, Vanderbilt, Clemson, Colorado College, and Carleton. They described Guilford students as much more serious than those at Colorado College; they are not grade-grubbers and they don't cheat, as students at Emory did; they don't mind working at something they're interested in even if it means a low grade; they will try things; they're outspoken and thoughtful; they feel they have authority, and they challenge; they want to go to graduate school but it's not a track as it is at Carleton. And there's simply no comparison with the Clemson football factory, where instructors were under pressure to favor athletes.

Ten years later, Guilford students and alums were saying the same sort of things their predecessors said a decade ago; namely, that Guilford is a warm and accepting family and a mind-opening place of discovery where they've been pushed to go beyond what they'd thought they were capable of.

A sophomore girl, after saying Guilford students had a "genuine love for everyone," and that it had already caused her to change her major from biology to physics and Spanish, added, "What stands out most to me about Guilford is how we are encouraged to make positive changes in the community and the world. Everyone seems to have a cause and many people are actually making things happen. Most importantly, we are encouraged to make changes within Guilford itself. My first week here I met students who were musicians or contra dancers. A month after I first arrived we actually organized a contra dance on campus, with funding from the student senate. About a hundred students, faculty, and members of the community attended, and it was an amazing time. We've had a contra dance every month of the academic year since, for two years. Being an organizer for all of this has helped me to see what a difference I can make in the community, and is encouraging me to set larger goals in the future."

A sophomore from New York City, a high school dropout whose checkered background had included training to be a professional wrestler, said, "It's hard to describe all the things Guilford's done for me. Mainly, it's given me a chance. Other colleges accepted me but Guilford gave me a scholarship; they saw potential. I've gained a lot of confidence. I've learned how to incorporate spirituality into the way I see the world and have changed my ways of thinking based on things I've been exposed to here. Above all, the most significant thing is discovering music (because of a teacher). It has completely changed my life. Suddenly, I'm composing my own pieces. I think this has happened because Guilford gives you the freedom to explore. I'm now double majoring in music and political science, which Guilford encourages. I'm a better and happier person. Guilford's changed my life; it's changed my whole world."

A senior girl said Guilford had given her such excellent critical thinking skills that she cannot see a movie or listen to a political speech without analyzing it. Guilford "taught me to think about things on a deeper level. Also, I feel more able to stand up for the issues I believe in and to voice my opinion in an educated manner."

An alumna from the Ukraine said Guilford had "strengthened my integrity by allowing me to discover my identity—my own spirit. I was encouraged by professors who knew how to push me. Guilford made me realize you cannot find integrity, but rather integrity is a constant and unique journey for every person. Without Guilford I would never have understood how to take risks and pursue my real dreams, and therefore would never have been truly happy. I believe that taking risks and being happy and at peace with oneself is the truest mark of a successful life."

A junior girl from Virginia said Guilford "has changed me in more ways that I will ever know." The concern of a professor and her mentor even "helped me deal with my homesickness. Guilford has taught me to push myself both academically and artistically. My professors' pushing me has already asked me to go above and beyond what I thought was even in the realm of possibility." She added that the Quaker principles are "not overpowering but so important to what Guilford is and why it changes people. They allow you to be yourself and those around you are so willing to accept who you are and they encourage you."

An alumna who went to Purdue as a Ph.D. candidate in earth and atmospheric sciences had been a double major in biology and English. She said she'd been so well prepared that a professor told her to skip the master's part of the program because "my previous research was more complex and developed than many master's projects." A lot of credit for that, she said, should be given to the fact that "Guilford is a writing intensive school." Furthermore, she said, "I felt like all facets of my brain were constantly stimulated, as if my brain were working in overdrive."

An alumna from Canada who got into veterinary school, which is far more competitive than medical school since there were only twenty-two in North America, said Guilford "couldn't have prepared me any better; my professors were amazing, their enthusiasm was contagious."

A graduate working for his Ph.D. in English at City College in New York, became both student and teacher when he got involved in teaching inner-city high school kids. He keeps their attention with disc jockeys and hip-hop performers livening up his new form of social activism. In college, his big interest was English and he wasn't an activist, but the Guilford influence was at work and came out after he got to New York.

A 2002 graduate, a policy analyst for Business Executives for National Security, a Washington D.C. nonprofit reform organization dealing with national defense, said, "I don't think I could handle this job if Guilford hadn't prepared me so well to be a writer and an analytical thinker. My teachers really pushed me to go one level deeper, one question further."

Hendrix College
Conway, Arkansas

On a balmy April day, as one enters the fifty-acre enclave of masses of red and white azaleas, dogwoods, giant willow oaks, and manicured lawns that set off Hendrix's attractive buildings, the overwhelming impression is that this Shangri-la in Conway, Arkansas, thirty miles north of Little Rock, must be the most beautiful campus of them all. And inside this lovely setting is a warm community that offers an educational experience to match; one without peer.

No city street intrudes; the outside world is walled off by the trees and shrubbery. Even the parking is way out of sight. A walkway high over the street takes visitors to a 120-acre parklike expanse of recreation and sports facilities. There are tennis courts, intercollegiate playing fields, and a fitness trail in the woods. A giant indoor activities center has more tennis, as well as basketball courts and a Nautilus fitness area. Students said it is more used by the girls than by the boys.

Close by are the streams, lakes, forests, and hills of that out-doorsman's paradise, the Ozark Mountains, offering canoeing, whitewater rafting, spelunking, rock climbing, horseback riding, hot-air ballooning, hiking, and camping, not to mention some beautiful country. The college takes full advantage of this bounty with a comprehensive outdoors program for every interest and every range of skill.

These attractions are bonuses offered by one of the country's academic gems. It truly is a too-secret treasure that is both a financial bargain, with 92 percent of students receiving financial aid, and a great opportunity for a better educational experience than you'd find in the name-brand places. It really is a shame that this century-old college of 1,400 students isn't more widely known. Partly because it's in Arkansas and partly because of modesty stemming from its church origins (Methodist), Hendrix has blushed unseen rather than trumpeted its virtues.

Hendrix accepts 86 percent of its applicants, and in 2003, slightly over half of them came from out of state. This book has helped make people across the country aware of Hendrix's virtues. The middle 50 percent have SAT totals in the 1,250 range, which means a lot of scores are below as well as above. Half of those accepted were in the top half of their high school class, but that includes many small rural ones, so it is a good bet for B students with good programs from larger and more competitive high schools. And that also goes for C students who mean business.

There are no fraternities or sororities. As a student from Alaska said, "You make friends with people from different departments, different parts of the country, different cultures. Your 'group' becomes the whole campus."

Nearly 90 percent of the faculty hold doctoral degrees from the great American and European universities. All of the rest have terminal degrees in their fields. In the last decade, the faculty has grown from sixty to eighty although enrollment is only up by 10 percent. New majors have been added in international relations, anthropology, and computer science, while more strength and diversity have been added to existing fields. The student-faculty ratio has been lowered to 12–1, and the average class size to fifteen.

In 2002 and 2003, the college completed several new buildings. One is for the physical sciences and another is for the life sciences and psychology. Biology and psychology are the two largest majors. There is also a center for programs in literature and language, a new art complex of three buildings for art history and photography, one for two-dimensional art, and one for ceramics and sculpture. In the plans are two more additions: a multiple-purpose campus center that will be a student union plus, and a comprehensive wellness and athletics center.

To accommodate all this growth, the college has added new centers for the physical and life sciences as well as two new dormitories and six small residences housing sixteen to eighteen students each to provide opportunities for residential programs. It has installed a new pipe organ in a renovated chapel and has added intramural and regulation soccer fields to its already well-equipped recreation area.

Sixty percent of the graduates go on to graduate or professional school. And they are welcomed. They score in the ninety-eighth and ninety-ninth percentiles in the graduate tests because they've already been doing what graduate students do: research. Each year students accompany faculty members to professional meetings to present the results of collaborative student-faculty research. The chances of a student getting this kind of experience at a great university are close to none.

It should be no surprise that by 2004, Hendrix seniors won twenty-two Watson fellowships in that program's nineteen years, seventeen Barry Goldwater fellowships in that program's sixteen years, and, to me, the most impressive of all, six Rhodes Scholars. One in eight of the state's physicians went to Hendrix. And the National Science Foundation ranks Hendrix among the top fifty in producing Ph.D.s in chemistry, physics, and engineering.

All this is achieved in a warm community of learning in which minority students are an integral part, and campus employees not only call students and professors by their first names, but put on the Christmas banquet. Former president Ann Die had hired a catering firm so that the employees could come. But after one banquet, the employees said they could do a better job and took over.

Developing moral thinking is an important part of the Hendrix experience. A former provost said, "It is places like this that are incubating the continuity of democratic values." What he said is certainly true at Hendrix and at other colleges in this book. In 2003, students adopted a code defining academic integrity, along with penalties for infractions.

Hendrix knows, like other colleges in this book, that they must prepare students to live in a global rather than an American world. So, in every major they are encouraged to have a term, or more, abroad. For most of them it becomes the mind-opening pinnacle of their college experience.

The faculty is an exceptional body of teacher-scholars for whom teaching is an act of love. One of them, Dr. Thomas Goodwin, a chemistry prof, won the national baccalaureate teacher of the year award in 2003. Some of them had planned only to start their careers at Hendrix and then move on to research institutions, but found that their lives had been changed.

A music professor said, "I came out of an undergraduate education [University of Texas] not much different than when I went in, except that I had a lot more knowledge. What's amazing to me is that the kids who come in here are unrecognizable when they leave. They learn to cope with challenges and to understand other ways and points of view, partly because of the foreign programs." To which another professor added, "I told a kid just today, 'You couldn't possibly have done something this sophisticated six months ago.'"

Collaborative learning is emphasized. Built with this idea in mind, the new library has small study rooms where little groups can work together. There is no cutthroat competitiveness.

As at other colleges in this book, the faculty's enthusiasm for their students is one of the two main reasons they have stayed at Hendrix instead of moving on to a university. The other is the faculty belief in a shared enterprise and the strong sense of fellowship. A history professor recalled, "I was only going to stay three or four years, and mine is the standard story, and it's the students, it's not the Arkansas climate. One of my students is a combined physics and history major, another designed his own interdisciplinary major. They're interested in many things, not just preprofessional or vocational."

A music professor said he came twenty years ago not intending to stay long, "but now you couldn't blast me out of here. The commitment of the students was a new world for me. Students are interested in music who aren't music majors. Both students and faculty are interested in worlds other than their own. The collegiality here was unbelievable; no factions at all, no infighting. This is a more appropriate kind of education; you get opened up earlier and specialize later."

A biologist who had come to Hendrix as a temporary stop on his way to being a researcher summed it up with, "I was blown away by the collegiality, a feeling that there was something special happening, that everybody was in this together, that they really were changing students' lives, and that that was something important—the most important thing you could do with your life. I've now been here twenty-seven years. We don't have disciplinary problems; they attend class. We've got good people, good counseling, and a positive atmosphere, and this is critical to a student looking for a place. We have very high standards and I think that is why our students are so successful in graduate and professional schools—that and collaborative learning and critical learning."

Freshmen have a two-day bonding and orientation campout with faculty members before the fall term begins. The school year has three terms of three courses each, so students can concentrate their energies. They start their Hendrix Odyssey, as the college calls its new plan, with Journeys, an interdisciplinary course that explores the life journeys of people in several different cultures. This is followed by Explorations, a sophisticated orientation course for the liberal arts and success at Hendrix. There is a required course, Challenges of the Contemporary World, which is just what the title says it is. There is also a capstone experience that can be a comprehensive examination or any one of a number of other scholarly or creative projects. The Odyssey also requires an approved activity in at least three of the following six categories: artistic creativity, global awareness, professional and leadership development, service to the world, research, and special projects.

Off-campus study opportunities are many. There's a Washington Semester Program, a Hendrix-in-Oxford Program in England, and many others around the world. Students interested in marine biology can take courses in the Gulf Coast Research Laboratory in Ocean Springs, Mississippi. Often these are heady experiences the student couldn't have imagined having when he was a freshman. For instance, the high point of one political science major's college career was a summer internship in the White House where, among other things, his duties included the exciting work of drafting political speeches.

Hendrix is an easygoing, unpretentious, democratic place. A senior from Missouri headed for medical school said she had been "charmed by the people and by the community atmosphere," to which a freshman added, "this is a really unique community. You can relate to your profs; they are your friends and they are involved in the volunteer programs." (Long before she's a senior I'm sure she won't try to modify "unique.") A senior from Texas called it the most welcoming and friendly place he had visited, noting that after he got here he found the work "challenging."

They all talked about how important their out-of-class experiences had been to them. Some mentioned activities and some the excitement and broadening experiences of the foreign-study programs, but the common thread was that getting involved was essential to getting what you should out of the experience. "This is no place where you can fall through the cracks," one student said.

The kind of person who should come here, they said, should be willing to be involved in the life of the community, be "open-minded, accepting, and willing to grow, because this is a most diverse place." He especially should want to take an active part in his own education. This was not the place, they felt, for anyone who wouldn't be happy in a completely unpretentious place. It's not for the fast-track person.

Little Rock is only thirty miles away but students and faculty felt like the richness of the campus cultural programs, the variety of activities, and the limitless outdoor attractions were more than enough compensation for not being next door to a major metropolis. There is a good cultural life on campus. The generosity of foundations has enabled the college to put on some first-rate festivals.

This is an ideal place for African-American students. They are very active. They have a pep music group that plays at games, and a choir. As one said, "I know that I can do what I want at this school." An African-American sophomore said that she came here because "I was ready to take on a challenge, academically and socially; a positive challenge." And she's glad she did.

At first I was a little puzzled that none of the African-American students had mentioned Hendrix's charismatic African-American English professor, Dr. Alice Hines, the kind of teacher there should be more of. I concluded they didn't feel a need to mention race any more than she had in lovingly relating the successes of some of her late-blooming students. She didn't mention color until I asked whether the African-American students felt they were part of the community. "Absolutely!" she said. "Black students are very active at Hendrix and are part of the community. When they come here they know where they're going; it's not a new culture, and they're self-starters."

Like some of the faculty members, I was unexpectedly blown away by Hendrix. It is an exemplary college and teenagers of a wide range of abilities and interests would find this a very happy fit socially. It is a far nicer and more sophisticated place, besides being infinitely more exciting academically, than the retreaded teachers' colleges that are now universities in most states, or the state universities. There should be at least one college as good as Hendrix in every state.

Ten years later, students and recent graduates say that Hendrix has changed their lives for the better.

A 2004 graduate, a Fulbright Scholar, said, "Hendrix College has been an amazing influence on my life. The students were more intellectually curious and open-minded than at other colleges, and much less pretentious, and a welcoming environment for gay students." He was one of several who called foreign-study terms their best experiences. He said, "It forced me to look at American culture from an entirely new perspective."

A rising junior said, "Being a biology major in a world-culture class taught by a religion professor was one of the most rewarding experiences of my life. The last two years have been the best of my life, but they'll have to compete with the next two."

A rising sophomore said Hendrix had taken "a rough, careless student and made a dedicated scholar. Hendrix has an incredible ability to provide for its students whatever it is they need to expand and grow, and isn't that what education is about?"

Two alums in top graduate programs, who'd been hotshot students in high school, said Hendrix was the best undergraduate experience they could have hoped for, that they "were challenged daily by professors who truly cared about the growth of their students."

A classmate said the foreign terms had made her realize who she was as a global citizen and thus became more accepting of other cultures and people.

A freshman girl said, "Never in my wildest dreams could I have imagined I would be able to seek advice from what I consider the greatest minds in the country, and they are also asking about my life and opening their office doors and their homes to me and my peers."

A junior from Houston said, "I know this sounds really cheesy, but coming to Hendrix has made me a better person. I went to school with kids who got brand-new Mustangs for their sixteenth birthdays. I had to have the coolest clothes, the newest shoes, etcetera. At Hendrix those things matter much less. I can honestly say that I am much less materialistic because of my time at Hendrix. My confidence level has increased exponentially due to my experiences here."

Lynchburg College
Lynchburg, Virginia

Lynchburg College is a 214-acre spread of exceptional beauty, complete with a lake and a view of Virginia's Blue Ridge Mountains, that is no longer a traditional little Southern college. In its rebirth it is making productive citizens by taking average students and developing in them powers they didn't know they had, with a special emphasis on minority students.

Seventy percent of the 1,850 full-time students are from New England, mid-Atlantic, or midwestern states. Their SAT totals are in the 900 to 1,300 range, half of them are in the upper half of their high school classes, and about 75 percent of the applicants are accepted. Students dress neatly. They are more conventional, nice-looking teenagers happy to be on this nice campus. And at Lynchburg they're in a community that operates on a student-run honor code.

For freshman who had high grades and SAT scores, advanced-placement courses, and extracurricular activities, there is a Westover Honors Program that provides special programs, lectures and trips, independent study in their senior year, and their own dorm suites.

Lynchburg is something of a financial bargain; Virginia provides tuition grants to state residents; aid is given to those in need. The college also offers a variety of scholarships out of its own funds, as well as all of the federal grant and loan funds. Ninety-six percent of the students receive some financial aid.

Twenty years ago the faculty saw that the job the college was doing had to change if it was going to prepare people to live productive lives in a new kind of world. Lynchburg brought back Great Books courses to encourage students to think about life's and society's problems; it required writing and speaking across the curriculum to equip students to communicate their ideas clearly.

What might seem a nonacademic wrinkle was also introduced. It is an Outward Bound–type Adventure Program with a challenging rope-climbing course that the freshmen have to negotiate. The college calls this "another form of education," because as in Outward Bound, surmounting obstacles raises one's self-image and builds self-esteem.

More important, the college committed itself to a change to attract more minority students and to help them succeed, which it has been doing. By 2004, Lynchburg had 15 percent multicultural students and 90 percent of those in the class of 2005 had become juniors. Many others have gone on to graduate and professional schools. One of several efforts responsible has been a Connection Program to help with the transition to college life. In this, thirty upperclassmen act as mentors and big brothers for groups of fifteen freshmen each. Another is a staff that gives special help to those taking "killer" courses, such as chemistry or math. And there is a general writing center for students who want help.

These good things had their beginnings in a faculty with vision, working with the late Dr. George Rainsford, president for ten years. When I visited him in 1994, he talked about his ideas of what a college must do in the new millennium. First, he said, in the next several years, one out of three people in this country will be of a minority. This means colleges must be helping minorities become equally prosperous parts of the family. Second, he said, every student will need more sophisticated preparation to be able to compete in a more complex and global economy. Instead of becoming a repository of soon-to-be-obsolete information, every student needs to be able to think, to see connections, to organize and to use information, and to write and speak clearly. And Lynchburg has been doing a good job, as you will see.

A lot of other good things have been happening in the last ten years. In 2001, a communications professor was named Virginia Professor of the Year, and in 2003, a nursing professor was one of four in the country named Outstanding Professor of the Year.

Lynchburg also became one of forty colleges supported by the Bonner Leaders Program to produce people "who will transform the lives of their campuses and communities and the world through service and leadership."

The college has a new 470-acre nature-study center, a tremendous academic asset that will enable all students, not just the environmentalists or scientists, to see the interconnectedness of things. It has two lakes, wetlands, a mile-long stretch of the Otter River, as well as grass and woodlands. It also has a new building with research labs, classrooms, and a pavilion for outdoor lectures, classes, and social activities.

On the campus are a large new classroom building and five townhouses for upper-class students so that more than the current 85 percent can live on campus and be involved in activities.

The faculty, having decided to require writing across the curriculum, realized there had to be something meaty to think and write about, so they introduced Great Books courses, now called the Lynchburg College Symposium Readings (LCSR). And they're not just lectures to passive listeners. At least 20 percent of each course must consist of writing. A program evaluator from Harvard reported that he was amazed to see "a literate, scholarly paper using a classical source emerge from a course on a subject like accounting."

The Communications Studies Program argued that speaking was as important as writing, so many classes became oral presentations by students instead of lectures by a professor.

Every student has to take six courses that deal with some of society's major concerns. It starts in the freshman year, so that the student gets to know John Locke, for example, all the way along. And the senior year LCSR course is a capstone to pull together the thirty-two courses he takes in his college career.

A college faculty often will accept change only grudgingly, but most of Lynchburg's is enthusiastic about theirs. They sit in on each other's classes—something that's a no-no at most institutions. They have discussions on what's working and what isn't. Some of them are elated about what it has done for their teaching as well as for their students.

A history prof said, "LCSR has shown me that lectures are not the most efficient way of teaching. Most of my classes now are conducted by questions; I only lecture when I'm introducing new material. The result is that I never know where the class is going. Furthermore, it has taken me from being isolated in my own discipline to seeing how it fits into the whole picture.

"In a model U.N. class where oral presentations are required, a very shy student had to talk, and it worked an incredible change in her. Group oral presentations are videotaped so they can see themselves later, how effectively they talked, and it's amazing how it builds confidence."

With obvious pride in what the new program was achieving, one prof said, "A few years ago, a boy who wasn't ready to work flunked out, realized after a term what he was missing, came back, graduated with honors, and won a major award as a senior. We're producing productive citizens!"

The faculty does business research and provides lectures for the business community. They also give people older than twenty-five a chance to complete or augment their education in a part-time program.

The hours of community service put in by the students have grown enormously and it is a large part of the college culture.

Lynchburg's students are heavily preprofessional, and a good many go on to get MBAs.

All of the students I talked to said Lynchburg was a place where you felt you should be involved and that if you weren't you were a bit of a deviate or a shirker. "This is not a wallflower school," as one put it, "it definitely encourages involvement." More than one of them said the whole attitude of the place had fostered independence and built their self-confidence. A couple of seniors said that as freshmen they'd been shy and afraid to speak out, but Lynchburg had helped them learn to assert themselves. "It helps in becoming your own person," added a senior girl.

Whether it's part of a nationwide phenomenon or a consequence of the new Lynchburg, the dean of students thinks the students here are less materialistic and more service-oriented than a decade or so ago, and also that they have a more practical, hands-on attitude.

Every student answered my stock question about whether they'd have good enough friends on the faculty to have dinner or spend night at their homes five years from now with emphatic responses like, "Sure, with lots of them," or "We have dinner at their homes now."

So far the Lynchburg approach has the full endorsement of its students. They agree with the college's claim that it is empowering them; they feel good about themselves and grateful for a confidence they didn't come to college with.

Ten years later, students are full of enthusiastic thank-yous to Lynchburg. They say that they achieved things they hadn't thought they were capable of, or sought "higher goals" because of the encouragement of their professors.

Frequently it was the supportive community, their internships or other off-campus experiences that changed their lives. Several referred to the college as "home" or "my family." One said her years at Lynchburg were responsible for her getting into law school and for her success in life. She spoke for others when she said, "I will be forever grateful."

A frequent sentiment from alumni was, "It was the best decision I ever made." One, a 1998 alumna, made an exception; she said, "except for marrying my husband." Most talked about their professors and their continuing friendships. One said her friends who'd gone to other colleges were "amazed that my adviser came to my wedding." Another spoke for several others with, "several remain an important part of my life today. They have become my mentors, advisers, and cherished friends."

A classmate said, "A great lesson I learned at LC that continued on to my current life was the ability to take advantage of any situation and excel past it."

Still another '98 alumna gave this testimonial: "Every woman has at least one person in her life she can point to as a source of support and encouragement, a force who pushed her always to do more so that she could eventually see her own strength of character, intellect, and creativity. I was fortunate to have an entire institution play that role in my life."

Undergraduates often spoke of Lynchburg "shaping the person I am today," always for the better. One said she now wanted "to make a difference in the world," and she doesn't get satisfied as easily as she used to. Another said the college prepares her to become independent and "an asset in the real world." A 2001 alumna had planned a business career, but "I left after four years knowing that I wanted to help other people."

A 1990 alumnus, an International Business major, in praising the marketability of his liberal arts education at Lynchburg, said, "who would have guessed that my presentation skills would shine because of an art class I had there. Who would have thought that an appreciation for the aesthetic could make such a difference? This is something a lot of my less fortunate colleagues are still struggling to grasp when their presentations simply fail to resonate the way mine do."

A 2001 alumna, now in a large public relations firm said, "Lynchburg college prepared me for graduate school and beyond. I did not struggle in some classes in my MBA program as some of my fellow classmates did. I had the background and knowledge necessary to succeed, academically and in business."

Millsaps College

Jackson, Mississippi

Few catalytic colleges are as good as Millsaps. On a day-long visit ten years ago, the sense of social responsibility, of family, and of mission and the desire to serve was palpable.

Today that is only part of the story. For one thing, it has 20 percent minority students, a figure that says much about its diversity. It has a master plan for its new facilities and for increasing the beauty of its 100-acre campus. And a capital campaign is raising funds for more financial aid, scholarships, new buildings and landscaping.

Perhaps its proudest boast is the all-purpose laboratory, a forest preserve of 4,000 acres in Yucatan, Mexico, owned jointly with Davidson College. Two Mayan ruins help make it a rich resource for just about every interest, whether it be archaeology, biology, the environment, demonstrating food production methods for the natives, economics, or history. In fact, the college magazine boasts, "Millsaps's sweeping vision for learning among the ruins leaves no discipline behind."

Millsaps was the first institution in the state to have a chapter of Phi Beta Kappa, the prestigious scholastic honor society. It has had five Rhodes Scholars. It is one of the sixteen colleges in the country and one of the three in the Deep South to have a Ford Foundation grant to prepare future college professors. The other southern schools are Eckerd in St. Petersburg and Morehouse in Atlanta. Its business program is the first in the state to win professional-association accreditation.

One great difference between a Deep South school like

Millsaps—or Hendrix in Arkansas, Birmingham-Southern in Alabama, or Rhodes in Tennessee—and a prestige school in the Northeast is that the kids you nod to crossing the campus or interview between classes seem so friendly and unaffected while kids at all the Northern schools are so cool and self-satisfied. (As a client there told me, "It's hard to be humble at Amherst.")

At Millsaps, the level of expectation is high, the grading is tougher than at many a prestige school, and 40 percent of its seniors go on to graduate or professional school. A school of 1,200, it has forty geology majors—an exceptional number—and fifty biology majors. There is no sense of competition or grade-grubbing; it is a collaborative learning adventure. Every student is actively involved; there is no way he can be a passive ear, as he would have to be at a university.

Millsaps takes 80 percent of its applicants, a third of them in the top tenth of their high school classes, about half in the top fifth, and 90 percent in the top half. Three-fourths of them have averages above 3.0 (B). The middle 50 percent have SAT scores ranging from 1120 to 1290, which means the other half have scores above or below those figures.

What all those figures mean is that while Millsaps will take B students and maybe some in the C range, the message to them is clear: Don't come to Millsaps unless you're interested in getting an education, which means work.

Millsaps students are not as affluent as those at many Eastern schools; 90 percent of them are on financial aid or get scholarships. Nor are they as affected. They don't exhibit the world-is-my-oyster attitude of many Ivy Leaguers. Faculty members and administrators describe them as ambitious young people who are interested in their education. Not only do many of them go on to graduate and professional schools, but many of them leave the state for greener pastures after graduation. The feeling I got was that what they wanted was not riches but a broader range of opportunities than the state offered.

Fifty-four percent of the student body come from thirty other states and eleven foreign countries, with Louisiana, Alabama, and Georgia providing most of the out-of-staters. Methodists, Baptists, and Catholics have nearly equal representation, and are trailed by Presbyterians and Episcopalians, and 15 percent of other faiths. Whatever their religious faiths or ethnic origins, all the kids I talked to were glad they came; more than one said, "This is my kind of school; it's so friendly and open," or "I've had opportunities here I wouldn't have had at other places." One fellow elaborated on this with, "You can get a Stanford education here at half the cost." I told him it was a lot better.

The able and enthusiastic faculty has national rather than regional roots. Its members not only earned their academic spurs in the nation's top universities but have also taught in them. But they prefer to teach at Millsaps, a conviction that comes through loud and clear in just about everything they say. Their sense of gratification and joy in their work is palpable; being on that campus is like a day in spring. (In fact, if visiting high school students have sense enough to see what lively, intelligent, and caring teachers these are, they'll look no further.) All this may sound a bit like hyperbole, but I've not been more persuaded by a school in many years.

As a former Brown faculty member said: "Here, the difference is that I'm given every incentive to improve my teaching skills, and [scholarly] publication is a way to hone those skills for use in the classroom. Millsaps offers a much more intimate relationship between the faculty and students. At Brown there was absolutely no incentive or pressure for me to work on my teaching. I'd go to my department chairman and say my class is getting too large and I need another one and he'd say what you need to do is to put in such qualifications that you can keep it low; schedule it at eight o'clock in the morning and put in a foreign language requirement. His approach was to limit the class so I could get my publications out.

"At Brown the classroom was only there to give some financial support so you could do your publishing. And that's why I'm happy here; it's an entirely different perspective. Here the people love to teach; at Brown they're being forced to teach. There are people there who do research well, but who cannot teach. That's why I enjoy it here.

"I see more growth here. Brown students are very highly motivated, but the lack of structure (no required courses) affects development of a good program. They have good creativity when they come in, but, having been selected for an elite group [Brown occasionally has been the most selective of the Ivies], they have no incentive to move beyond that. But these kids, by the time they finish, have a very similar type of creativity."

That statement eloquently summarizes one crucial difference between the university, whether prestige or pedestrian, and these high-quality places; these increase and improve the talents of youth.

Another vital difference is, as a business professor said, "We not only address their intellectual development, but we don't separate their development as a mature human being from the educational process. I do a lot of advising and I don't make a distinction between my function as an educator and my function as an adviser. And that makes a tremendous difference; they understand that actual development occurs in a lot of circumstances. In a university, they come to class and they want you to pour it in and then they go out. My classes at Alabama were three hundred; they're thirty here. I know them here; I didn't at Alabama.

An impressive English professor added: "We're asked to do something critical, and that's to evaluate a student's development, and there's no way under the sun you can do that with multiple-choice tests or by reading essays. I know more about my students than anybody at the University of Michigan, or the University of North Carolina, or the University of Alabama [all places where she has taught] would ever know about his."

There are two reasons why all this is true. One is the imaginative way the Millsaps curriculum probes the human experience, and the other is the collegial nature of the whole enterprise.

The goal of the curriculum, developed over two years by a faculty committee, is not the stuffing of young minds with facts, but rather the development of abilities that are going to be needed for the rest of their lives.

The new program, faculty members said, alters the model of liberal education. Instead of trying for coverage of history, philosophy, or some other subject with the narrative approach, it dissects a culture to help students see the big picture, to make connections, to use their imaginations and gray cells, and to make bold leaps—abilities they will especially need in the brave new world of unseen opportunities.

In four interdisciplinary, team-taught semester courses, freshmen and sophomores first take a topic of the ancient world, then of the premodern world, the modern world, and finally the contemporary world. They may choose courses in religion, history, fine arts, or something else, but all will be team-taught. For example, if an ancient world topic is theater, professors in religion, philosophy, and art would also be involved.

The other reason Millsaps is such a comfortable and effective learning place is that the faculty members talk to and learn from each other. This provides an implicit model for the students; they see professors getting each other's views, reading each other's work—sharing—and they do the same. It makes learning collegial rather than competitive.

Every morning, faculty teams discuss problems and listen to each other's presentations. "We all have a sense of where we're going; we all agree on the issues, which is wonderful," said one. "We're doing a better job of looking at a culture apart and see what's going on."

Whether it's the new curriculum or the perceptive way the faculty attacks it, they all talk of their excitement seeing in their students so much growth—in intellect, in self-confidence, and in the development of a philosophy of life or values. And the teachers feel privileged to be in on the magic.

The biology and chemistry teachers proudly displayed their new state-of-the-art laboratories and research facilities housed in an eye-catching structure that is architecturally distinguished and has a three-story rotunda grand enough for receptions. Any college would be happy to have either the building or the science evangelists within it, or both.

All science students get involved in research, though how much they do is pretty much up to the student. The opportunities are not only there but are being pushed in front of them. In the second year, everyone does a research paper, which is part of the school's heavy emphasis on writing. In the core curriculum, a paper is due every week. Each year, the Ford Foundation grant starts a dozen budding scholars on the path to becoming college professors. The college also invites students and faculty to apply for fellowships on which they work together for a year, both in the classroom and outside.

Many students echoed what a faculty member told me: "They are attracted to the college for one reason or another and they change. They get new ideas about what they think they want to do with their lives, and they change because of what they do and what they learn and what they hear."

Leaving his office, I chanced upon a heartwarming example of this. She was a senior, a French and biology major planning to work for the Peace Corps in French West Africa before becoming a teacher. She said Millsaps "has helped me see myself and has made me want to be a teacher rather than a doctor, because we don't have enough good teachers." The standards and the whole intellectual experience at Millsaps had opened her eyes to a great need.

Another example was a senior biology major who said, "When I came to Millsaps I didn't know who I was, and I just kind of stumbled around. But then some of the exceptional people here took me under their wing, and I've ended up with opportunities I couldn't imagine getting at other colleges. I'm doing research in genetics and assisting in teaching three classes this year under a Ford fellowship. My faculty mentor and I are going to write a textbook next semester based on our work together."

Others had good reason equally important to them; a sophomore English major said, "Everyone here is so nice and friendly, and it's so easy to meet people and get involved. I sure don't know of many schools where I could be a copy editor for the college newspaper my first year and work for the literary magazine."

And a junior English major agreed that Millsaps had given her opportunities to develop leadership skills and strengthen her self-confidence, as a resident manager and as president of the Black Student Association, among other things.

A clincher of sorts was provided by a budding intellectual, one of that rare breed: a classics major. Asked why he was at Millsaps, he replied, "It's my kind of school."

Every college has dissatisfied students and those who shouldn't be there, but I didn't run into any at Millsaps. The students I queried spoke with one voice, saying the same sorts of things the faculty members did; they liked it here and found it exciting; they talked to and learned from each other; it was so collegial it was familial and if they had to do it over again, they wouldn't be anywhere else.

Ten years later the comments of students and recent graduates were reflecting the same sense of social responsibility and desire to serve as in the mid-nineties. That surely will be true ten years hence, and well beyond. Also, the Millsaps reactions tended to be more serious than those in many of the other colleges.

However, the most senior alumnus, class of 1975, added the view that a Millsaps degree had a high market value. "Millsaps instilled in me a thirst for learning that has never stopped, and I still find that atmosphere on campus today. In addition, having a degree from Millsaps has enriched my reputation simply because of the incredible reputation the college has in the area. A Millsaps degree means so much to graduate schools (law school in my case), employers, and colleagues. I have found many doors opened simply because of my association with the college. Finally, Millsaps was rigorous, and I found I had an excellent preparation for graduate school because of my Millsaps experience."

A 2004 alumna in medical school said that as a result of her four years at Millsaps, "I am challenged to fight the comfortable temptation of complacency. I am prepared to analyze situations and environments and spark change when improvements are needed."

She wants to practice in rural Mississippi because there is such "dire need" there. And she hopes to treat her patients "holistically by ministering to their minds, bodies, and souls. By applying the lessons that have been embedded in my mind and heart by my Millsaps experience, I hope to respond to the call of social responsibility, engage in meaningful work, and strive to live authentically."

Alumni spoke of their "transformative experiences" at Millsaps, of having to confront presently held opinions with novel ideas and of having to think critically about them. One, planning to be a minister, and a top student in high school, had been advised, "to keep my head on straight" when he came to Millsaps, since "it had the reputation of being irreligious at best." Instead, he said, "I found church in the largest sense of the word, loving people engaged in a common task exemplified in the school's motto, *ad excellentum,* toward excellence; we are a people driven to excel." In his freshman year, it had been a shock to get a C on his first paper.

Although he'd been warned that Millsaps would destroy his faith, he said the opposite happened; he became "enthralled with the sacredness of other religious texts" which made him ask, "Why have I been so willing to limit God to one revelation, found in one set of scriptures, given to one religion?"

He added, "I was given new eyes to see my own tradition in a more meaningful way by asking the tough questions."

New College

Sarasota, Florida

f you are interested in learning for the sake of learning, in an honors college that has no required courses, an evaluation-based grading system, and that produces winners wholesale, try New College of Florida in Sarasota. You'll love it, as do nearly 700 others.

It is one of the five most intellectually challenging colleges (or universities) in the country. The others are Marlboro, Reed, St. John's, and one that's been labeled "a seminary for scientists," the California Institute of Technology.

New College was born in 1960 on 140 bayfront acres of the Charles Ringling and Caples estates as a private, innovative honors college. Fifteen years later, for reasons of financial security, it became the honors college of Florida's public university system as part of the University of South Florida. In 2001 New College regained independence while remaining part of the state system. The New College Foundation, the school's private, nonprofit fundraising arm, provides part of its support.

New College's evaluation-based system of grading has encouraged an educational virtue—breadth. Even though there are no required courses, students don't shy away from tough ones; there's no bugaboo of a bad grade on a transcript. Instead, in-depth faculty evaluations assay the student's strengths and weaknesses as well as the quality of his or her work. Gone are the flat A, B, or C labels.

Students and graduate schools both like it. One girl told me, "I'd like to put my evaluation on the wall." The graduate schools obviously are sold on it. A *Wall Street Journal* survey found New College seniors get into the top law, business, and medical schools at a higher rate than those of any other public institution except University of Michigan, and New College ranks thirty-first among the top fifty private and public feeder colleges in the country.

New College's educational plan is akin to those of Antioch, Hampshire, and Marlboro in making the student take the initiative in planning a joint venture whose goal is "excellence, creativity, and personal growth." The idea is to develop self-starters with the power to keep on growing; winners, in other words.

It is a plan that, as the late Eugene "Bill" Wilson, Amherst's longtime dean of admissions, said, "trains you for nothing and prepares you for everything." And that includes any career not yet invented. The proof is in its products. In its short life, New College has turned out numerous Carnegie, Fulbright, and Rhodes Scholars, corporate CEOs, Ivy League faculty members, an Ivy League dean, doctors, lawyers, economists, legislators, entrepreneurs, musicians, a music-school department chairman, composers, writers, a TV producer, and a South Pole explorer. A mathematician and a physicist have won the top awards in their disciplines, and another physicist teaches at California Institute of Technology.

The New College educational plan is simple and gives the student all the freedom of choice he or she can handle. It consists of "contracts" for seven of the eight semesters with each contract involving work in up to four different subject areas. There are also three independent study projects (one a year), a senior thesis, and an oral baccalaureate examination. A January term is devoted to independent research projects.

Everybody is happy with it; in fact, New College is a campus of people enthusiastic about their work. In two visits I didn't find a single dissenter. One girl who couldn't afford to return to Haverford for her sophomore year said of New College, "I love it more every day," and added, "at Haverford all those kids want to be is doctors, lawyers, or economists." One of three Fulbright Scholars in her senior class was glad that she hadn't been able to return to Sarah Lawrence. "Coming here," she said, "was my good luck."

And if this exceptional college is for you, they'll probably take you. They accept most of their applicants, as do Antioch, Marlboro, Reed, and St. John's, because someone not interested in this adventure doesn't apply.

About 92 percent of those who do have SAT verbal scores over 600, and 72 percent have math scores over 600. The average GPA is 3.8. But what really counts is whether learning for the sake of learning excites you. A solid GPA from a strong mix of high school classes said one prof, is more likely to indicate a good prospect than the SATs.

The costs make New College an academic bargain. Tuition

and fees were $16,473 in 2004 for out-of-staters and $3,240 for Florida residents. Room and board were $5,668.

Every one of the blue-ribbon faculty is a Ph.D. and an active scholar, but unlike a research university, the faculty at New College all teach full-time. Even the president, Gordon Michalson, Jr., teaches. The 11–1 student-teacher ratio doesn't begin to reveal either the quality or quantity of the one-on-one relationships this community of learning lives by.

Faculty members have won so many major cutting-edge research grants from federal agencies, and their mentoring gets so many students involved, that the blue-ribbon designation fits. Here are some of them:

A biochemist with continuing six-figure National Institutes of Health grants is studying earthworm stem cells in a quest that may help find cures for Parkinson's disease, cancer, and Alzheimer's disease. A physicist has a patent in the burgeoning new field of nanotechnology, making microscopically tiny objects of all kinds for major industries of the future. A psychologist has a grant to learn how the dolphins' sonar system works, how it "feels" or "sees" objects at a distance, and how it aids in communication. Her work has been the subject of several national television programs and magazine articles.

A National Science Foundation grant is funding a mathematics professor's work on computer software to help students learn abstract concepts in mathematics. The U.S. Education Department is funding a physics professor's groundbreaking work using spectroscopy to date and analyze some of the nation's most valuable works of art without having to disturb the paintings or sculptures to take samples.

The college itself has a federal grant for its marine- and environmental-science labs to work with schools and community groups, studying the implications of waste water management on business and the environment in the state.

A charismatic music professor's story typifies New College's spirit of adventure. Most of his majors did not come to college intending to major in music, but now several are composers, performers, and directors thanks to the school's affiliation with Sarasota's thriving arts community. Through an association with the Florida West Coast Symphony, New College students gain the opportunity to have their original compositions performed by one of Florida's leading orchestras. Unique opportunities like these lead New College students to a colorful choice of majors. During my visit, one young woman had a double major of music and physics; another had French and music.

Two professors have turned down offers to go to Ivy League universities, as has President Michalson, a philosophy-of-religion scholar renowned in his arcane field. He said no to a prestigious offer from Brown University out of a sense of mission. The faculty unanimously elected him president when the college became independent in 2001. Nor does he lack for student admirers. One girl beamed as she said, "He always stops and talks when he meets me on campus, and his classes are wonderful."

New College has a broad array of foreign- and off-campus-study opportunities and internships, and it encourages and actively helps students to take advantage of them. Many also do research terms off campus.

Student life on this semitropical, waterfront campus is informal, and the activities, whether political, religious, artistic, academic, or other, are student-initiated. Sports are recreational and the facilities are varied. There are basketball, tennis, and racquetball courts, a volleyball pit, a multipurpose field, a running path, a twenty-five-meter swimming pool, and a state-of-the-art fitness center. Sailboats, sailboards, and canoes also are available to students free of charge.

What's more, Sarasota is a city noted as a cultural center for theater, art, and music, as well as for its beautiful public beaches. Here you may, if you wish, complement the intellectual life with as much cultural and recreational life as you want.

. . .

Note: This is New College's debut in this book, so there can be no "Ten Years Later" section. However, in 2005, I attended a pre-commencement reception for seniors and their parents, one that gave a feeling of near-euphoria unlike any I'd seen before. Parents weren't just relieved their sons and daughters had gotten their degrees. Every one I talked to was enthusiastic about how much New College had changed them. And they weren't talking about four years of maturing; they were talking about how pleased they were with the kinds of people their children were now. It was more than palpable, it bubbled out, and it made me feel good.

Rhodes College
Memphis, Tennessee

If its elegant, Oxford-like campus of lovely grounds and collegiate Gothic buildings with leaded glass windows were transported from its residential area in Memphis, Tennessee, to a town in New England, Rhodes College, formerly Southwestern, would be as selective as an Ivy school. But so long as it isn't, it will have to be satisfied with being better than an Ivy.

The catalog says beautiful architecture "inspires and broadens the mind, expands the consciousness to beauty and harmony and reminds the community of the history and breadth of learning, shapes the quality of education, and provides students with a constant vision of excellence." Or, as Winston Churchill said, "First we shape our buildings, and then our buildings shape us."

Not only does the campus have an architectural unity that is probably unique, but every stone of its many buildings comes from the same quarry, because a long-ago president accepted the quarry as payment for a debt to the college. Fourteen of those buildings are in the National Register of Historic Places.

The new center of the campus, opened in 2005, is an imposing $42 million library with a media center, peer-tutoring space, a teaching and learning laboratory, group-study rooms, and hundreds of carrels for laptop use, among other things.

Two more important facilities have been added since my last visit: a comprehensive sport and recreation center added to the gym, and attractive apartments for 200 juniors and seniors to keep them on campus.

Rhodes also has several new programs to expand the college's emphasis on community service. One is a center for "research and education through service" to "translate academic study and personal concern into effective community leadership." Another is an institute for regional studies using the Memphis region as its laboratory. The college also gives fifteen scholarships a year to students who make a service commitment.

A partnership with St. Jude's Hospital seeks to create research opportunities for every science major.

Rhodes is more selective than most of the colleges in this book; while it accepts about 70 percent of its applicants, 62 percent of them had grade point averages of 3.5 or better, 45 percent were in the top 10 percent of their high school classes, and 90 percent had averages of 3.0 (B) or better.

The middle 50 percent had SAT verbals ranging from 590 to 700, and math scores from 600 to 690. Half of them had SAT totals under 1,280. But figures don't tell the whole story. As David J. Wottle, Dean of Admissions and Financial Aid, said, "No grouping of numbers can adequately convey the importance we place on the subjective criteria . . . counselor and teacher recommendations, a personal interview, the application essay, and extracurricular involvements. We want," he said, "a very motivated and diverse group of talented students." About 90 percent return for the sophomore year and about 75 percent graduate in four years.

Most of the students come from the southeast or southwest but the college is seeking and getting more diversity. It has 12 percent minority students and about 3 percent foreign students. While Memphis has a large African-American population, the competition for its college-going teenagers is cutthroat; colleges across the country are bidding top dollar for every one of them.

Rhodes cost a total of $31,000 for 2005, including incidentals, but three-fourths of the students get financial aid averaging $19,000. Also, half get merit scholarships that average $11,000. Merit aid is in addition to need-based aid, and all aid is for four years, assuming the student is in good standing.

For decades, the college was sunk in anonymity as one of sixteen Southwesterns. Then in 1984 it broke out of the mold not only with a new name—honoring a former president—but with a campaign to let people know how good it was. The matter-of-fact, unprepossessing 1984 catalog says not a word about the beauty of the campus, the school's high mission, or its top quality. The current catalog casts the old modesty aside to proclaim these virtues but, unlike other colleges, it makes good on them. As a maverick prexy in the roaring '50s said, "If the Federal Trade Commission ever started prosecuting colleges for false and misleading advertising, there'd be more college than corporation presidents under cease-and-desist orders."

Many of Rhodes's students have the look of people accustomed to its expensive beauty. For one thing, the hairdos and handbags are clues that fewer of these kids are on financial aid than at Millsaps or at many midwestern colleges. The figure is just over 40 percent, or a little better than half that at Millsaps. However, Rhodes offers so many merit scholarships in which need is not a factor that the percentage getting some form of aid jumps to over 70 percent. This almost puts Rhodes in a class with that nonpareil men's college, Wabush, where half of the students get merit scholarships and 93 percent get need-based aid. It makes Rhodes a prime prospect for high school seniors looking for merit scholarships.

Slightly more than half of the men and women belong to one of the six fraternities and seven sororities, but it is not necessary to be Greek to be a big shot on campus or to have a good social life. One reason is the students do not live in the fraternity or sorority houses; everybody lives in the dorms. The student body is, as one faculty member said, "middle-of-the-road conservative." But on my first visit twenty-five years ago, what had made an indelible impression was how accepting and friendly they were. At a time when African-American students on many campuses in the North were segregating themselves, those at Rhodes told me they were contented members of a single social group.

A clue to the students' mostly middle-class origins is what faculty members say about them: "They expect to be cared for—a sense of entitlement," or "They could work harder." Still another was the note I saw on a professor's door: "Dr. Haynes, I need to have a meeting ASAP. Please give me a call at 3204. Ralph." While such a note may convey a perhaps irritating sense of entitlement, it also suggests that faculty-student relations are close and easy. Just imagine a student daring to do that at any large university.

Professor and former academic dean Marshall McMahon, who has won an outstanding-teacher award, said that the fact that more Rhodes students have educated (and affluent) parents than at places such as Rutgers or Florida, where he had taught, explains the sense of entitlement. He also made two important contrasts with the larger schools. For one, the bottom one-third in ability at those universities don't get into Rhodes, so it can focus on the problems of the rest, "and they can't fall through the cracks." A student would have to hide, he said, to avoid getting help. The other is class size; they are fifteen or twenty instead of 150 or 200. "So, this is a great place to learn; there's a lot more student contact. And you get kids who see the light come on."

Asked if he thought Rhodes had an impact on them, he said, "Unquestionably. There is a community of scholarship among the students. Even in their social life, it's hard to get away from their common purpose. When you're out on Saturday night, you get conversational exposures to the ideas or problems discussed in class. Life is a learning experience. At Harvard, students are taught by students. Here they're taught by scholar-teachers. I repeat: this is a great place to learn."

But that is only part of the picture. A professor who gave up a rich research fiefdom and a larger income at the University of California at Los Angeles to come here "to teach and to talk to students," said: "Here they're incredibly polite to each other and in class they help each other. They are remarkably honest. I've never been at a place where the honor code was as effective in bringing about the sense of values it was intended to, and it is student-administered. In one case, a student was exonerated, so it works very well; it's not just punitive. There was cheating at Gettysburg [where he also taught] on exams and plagiarizing of papers. There is a striking quality here and a high level of expectation. There is definitely more interest in learning here than at UCLA or at Gettysburg. At UCLA they were much more focused on what they wanted—the job or career. And there's a seriousness of purpose here that was lacking at Gettysburg."

The institution planned it that way. And here is where it bests an Ivy. It hires faculty members who believe in "lives of faith and service, and that a liberal education is the best one for all of life." And it requires every student to take one of the two four-semester sequences intended to make them examine, and strengthen, their values and beliefs. One is The Search for Values in the Light of Western History and Religion, an interdisciplinary exploration taught by profs from the religion, philosophy, history, political science, art, English, humanities, Spanish, and German departments. The other is Life Then and Now, a study of the Hebrew-Christian tradition which is taught by members of the religion, philosophy, and English departments.

While Rhodes, like most private colleges, is church-affiliated (Presbyterian), its emphasis on an examined and moral life is the only clue a student would get. There is no denominational tinge, and people of all faiths or no faith feel equally at home.

Aside from the core courses, students have a panoply of choices: traditional majors or interdisciplinary ones, internships in many different fields that may open career doors, and a variety of foreign-study experiences—including, of course, a term at Oxford.

What Professor McMahon had said was spelled out in detail by a chemistry professor who had taught at the University of North Carolina and at the University of California at Irvine. "I know four hundred students by name; I've got thirty students coming to a Christmas party tonight. Seventy-five percent of the chemistry students do research, both in the academic year and in the summer. To be alone in a place like this, you'd have to work at it. My own child is a senior here. The individual attention he gets, the quality of it, and the students' appreciation of it—I literally could not ask for more."

The psychologist who had left UCLA added testimony that is particularly relevant for preparing for a new and different world. He said the kind of education needed today is not possible at a place like UCLA because, "If you're going to make a career contribution, you have to find out what your interests are; the ball has to be put in your court. That kind of interaction—dialogue, questions—is necessary, and I can do that now; I can talk to them here." In fact, it was a visit in which he saw what kind of learning community it was that sold him on rejecting a research empire to teach at Rhodes.

A similar approach had been made by a business/economics professor. He'd had tenure at Vanderbilt, had quit to run the family's national petroleum business, then wanted to return to teaching. Asked why he didn't go back to Vanderbilt, he said, "The kids are the same at Vanderbilt and here, but you can go through Vanderbilt and never write a sentence or see a prof. I wanted contact with students. And that's precisely why I am here. And here they learn to write."

According to another economist who's been at Rhodes for twenty years, its students have changed a little bit. He perceives them as better students, more like good consumers, and there's a sense of community in spite of fraternities and sororities. But in the matter of community service he sees no change, because "We've had a long tradition of community service with an established program, and a large percentage of the students are involved."

He also said that the honor system has a lot to do with a major objective: "We hope to make them responsible for their own actions." The way the economics/business faculty handles its internship program also has a lot to do with that objective. "We don't just send them out," he said. "They have to do résumés to show what they've done and what their objective is. There is lots of economic theory in our joint business-economics major, and every major has to do a research paper and present it to the class."

About 35 percent of Rhodes graduates go on to professional or graduate school, with medicine, business, and law accounting for a large share of them. The acceptance rates in all fields are near the ceiling. In the last ten years, Rhodes has had sixteen Fulbright Scholars and six National Science Foundation Fellows. Since the prestigious Rhodes Scholars program was founded, the college has had six win that honor. Its literature boasts of being in the top 20 percent of all colleges and universities in the percentage of graduates who later get Ph.D.s in the humanities and social sciences, which puts it in good company, if not in the top fifty.

As at many other colleges, there are fewer business and more English majors these days. Theology, psychology, and letters divide up a quarter of the majors.

As at Millsaps, Birmingham-Southern, Guilford, and Eckerd, one gets an unmistakable sense of a quiet live-and-let-live atmosphere. A biology prof observed, "We are not venturesome. Southern educational systems don't put out the product others do. Our students often come not well prepared, but they have two years to overcome it." They tend, he said, to be bright, middle-of-the-road conservatives. Fifteen of them in his department are doing research with faculty members, and three of them were coauthors of an oral presentation at a national professional meeting.

Rhodes's students are also comfortable in the assurance they're in a top-notch school; they're not frustrated rejects in a fallback college. The editor of the school newspaper, for example, chose it over Bowdoin, Carleton, and Haverford, and he would do it again, even if he thinks that not enough of his peers are interested in the life of the mind. But then he's a philosophy major headed toward the academic life, and his reservations were the only ones I ran into.

The son of a faculty member said he had tried "an eastern college" for his freshman year and switched to Rhodes, even though his father was there. As at Millsaps, some said their southern high schools had not prepared them for the rigors of a place like Rhodes. Everyone I talked to was glad he or she was at Rhodes and gave the impression that being there was a star in their crown.

The stately beauty of the campus and the smiles one gets walking from one imposing building to another convey a sense of stability and civility. The people are just as friendly as they were ten and twenty years ago. It would be difficult to imagine a sit-in blocking the administration building, a mass protest, or graffiti on a wall, much less a revolution. The nature of things wouldn't stand for it.

First-rate, caring scholar-teachers are the hallmark of the colleges in this book, but I was especially impressed with the ones I talked with at Rhodes. The college awards rich monetary prizes each year for outstanding teaching, for research and creative activity, and for service to the school. It is one of those few colleges that gives what it proclaims in the catalog in full measure to its lucky students.

Ten years later, alumni in many different fields brag that they top the competition or find graduate school easy because Rhodes instructors had taught them how to think, how to write, and to demand the best of themselves. In the process, they became close friends.

A thread that runs through their testimonials is the number who had no idea when they came to college that they could achieve the things they did, whether it was a creative, research, or learning triumph or some athletic or extracurricular accomplishment. And this kind of tribute came as often from the kids who'd been whizzes in high school as from those who hadn't. One of them made Phi Beta Kappa, something she couldn't have imagined as a freshman.

They also were sure that no other school could have given them the same kind of you-can-do-it confidence that the "incredible role models" at Rhodes had made possible. This sort of thing was voiced by alumni of other schools in this book.

Several had been affected by Rhodes's heavy emphasis on service. One mentioned especially the good work sponsored by the college at St. Jude's Hospital.

A 1996 alumnus, a Ph.D. in educational leadership, was told by the financial-aid director, "You get in, I'll find a way to get it paid for." He got a Bonner Foundation Scholarship for community service. "My advisers helped me see all that I could achieve. Now my goal in life is to help students the way they helped me."

A 2002 alumna wrote, "As one of the few Jewish students there, I can say that Rhodes was one of the most accepting and diverse places I've ever had the pleasure of spending years of my life." As for the faculty, she said, "The open-door policy helped us form lasting professional relationships with our professors. I am still in contact with several of them six years after graduation, a testimony to how involved they are in our lives." Her younger brother and sister followed her to Rhodes.

Many others said they still were close friends with their professors and call them "brilliant," "unmatched," "amazing," and similar superlatives. Often they give Rhodes and their professors credit for finding themselves and for their success and satisfaction with life.

A 2002 graduate and an aspiring writer said her advisers "have become permanent guides on my life journey." Another, the Phi Beta Kappa with a meteoric career only two years out of college, said it was her professors who gave her "confidence I never imagined possible" to hold a responsible museum job, write for its magazine, and then become assistant to the chief curator of an organization that puts on major exhibitions.

A 2004 physics B.S. who thinks of his teachers "more as

family than faculty," wrote that "because of their support and encouragement I was able to win a National Science Foundation Graduate Fellowship this year."

A young Air Force major from Minnesota, class of 1995, called Rhodes "an institution without peer in providing a liberal arts education where I had every opportunity imaginable to define myself. 'Know thyself' is not just a catch phrase from a Greek philosopher, it is the key to living a productive and satisfying life. I can't think of a single classmate whose life wasn't changed positively at Rhodes." He called it "this gem of a college in Memphis where the faculty is unmatched." He had played lacrosse, sung in two choirs, was in Air Force ROTC, was in student government, worked a student job, went to Bible study, and served as a resident assistant while taking a demanding course load. This, he said, was typical of Rhodes students, and the college encouraged such involvement.

A 1998 graduate said, "When I went to graduate school [Washington University in St. Louis] I realized what a fine education I had received at Rhodes." Writing papers and taking tests were easy for him, but his classmates from large universities "struggled." But there was a dark side: He never met his adviser; "He emailed me twice in two years. He was an award-winning scholar with four books and a vitae to prove it, but he never would have known my name if I had walked into his office." He got "the experience of a lifetime" at Rhodes, "but when I chose a [top] graduate program based on the [*U.S. News and World Report*] rankings, my experience was less than ideal."

A 1994 graduate, a Ph.D. in theater, said, "Rhodes provided me a place to address spiritual questions and ultimately come out as a gay man. The latter was sometimes rocky given the administration's policy not to recognize the Gay-Straight Alliance I founded. Nevertheless, there were numerous faculty, staff, and students who were supportive and encouraging. It was a true joy to attend a college where faculty, staff, and administrators take an active interest in students' lives."

A pastor in a conservative church, who graduated in 1992, said, "I entered college with a conservative, Christian, and evangelical world view. The good news is that I left college four years later with this same world view, except much stronger for having had this philosophy challenged by many who did not share this world view. I did not ever feel chastised or uneducated for holding this world view."

A 1996 graduate and actor who had "just got into a top-level graduate program" wrote that Rhodes "is a wonderful place that teaches us to be who we dream to be and accepts us for what we are while we are there."

And a 1997 alumna wrote, "Everyone says graduation day is one of the best days of your life, but for me it was one of the hardest days of my life, as I was walking away from a place that had been my family for four years."

Antioch College
Yellow Springs, Ohio

Antioch is in a class by itself. There is no college or university in the country that makes a more profound difference in a young person's life, or that creates more effective adults. None of the Ivies, big or small, can match Antioch's ability to produce outstanding thinkers and doers. A handful of distinctive and distinguished colleges—also in this book—have equal but different effects.

I wrote that ten years ago, in 1996. It is still true in 2006 and will be true ten and twenty years hence, because colleges with missions don't change. For decades this yeast of American higher education in charming Yellow Springs, Ohio, with a 1,000-acre nature preserve next to its 100-acre campus, has produced higher percentages of future scientists and scholars than any Ivy university except Princeton. When it comes to the country's top achievers listed in *Who's Who in America,* Antioch shows a higher percentage of alumni than some of the Ivies, most of the major research universities, and all of the Big Ten except Northwestern. It also has better medical- and law-school acceptance records; for a couple of years running, its medical school acceptance rate was

100 percent. As a medical school dean years ago said, "Antioch students know how to think."

Antioch has as many MacArthur Fellows as Princeton has—seven. But Princeton is ten times the size of Antioch and ten times more selective. Princeton skims off about 12 percent of the top high school academic achievers. Antioch takes about 80 percent of all who apply and doesn't even use the SATs or ACTs.

What does all that say about grades, scores, and selectivity? As measures of a human being they're phony. Antioch proves it.

You will not find the words "grades," "grading," or even "evaluation" in the catalog, nor a degree requirement section that says you need a 2.0 average to graduate. Students do get written evaluations from their instructors, which several valued because "they go beyond grades."

What makes this so impressive is that most of Antioch's 700 undergraduates couldn't get into the very selective schools.

What makes little David so mighty? The central reason is that the power of an Antioch education focuses on the student rather than on the curriculum. It is entirely possible that no two students will have identical programs.

In the 1920s Antioch pioneered a challenging, maturing Outward Bound–like adventure of classes interspersed with real-life jobs. Today, each student spends six quarters in these co-ops. Other colleges have cooperative education programs, but they're simply not the same animal; they're just vocational internships. Here, most jobs, especially during freshman year, will be unrelated to majors, but students learn how to find their way in a new city or country, how to budget their salary to eat and pay the rent, and how to fit into a group of workers. As one student said, "Classes involve ways of looking at the world, and co-ops involve ways of dealing with the world." The effect is powerfully synergistic; one complements the other and the result is magically greater than the parts.

Twenty years ago, and also last year, these kids were saying the same things: "I could survive, I could cope and meet the challenge anywhere or in any situation." Or, "A Princeton grad may have memorized more things, but I feel I can think better."

That's not surprising, for as undergraduates they are the most independent, uppity, tell-it-like-it-is student body on the face of the earth. Those brash qualities reflect an attitude toward truth, for they are without arrogance and their protests may be environmentally considerate. A feisty client of mine gave vent to her demands on the administration building sidewalk, but in chalk—the rain would wash it clean. They are friendly and without pretense. Their dress so testifies; it is unconventional, as one might expect in a family of individualists. They are not slobs and I saw no green hair, but a conservative southern girl would know her lipstick was out of place here.

Antioch is a democratic community. Students have a voice—a strong one—in the governance of the college, and they exercise it. During a visit twenty years ago, I attended a meeting on cafeteria prices that might have drawn four or five students at other places, but that brought a hundred crowding into one room to hear the student chairman tell the cafeteria manager, "Now Jack, we're not asking for answers; we're demanding them." I must have talked to at least fifty students then, and every one of them had some criticism or suggestion for betterment. Implicit in them all was a possessive loyalty that brooked no excuse for imperfection.

Twenty years later, students were just as feisty and just as sure they were running the place. Antioch's conduct rules for dating, which require permission to be asked for every touch or kiss, is an example of how different Antioch is from the world of other colleges in which speech and conduct codes are imposed from above. It is a student creation built on lessons they learned from an earlier, failed code of no-nos that was also their work. Then-president Al Guskin said, "I knew the first one—a policy of prohibitions—wouldn't work, but they had to live with it, find that out, and they changed it to one of mutual consent that would."

One measure of its effectiveness is that the dean of students says Antioch, of all places, is more at peace than any place she's worked. Another is that other institutions searching for solutions, including Harvard, Yale, Stanford, and New York University, have been asking Antioch how they do it.

The reason it works is that at Antioch—as at Reed, Hampshire, and Marlboro, communities most people would consider far out— there is no peer pressure to conform. Every person is respected as an individual. Antioch was the first college to have open dorms forty years ago, but when I first visited there, both girls and boys said they felt no sexual pressures whatsoever, and assured me that "anyone who's into drugs isn't going to hack it here."

In more than thirty-five years of advising, I've had the secret wish that everyone could have an Antioch-like experience, even though I know it wouldn't be possible. Usually it takes a person who is, or who has the potential to be, self-reliant, independent, and self-motivated. They should also have sharp antennae. Most adolescents don't fit these categories; as a physics prof friend said, "Most teenagers have a planning span of about ten hours." But they do tend to be adventurous, and as a longtime prof said, "Antioch is a wonderful place for people who are adventurous and willing to take charge of their lives, or who can become so."

Antioch graduation requirements include courses giving the framework of liberal education, a cross-cultural experience among their co-ops, and conversational mastery of another language. Otherwise, there is great freedom of fashioning one's own pro- gram as a course or a job experience changes him or her from an art major to a psychology or a philosophy major.

Every other quarter, working at a job is a maturing experience that makes Antioch classes unlike those anywhere else, even at Hampshire. "Antioch students will challenge you. They've had real jobs where they have been responsible for themselves," as one prof said, "and then they come back and want to see how what they're doing in class relates. So it's hard to walk into class and say, 'Here's what happened.' They'll say, 'How do you know, what is your source?' And they'll do it all in perfectly good humor." A psychology prof added, "They really challenge you. I was interested in research but can't get away from teaching here; it's too exciting."

A class may strike a visitor as some chance gathering of colleagues on a first-name basis, one where anything goes. On a September day in a French class where everyone had a cold, and all were lounging on the carpeted levels of a tiny amphitheater with no chairs, one student went out and got a Coke, another left and came back with a roll of toilet paper, and the instructor was the first to ask for it so he could blow his nose. A boy started to ask a question of a girl who was asleep and the instructor said, "Oh, don't bother her; she probably didn't get enough sleep last night." And later a Belgian assistant demonstrated proper Parisian propriety and provincial slouchiness in the wearing of a beret. Unconventional? Disorderly? Yes. Involved, happy, effective? Yes.

The co-op is one of Antioch's principal special ingredients. A staff of six faculty members helps students connect with jobs. Antioch has been doing this for eighty years, so its contacts are worldwide and growing. It also now uses the Internet in its placements. A job might be anywhere and involve doing anything, but it has to have specific duties: It has to be a real job. Later, jobs that are more sophisticated often lead to careers or to graduate schools. The other side of the coin is that because learning is negative as well as positive, a job experience can show a student he or she is really not interested in this kind of career. The pay is usually the prevailing wage. Many work on low-paying jobs or on unpaid volunteer assignments because they have their hearts in the missions.

After four weeks on the job, each student must write a report, partly for the benefit of others who might follow, and partly so that he can think about what the experience is doing to or for him. Also, most majors require the student to complete at least one independent-study course while away on a job. Such courses are designed to help make connections between theory and practice. An example might be studying moral decision-making while

counseling in an abortion clinic, or child psychopathology while
working in the juvenile ward of a state hospital.

What's more, classroom faculty are sent along with the co-op
faculty to visit employers and students on the job, and, as psychology profs Patricia Linn and Katherine Jako reported in a
study of the co-op program, the teacher may get an eye-opening
appreciation of the student that he didn't have in class. One, for
example, watched a student who had been tentative and uncomfortable in class take command to restrain an emotionally dis-
turbed child about to injure herself. At the start of each term,
co-op faculty hold swap sessions for returning students to share
experiences. Not only do classroom teachers often get to see their
pupils in a new light, as effective doers, but the students' real-life
job experiences often bring an immediacy and relevance to classroom discussions.

There is also the magic of serendipity. Even when students opt
for jobs requiring physical labor or ordinary office skills, they often come back after only three months more self-aware, responsible, and mature people. "And it's amazing how they've grown in
wisdom," the psychologists said. "These subtle forms of integra-
tion of co-op and course work are hardest to describe, but they
may be the most central to student development."

At Antioch, even the president, his dean of faculty, and half of
the administrative officers teach. They want to keep in direct contact with students, and the college's educational mission. Sixteen
faculty members have been added, as well as a director of academic
support services, to provide assistance to students with learning
disabilities and any others needing help. There is a four-week summer program, Accelerate into Antioch, to help entering students
prepare for the challenge of full academic load in the fall term.

The calendar is being changed to trimesters, and the summer
term will be on the block plan: three blocks of one course each. The
idea is that some subjects, such as theater, will profit from this for-
mat. Distinguished guests will be brought in for the summer term.

Many faculty members at Antioch would refuse jobs elsewhere at more pay; indeed when the school was having a major financial crisis years ago and the job market was good, many stayed. All of them talked as if they were boasting about their own kids. One who stayed, Prof. Steve Schwerner, summed up their views of the students: "There is much diversity here. In one class I have a descendent of William Bradford [governor of Massachusetts Bay Colony in the 1620s] and a girl from Nigeria; whoever they are, they all challenge. Antioch prepares them for a new world. It gives them versatility, resourcefulness; they land on their feet no matter what happens. They also challenge each other, they take risks, they ask the difficult question, and out in the world they say, "Why can't this be?"

Every student I talked to was glad he or she had found Antioch, because they were sure there was nothing like it. For one girl, the Antioch experience had been a full conversion. Reading about the college's record in producing Ph.D.s had attracted her originally, but on a visit she was deflated to learn it had none of the trappings of a "real college," such as football teams or fraternities. But such things were not priorities for her.

Several seniors were headed for graduate school; some were going to take a year off and work before deciding. When they were asked what Antioch had contributed to their experience that they didn't think another place would have, they said such things as:

- I have the ability to adapt and thrive.
- I know how to go into different situations and cope and make it pay, take lessons from it, set my own goals, and be able to teach myself.
- I have an integrated sense of where I fit in.
- You can find yourself. It's a lot of excitement. You get out and get experiences and you say 'I'm on the wrong track.' You're a participant in your own education. You're learning how to adapt in a situation you've never been in.
- You're learning how to become confident in your own ability to take control of your experiences.

- You go over to the professor's house for conversation, and a class is conversation. The professor is on the same level. That's what I really like more than the co-op.

The kind of person who should come to Antioch, they said, is one who is open-minded about both ideas and experiences.

Years ago, when Antioch's administrators seemed to be doing all the wrong things, the college was in financial crisis, and the trustees even let one president operate absentee-fashion from New York, clients would ask me whether it would still be in business in four years. I'd tell them that if it really was life-threatening, some foundation would come to the rescue, because this country could not afford not to have an Antioch. As for leadership problems, many of the best colleges have survived ambitious or mistaken CEOs, and are doing so today. They survive because the ethos of a place is what animates it.

However, Antioch was fortunate after that period in having as president Al Guskin, a man of humor, vision, courage, and candor. His analysis of what Antioch does was right on the mark: "The power of this education is that it creates an environment for profound student learning even when the components are not done very well by the college. For, and this is humbling to an educator, the focus on student learning creates such a strong force . . . that it overpowers the problems in the program itself. I remain very impressed, as an educator and a parent of a graduate, with the power of our graduates. . . .

"My belief is that our education works so well because it develops a creative tension between structure and freedom, between the intellectual and the experiential, between learning and doing. This balance or creative tension releases enormous energy within the students and allows them to feel a sense of effectiveness, competence, and personal power which permits them to learn about themselves in ways that previously they thought were unimaginable."

It is also important, as he points out, that Antioch "gives a shield of protection" to let them take risks; it gives them confidence. It is such a profound learning experience. And Antioch is more important in the 2000s than it was in the 1900s.

Ten years later, Antioch is doing some good new things academically, and is writing a happy chapter in a financial story of great irony.

Back in the 1920s, Arthur Morgan, a noted engineer and the president who developed Antioch's co-op plan, turned down GM chairman Charles Kettering's offer of one percent of General Motors profits because he feared it might become the wrong kind of influence. Had he accepted, Antioch today would be the richest college in the land.

But in the new millennium, a modest capital campaign for $65 million began so successfully that the goal was raised to $80 million and then to $100 million, and the college had a balanced budget for the first time in thirty years.

One of several results of the new prosperity is that 90 percent of the students get financial aid and the average package is $19,000.

Academically, Antioch has installed its own unique version of freshman seminars, which will be a single shared intellectual experience rather than letting freshmen choose from a variety of topics.

Now there is writing across the curriculum, even in math and the sciences. If they need it, students have a support staff to help them meet the heavier writing demands. There is also one for students who have learning problems.

But the really important things remain the same, as the testimony of students and recent alumni attest.

They are saying, as they did decades ago, that Antioch changed their lives, it has opened their minds, made them think, and made them into accomplished and confident self-starters. They all give the sense that they not only can cope in a changing world but would be able to land on their feet if times got bad.

For example, a 2003 graduate said, "The relationships I had with faculty, staff and other students helped bring out the strengths, gifts, and talents within me waiting to come out. Antioch gave me the opportunity to learn how best to use my resources in any circumstances, no matter how challenging a place I find myself. Moving through Antioch allowed me to pursue my interests and call it college."

A member of the class of 2007 said Antioch's effect is quickly felt: "Going into Antioch, I thought I knew myself. I was sure of who I was and where I wanted to go with my life. Within two months I knew that I was wrong. Everything I believed in and stood for was challenged, and I am thankful for it. Even though I've been at Antioch for only eight months, my life has changed. My perspective on the community and the people in it is altered in ways that I did not know existed."

Beloit College

Beloit, Wisconsin

If product research had ever been done in higher education, today's college scene would be turned upside down. Beloit, and a few others like it in this book, would be at the top, and the very selective elites at the bottom. Also, there'd be little need for a book such as this, because people would know Beloit is a happy place that multiplies talents.

Since record-keeping was started in 1920, Beloit has consistently been one of fifty colleges producing the highest percentages of the nation's future scientists and scholars. That also applies to achievers and contributors to society.

Even more to the point, it has been doing this for nearly a century with an inclusive mix of academic abilities, whereas some, such as Amherst, Wesleyan, and Williams, skim the academic cream. What's more, Beloit gets 94 percent to 97 percent of its freshmen back for the sophomore year, which is at least as good as the status schools.

It is also among the top twenty of the nation's 3,000 colleges and universities in the percentage of alumni who contribute financially. This is one of the consequences of Beloit's sense of community. One student described it as "so tight it's tremendous," and another called it "incredible."

Beloit does have fraternities, to which about 11 percent belong, but they do not Balkanize the campus or affect the social scene. Instead, they are leaders in community service.

Only in the first of three visits since the early seventies did I hear even two complaints; one said the "Beloit Plan" of that era interrupted friendships because it mandated an off-campus term in midcareer. The other was a fellow who caught up with me in midafternoon to say in a low voice, "I understand you're looking for bad things about Beloit." He didn't like one of his profs. Otherwise everybody said Beloit was a happy place and a community.

Sixty-three percent of graduates go on to get graduate or professional degrees, which puts the school among the top fifty in the country. And when it comes to producing future Ph.D.s in sociology, anthropology, geology, and foreign languages, it's in the top 15 percent. When *Who's Who* is used as an indicator of major contributors or achievers across the board, Beloit again appears among the top fifty. Several years ago Standard & Poor's did some digging to find out what colleges produced the highest percentage of corporate executives, and again Beloit was among the top fifty of that group. Only twenty-one colleges can claim to be in all three listings. (The others are Amherst, Bowdoin, Carleton, Colorado, Davidson, Denison, Grinnell, Hamilton, Haverford, Kenyon, Macalester, Middlebury, Oberlin, Occidental, Pomona, Swarthmore, Union, Wesleyan, Williams, and Wooster.)

What Beloit turns out is a better, more effective person, and one who tends to go on getting better. And it takes B and C students.

A cognitive psychologist says, "Our faculty are passionately devoted to students and will go the extra mile to engage students in the intellectual conversation that leads to true learning. Students and faculty get to know each other very well. You can hear the pride in a student's voice when she says her adviser made a special effort to attend a play she was in, or spent hours helping her refine a poster for her seminar presentation." Or, when a student was told he'd been assigned Dr. Steven Wright as his adviser, he said, "Oh, I know Steve." Dr. Wright had seen the student's family on campus and had taken them to lunch.

Beloit has a program that creates a sense of belonging, and that provides a way to help adolescents confront problems, air frustrations, and make choices at the critical periods of their first two years. It's more than a successful plan; it's palpable in the atmosphere, in the attitudes of faculty members and administrators, and in the way the students talk about their lives here. And while a statistician would say my sample is too small to be significant, over a thirty-year period I have received some euphoric notes from freshmen excited by the diversity of their classmates and telling me how wonderful their profs are. To me it's significant because it takes a lot to bestir a teenager to write.

Many colleges have tried various freshman-orientation schemes preceding the fall term, and with varying degrees of success. Beloit's—as its retention figures show—has been a resounding triumph. What they call the First-Year Initiatives program begins ten days before classes, continues through the fall semester as a for-credit seminar, and becomes more of a social group for the spring semester. In the second year it does a sort of metamorphosis to combat a condition eternally endemic in the collegiate world: sophomore slump.

In the area of advising, where nearly every college, good or bad, falls on its face some or a lot of the time, Beloit has achieved the best kind of in loco parentis, supportive and thoughtful but not intrusive. But that is only half a program that gets students and teachers involved intellectually, with each other and in their various groups.

On arrival, each freshman chooses a seminar group of fifteen that will explore some aspect of a common theme as his first intellectual adventure. One year it was Continuity and Change, which suggested such questions as, "What is the effect of the past on the present?" "Where do we adapt and where do we adopt?" "Do we own the past or does it own us?" Each seminar is supposed to suggest two lines of inquiry: how the here and now affects the future; and a sense of cultural pluralism and global awareness. While there are common tests or readings, each group has a leader who brings his particular expertise and viewpoint to the discussion, whether he be a physicist or a philosopher. The idea is to keep the seminars nondisciplinary; hence the leaders' fields are not identified, and prospective psychology or economics majors can't pick their particular specialists.

The term "leader" is used rather than "teacher," "instructor," or "professor" because it means just that; he or she is only the leader of a cooperative academic experience that stresses the sharing of ideas and acceptance of responsibility for mutual growth. It encourages students to engage actively in inquiry and analysis. It also stimulates the setting and pursuit of personal goals, self-reliance, and the taking of initiative in achieving worthy ends. Naturally, it seeks to introduce the satisfactions of the life of the mind.

The leader will also be that group's adviser for the next two years. Judging from what students proudly told me, as it has worked out, the label "adviser" doesn't cover the multifarious roles of confidant, counselor, and friend each leader fulfills.

As the seminar goes into the fall semester it is beefed up by out-of-class group assignments, such as community-service projects, which help build on the sense of cooperation and tolerance fostered by the emphasis on group learning. There is also much writing. The seminar is the start of a strong writing program that features a drop-in writing house with talented instructors, and provides the help that is often needed to back up the college's carefully planned program of writing-intensive courses.

In the third or fourth week of the spring semester, each group has a social event, about midterm there is a Great Lecture, in the twelfth week a "reunion" meeting, and near the end of the semester a major Rites/Rights of Spring blast.

The sophomore-year program, starting with a six-day preterm seminar, seeks to combat the affliction that causes many a youth to worry about lack of direction, to feel frustrated about having to make a decision about a major, and in some cases to wind up not doing well or withdrawing from school. Many colleges, in fact, have greater attrition after the sophomore year than after the freshman year. The fact that one of Beloit's own deans had been a victim of sophomore slump and a dropout had a lot to do with Beloit's 911-type answer. A unique part of the sophomore year program is the Sophomore Retreat. Students and faculty spend an entire weekend discussing careers, aspirations, problems, and choice of a major, and generally planning their futures.

Instead of getting so much nurturing, sophomores work more independently but with specific support from faculty and staff to confront such problems as committing themselves to a major, deciding whether they want an interdisciplinary minor, exploring off-campus study programs, internships, and field experiences, or completing their Comprehensive Academic Plan. The CAP is just what it says: an outline of the student's general direction, including specific courses, internships, or special projects for the rest of his college career, and possibilities for life after graduation.

The sophomore's seminar is an intensive one titled Crisis, Conflict, Consensus that challenges their skills in research, analysis, and presentation. The specific topic is announced on the first day. Students work in groups of ten to attack the topic problem. Each group represents a region of the world. Faculty, staff, and invited guests serve as resource persons or in other helpful roles.

After the fall term begins, there are Exploration Weeks during which the various departments hold informational meetings with outside speakers, symposia, and social events. Later comes a two-day retreat for more exploration with alumni leading workshops on career directions and planning, with entertainment and social activities added. Still later comes Declaration of Major Day, when departments hold open houses to answer questions and to help the sophomores complete their Comprehensive College Plans (CCPs). I know of no public institution that displays such empathy, and the thought of any university showing such concern is beyond imagination. Beloit's caring may be one reason why complaints are so rare.

Beloit's charming campus is probably the only one in the country where several Indian burial mounds provide its distinctive decorative features. This is almost as if nature and fate had decided it, for Beloit's Logan Museum of Anthropology owns the largest archaeological and ethnographic collection of any college in the country, and much of its collection was provided by Beloit's own Roy Chapman Andrews, the most famous archaeological explorer of the twentieth century. (Rumor has it that he was the model for the film character Indiana Jones.)

That helps explain why Beloit is an outstanding producer of people who go on to get Ph.D.s in anthropology. It doesn't explain why it is one of the top fifty in foreign languages and international studies. One of the reasons for that is its membership in the Associated Colleges of the Midwest, a group of fourteen colleges that has pioneered study-abroad programs. The ACM has programs in London, Florence (one in art history, one in humanities), Hong Kong, India, Japan, Russia, Costa Rica (one in Latin-American culture, one in advanced field studies), and Zimbabwe. ACM also has a rich array of domestic off-campus programs to fulfill almost any interest, from nuclear science programs at Oak Ridge National Laboratory, to environmental and nature terms at their Wilderness Study Area at the headwaters of the Mississippi, to urban studies, to research programs in the humanities. In addition, Beloit has seventeen study-abroad programs of its own. It is not surprising that by the time they graduate, more than half of Beloit's students have had some kind of off-campus study or internship, in this country or abroad. Also, over 80 percent of graduates have completed an independent study or special project.

Beloit is also a founding member of the International 50, a group of colleges distinctive in their interests and achievements in international studies. This group produces foreign service officers, ambassadors, and people who get doctorates in foreign languages and international studies at four to six times the rate of major research universities. In 1991, Beloit hosted a meeting of the 50 to exchange ideas and suggest plans for cooperation in furthering such studies.

As at other good colleges, Beloit's students are heavily involved in their own education. Each presents an individual project in open forum and submits to questions from other students, faculty, and staff. Some projects have been good enough to be accepted for academic professional meetings. I was there on a report day and at any one time there'd be at least half a dozen faculty and administrators (including the president) and twenty or thirty students—depending on the topic being presented—most of them eagerly asking questions.

Furthermore, all of the science students do undergraduate research, and the emphasis is on graduate rather than medical school, which means that it is scholarly rather than job-oriented. It is not unusual for students to be coauthors, with faculty members, of papers presented at professional meetings, and occasionally of a book. It would be unusual for an undergraduate to have this kind of excitement or get this kind of recognition at a university.

Beloit has always produced a disproportionate number of writers, and one reason is the attention given to writing. When Dr. Steven Wright, a friendly English professor, hands back a paper, the student gets not only marginal notes but a full page, single-spaced, of critique. "I walk them through it," he explains. At Beloit, the profs' first interest is teaching, not their own publishing.

At many colleges and universities, honor students find they can't get into honors courses—I've heard such complaints not only from prestige universities like Michigan, but from prestige colleges like Williams. At Beloit, teachers often give a tutorial to satisfy one student, or may arrange an independent study plan.

It would be easy to think the students were on the college's payroll with statements like these:

- In every class, I've come out a better thinker, a better person, and a better writer. Beloit is open to letting you try new things.
- I've gone to lab at 10 p.m. and a prof helped me because he cares so much. Someone's always there.
- Students are on committees with faculty, and they listen; and they're on the Academic Affairs committee.
- I've learned as much out of class as in class. The sense of community here is incredible.
- If you want something to happen you can make it happen, and they'll go out of their way to help you.

Every last one of them would pick Beloit again and hope their kids would too.

For those who might long for privacy as well as diversity, Beloit is the right place. It is a place to develop a strong sense of identity.

Beloit reminds me of a long-ago billboard ad for Chevron gas that read, "Fits any size tank." I talked to whiz kids from magnet schools like the intellectual, science- and math-oriented Thomas Jefferson High School of Science and Technology in Fairfax County, Virginia, which are tough even for whiz kids to get into, and they felt as fulfilled as any of the others. And when one considers that Beloit takes most of its applicants, who represent a fairly wide range of academic ability, and out-produces very selective schools in graduates who make significant contributions and achievements, that testifies to what good teachers have always known: that a mix of abilities produces a good synergy; it also says something good is happening in and out of its classrooms.

Traci Kyle, a student who was dissatisfied at Wesleyan and decided to try Beloit, restates a forgotten verity that should comfort those who think that because an Ivy has more high-ability students, it offers more learning or intellectual challenge than a good but less-selective school. Here is what she has found: "I was at Wesleyan three semesters and I liked the kids a lot but I wasn't happy on a day-to-day basis. The professors were inaccessible and there wasn't much personal attention, so I took a leave of absence to go to Beloit for a semester and I liked it, and then I took another, and I think I will stay.

"I didn't know what I was missing; the professors here are right there when I want them, and in abundance. They are open; they are friends; they are wonderful. The students here are more laid-back and they care more about things. The Wesleyan students are incredibly bright. For the first time I didn't feel I was the smartest; I was just average and it scared me to death. But they tend to have tunnel vision; they don't realize there's more to life [than schoolwork]. At Beloit, students are developing in more ways. I didn't realize what I was missing; it was only when I got away that I realized it."

When I asked her if she felt the atmosphere at Wesleyan was more intellectual, if there was more discussion about what went on in class, she said, "At Wesleyan there are more conversations about what went on in class; at Beloit it depends on the group; you find your own niche."

Many professors I spoke to agreed that a mix of abilities produces a more intellectually stimulating class of students who are much more willing to ask questions. When I asked Traci if she would agree, she said, "That's definitely true. People are so open at Beloit, I don't feel embarrassed about asking questions. At Wesleyan it was stifling. I find I learn more at Beloit, even though it doesn't have the prestige."

Also, because Wesleyan has 3,400 students, freshman classes are large, with 100 or so students. There was not nearly as much writing required as at Beloit and not nearly as much personal attention. Papers, she said, would come back "with only a few comments and those the negatives—it was minimal. At Beloit, the professors give us fifteen- or twenty-minute conferences every week and two- or three-paragraph write-ups telling us where to go."

At Wesleyan the sense of community "is not very strong; there is a concerted effort for everyone to be his individual self; there is no strong sense of place. Here, everyone is fiercely proud of Beloit. [As the Chevron ad said] it does fit any size tank. You would have to work hard not to fit in at Beloit."

Ten years later, seniors and recent graduates are saying just as emphatically that Beloit has changed their lives and often their intended directions. One graduate said that she had become a classicist instead of an archaeologist largely because her adviser had helped her learn Greek over the summer. Others said it was a place of "such good feeling" that students and professors were on a first-name basis. Another said it had been described to her as a place where "everybody was happy to be," and she added, "I couldn't find a better description."

Practically all of them talked about how much they valued their study-abroad terms. They used terms like "amazing" to describe their variety and the way their minds had been opened. They said their values had been affected; they'd learned to think and to have confidence. One said, "Beloit produces amazingly strong individuals who are ready to go out and do something they love to do."

A senior and former client who worked a year after high school bubbles with enthusiasm. She says students feel strongly that an honor code not only is unnecessary but installing one would be an affront.

The mix of abilities and the diversity, she continued, make class discussions the places "where you learn it after you've done the reading, and wonderful teachers are eager to help you. What's more, if you want to get something done, you can do it; the college will help you." She knew: In her junior year, she organized a folk-and-blues music festival, complete with big tent, several bands, and candy-cotton and popcorn machines, for which the college gave her a $14,000 budget. It was a smash.

Her mother says Beloit did a lot more for her than the University of Virginia did for her older sister. At UVa, she said, "kids were consumed with grades." Also, after four years, the older sister can't find a job in her field, art history, and has had no help from a single faculty member. Also, the younger daughter had suffered from a learning problem until she got to Beloit, where "her brain just took off."

A girl who chose Beloit because of its strong dance program called it "a place where mistakes and challenges are examined and used for an opportunity to grow."

A sophomore, talking about her rigorous experience, said, "You'll never stop writing papers if you come to Beloit. I have a friend who had to write a paper for his calculus class."

Cornell College

Mount Vernon, Iowa

Speaking at a Midwest counselors' convention many years ago, I said, "Cornell College will give your advisees a better education than Cornell University. The college's students will be actively engaged in their own education, not passive ears. Its able professors are there because they love to teach, and their research keeps them on the cutting edge. In the university the reverse is true; teaching undergraduates is a nuisance chore that helps fund research and the professors do little or none of it."

Seated next to me was Cornell University's admissions director. He treated it as a joke. But it was true then, is true now, and will always be unless there is an earth-shaking change.

Since Sputnik, the university has become a research institute, grubbing for grants and prestige, and to hell with the undergraduate. He simply is cheated.

In the new century, Cornell College has added many attractive features to its already-lovely rolling 129-acre campus with a lake, 200 miles west of Chicago.

There are new facilities for the fine arts, including a new theater, art gallery, ceramic and sculpture studios, a kiln, and major renovation of other buildings.

A pedestrian mall now spans the campus, plush new suite dorms and interest houses have been added, and a major expansion of the student center is in the works.

It is the only entire campus in the country to be included in the National Register of Historic Places, and even some of its modern facilities, particularly the Life Sports Center, are breathtaking. That structure, which serves the community as well as the college, has five basketball courts with movable bleachers, a six-lane, two hundred-meter track, four tennis courts, five volleyball courts, four racquetball courts, golf and batting cages, weight training, wrestling and training rooms, as well as locker rooms. The twenty-five-meter swimming pool has submerged observation windows in addition to seats for the spectators at swimming meets and water shows. Outdoors it has the football stadium, the baseball diamond, open practice fields, six tennis courts, and a six-lane, four hundred-yard crushed brick track.

This college of 1,200 with its distinguished history and bright present, takes two-thirds of its applicants, whose SATs range from 1100 to 1340. They come from all fifty states and twenty foreign countries; only 30 percent are from Iowa. While they're in school, three-fourths of them get financial aid, and the upper third get scholarships ranging from $10,000 to $20,000 per year. And when they graduate, three-fourths of them are headed for graduate or professional school. Cornell is one of the principal seedbeds of the nation's scientists and scholars; it is in the top 12 percent of the private colleges. What's more, only 44 of the 2,000 four-year institutions have higher percentages of alumni in *Who's Who*.

The Block Plan sets Cornell apart. Cornell and Colorado College are the only colleges using this intensive learning method. With this approach, a student takes one course full time for three-and-a-half weeks, has a four-day break, and then takes another course. In each block he will do a semester's work. Over four years there will be nine such terms and a student's course work is completed in eight. So the college lets him or her take the ninth term tuition free, and he can take any courses he wishes.

A student spends three to four hours in class each day, Monday through Friday. A day might be divided into classroom time and conference time; lab time and lecture time; independent research and group project work; on-campus and off-campus learning. Like the students, the faculty teach one course at a time and switch courses every three-and-a-half weeks. After 3 p.m. every day, everyone is out of class and free to pursue extracurricular interests.

Both students and faculty are enthusiastic about the Block Plan. It lets students concentrate on one thing at a time, makes possible more intensive contacts with teachers, and is conducive to group learning.

Cornell's first student, in 1853, was a woman, and it conferred the first college degree given to a woman in Iowa. It was the first college or university west of the Mississippi to grant women the same rights and privileges as men. It also was the first in this country to give a woman a full professorship with a salary equal to that of her male colleagues. About that time it established a music conservatory, and many Metropolitan Opera stars have performed here. The first college literary society west of the Mississippi was established here and Cornell has always turned out a fair number of writers. It has also produced many scientists and educators, one of whom was Dr. Lee DuBridge, the physicist who helped develop radar, was science adviser to presidents Truman, Eisenhower, and Nixon, and served as longtime president of California Institute of Technology.

In the sound-body department, no other college in the country has this record: Cornell had athletes in every one of the Olympic games from 1924 to 1964. Eight Cornellians were members of the Olympic wrestling teams, twenty-five have won national championships, and in 1947 Cornell won both the AAU and the NCAA national championships in wrestling. And all this was done with genuinely amateur students.

Then why isn't Cornell better known? Developing either writers or wrestlers doesn't generate publicity; and like many other good colleges, Cornell did not exploit the admissions frenzies of the sixties and seventies to tell the country about its virtues.

Perhaps because he was educated by the university system—Michigan and Northwestern—Dean Dennis Damon Moore was full of superlatives about Cornell students and what the Cornell ethos does for them. (He had five job offers before he chose Cornell.)

"I found Cornell students to be just plain nice kids." The dean described them as not independent when they come, "but they are willing and bright and they do good work" in a program that powerfully changes them. But lest his words give the wrong impression, he cautioned that Cornell is not a place for people with learning disabilities; the demands are too rigorous.

Unlike those at many colleges, he said, students are not career-oriented; they are here for an education. Also important is the fact that for 90 percent of them, Cornell was their first choice. That means there's no morale problem as there is where many students feel they're some other college's rejects. It also undergirds the sense of community, because this is the place they all want to be.

To give a sense of what the students are like, Dean Moore told of a block English course he gave for students who wanted to do more writing. Taking it was entirely voluntary and it was given off-time, but "every student turned in every paper. It was a true group momentum. There are nice, sweet, interested kids who put out."

He was just as enthusiastic about the faculty, which he called "terrific." They are continually talking about teaching, he said. They attend brown-bag lunches, which are not command performances, and may show how they conduct a class, as when one gave thirty-five other fascinated professors an art lesson. There are student evaluations as well. "The rewards for teaching here are great," he said.

Although adoption of the Block Plan at first caused a generational split in the faculty, as it did at Colorado, everyone now thinks it was the answer. The dean called it "total immersion, like a graduate experience." A political scientist, who has also taught at Grinnell and Princeton, summed up the enthusiasm of several others when he said: "It engages like no place I've ever known. It has dramatically changed my classes and liberated them. I couldn't teach a semester class the same way. It's motivational magic. Attendance is very high. There are no long-term deadlines ten weeks off. This is their only course and it concentrates attention; every student in my class is a political scientist."

Another said, "The ethos here encourages questions; the students are very open, and where everyone in the class is concerned with only one subject for nearly a month, students just pull together. This plan helps the B and C students because they have time spent with them. And it's good for everybody because there's no place to hide."

There is not only much discussion in these long classes, but also much writing. And like converts testifying to their new faith, these men and women from the country's greatest universities talked with pride about how well the graduates of this program and this college do in graduate school or in the corporate business world. They succeed because they have learned to think and to write clearly, and because they have learned to see and to tolerate other positions.

A psychologist educated at the universities of California and Wisconsin said, "We need to protect the choice between the large and the small school." In other words, the consumer should know enough about himself and the real differences in the schools to make a fruitful choice.

All of the students I talked with, who were from many parts of the country, were no less enthusiastic than their teachers about their college, the Block Plan, the warmth, and their friends the teachers. Some used words like "terrific" to describe their professors; every one of them said if they came back years from now they'd have dinner or spend a night at a faculty member's home, often adding, "We have dinner with them now."

Another thread running through their comments was that Cornell had changed them by making them more open to the views of others and by making them examine their own beliefs and values.

For many of them, the Block Plan and the welcoming attitude of Cornell students when they visited were the things that make them choose it over more selective colleges or universities. Typical was the answer of an African-American junior from Chicago, much courted by colleges as both a National Merit Scholar and a good football player. He said a visit showed him how friendly everyone was and how appealing the Block Plan was. It convinced him he could get involved, play football, and major in biology too.

What Dean Moore had said about Cornell being a first-choice school was borne out in student reactions: Every person I talked with was glad that he or she had come and wouldn't attend any other place. Some who'd had other offers chose it because they were made to feel welcome here, in contrast to what they called "a certain arrogance" at the very selective colleges.

A young client of a dozen years ago, whose father was a major newspaper executive in Los Angeles and who in his undemanding high school had been interested only in redoing old cars, went to Cornell. Four years later I got this telephone call from him: "When I came to you four years ago, I had no idea I could hack it in college, and the first year at Cornell I didn't like it, but every year I liked it more, and now I think there's nothing like it. I wanted you to know that I've just been accepted for a Ph.D. program in history."

That never would have, and never could have, happened at Cornell University or any other university, even if he had been able to get in. This is what Cornell College is doing for each next generation and, therefore, for society.

Ten years later the 25-year-old Block Plan is a principal Cornell virtue for many students; one called it "a fantastic system, and I cannot imagine going through school any other way."

Another widely shared opinion was the testimony of a student who said, "The professors here are like an extended family to me; they aren't trying to weed out the best, but to teach and nurture everybody along the way. They want to see you succeed and they do everything they can to make sure you have the opportunities to do so."

A junior said, "The people at Cornell are the most amazing friends, professors, and leaders I've ever come across. People are passionate about Cornell. Students and faculty alike are always supporting each other in one way or another. You can be whoever you want to be here; people don't judge you, or care what your grades or your GPA are. It's a fun place too. Cornellians work really hard during the week and party really hard on the weekends. So how has Cornell changed my life? One sentence can sum it up. I have found out who I really am."

In her first job interview, a 1995 alumna cited the Block Plan as evidence that while she didn't know the first thing about the firm's information technology, she could "think for myself, learn faster than anyone else you could hire, and I could be here tomorrow." Out of 125 applicants, she was one of a handful hired.

An alumna in law school said, "I usually have fewer pages of reading than I did at Cornell, but the reading is much more dense. The critical reading from my classes at Cornell made it easier to adjust to the demands of law school."

A forensic scientist for New York City said, "For me, Cornell was second to none when it came to personal interaction. Cornell is not a typical college; it attracts students who want to be challenged. It is truly one of a kind."

A junior who called his teachers "amazing," said, "There aren't any professors at Cornell; there are, however, passionate, intelligent individuals who care about their students and want them to achieve their goals."

A girl who'd been a straight-A student in high school found the pace and demands of the one-course-at-a-time so great they "made me improve my time management and organizational skills." Another said, "Cornell is perfect for me, and I probably would not have found it but for you."

 ## Denison University

Granville, Ohio

Denison, with its lovely, shady spread in the New England–style village of Granville, Ohio, has always been the image that comes to mind when I think of a beautiful college campus. That is as it should be, because it was designed by famed Frederick Law Olmsted, who did the campuses for Wellesley and Stanford, as well as Central Park in New York City. Now its power to change young lives equals its beauty.

Denison has had a long history of producing distinguished citizens, scientists, and scholars but when I first visited there in the late seventies, it had the reputation of being a backup school for easterners, fraternities and sororities dominated the social scene, and the atmosphere was distinctly preppy. Nearly every minority student I talked to was angry and alienated.

Then in the eighties, Dr. Michele Tolela Myers became president, and in ten years changed the whole ethos of the place. Many scholarships for outstanding students, an honors program for all who qualified, and exciting new academic programs attracted serious and idealistic students, crowding out the less serious who made trouble in and out of class. She also made it much more diversified.

She ended the laissez-faire attitude toward fraternities, reined

them in, and held them responsible. She also made them nonres-
idential (sororities already were) and that marginalized them.
When I visited there in the mid-nineties, two seniors told me
their fraternities were not nearly as important to them as they had
seemed in their freshman years. An English professor described
the change: "Ten years ago a fraternity man would slouch down in
the back row with his baseball cap on backwards with an 'I-dare-
you-to-teach-me-something' attitude—if he were awake. Now he
sits in the front row and participates." Also by the mid-nineties,
15 percent of the students were persons of color, and every one of
them I talked to said they couldn't be happier.

Now Denison has become even more of its new and better
self under President Dale T. Knobel who is committed to Denison's mission. His job is made easier by some underground network that draws certain kinds of students to certain colleges, and
Denison is attracting a considerably more idealistic type. There is
ample evidence of this in the euphoric "Ten Years Later" section
at the end of this chapter. And no matter what a student's interests are, he has so many rich choices and so many off-campus
study terms (there are eighty foreign choices), internships, or research opportunities, solo or with a professor, that he can find just
what he wants and find it plenty challenging. And such opportunities are for everyone with the desire, not just for the top students. That's because Denison faculty members push all their
students to excel, not just the best ones.

A prime example of the new choices is the 350-acre biological
reserve and field station. It is not only a boon for the science students, its environmental-studies major attracts faculty from every
division who want to bring their subject matter and their students
to it.

This is only one of Denison's new attractions. Among the others are an impressive new biological-sciences building, an immense two-acre Campus Common, and new apartment-style
residences to ensure that students live on campus. There is also a
science-fiction type digital-media teaching facility in which lights
and sounds bring the audience into the actor's mind.

A rigorous exploration of the interconnections of political science, economics, and philosophy provides the theoretical foundations of political and economic thought. Course work in each of the three disciplines, plus a senior research project, require so much work that it is in effect a double major, and anyone in it may not take another major or a minor. But students who finish will be equipped to work for fellow alumni like Senator Richard Lugar of Indiana, or to become senators of broad understanding themselves.

If they'd rather seek their fortunes abroad, an international-studies major will fit them to work in many areas of Europe and Asia. But it isn't a snap; they have to study the languages as well as the histories, cultures, and economies of each. For the many who long for an off-campus study term in almost any field of interest, whether in this country or abroad, Denison, as noted, offers eighty programs, several of them in cooperation with the other good colleges of the Great Lakes Colleges Association. Each year more than one-third of the junior class takes part in an off-campus study program.

Something is indeed happening when the college graduates 75 percent of its freshmen in four years, nearly double the national average, and 78 percent in five years. The percentage of freshmen returning for their sophomore year has risen to about 88 percent, and what is more telling, every one of the African-American freshmen returned. That probably wouldn't have happened fifteen or twenty years ago.

The percentage of skeptics in a faculty usually is a good deal higher than in a school's general population, but among Denison's professors I found a general agreement that this was a changed Denison. One volunteered this estimate: "If there's a place where students and faculty work better together, I don't know where it is." Another, a Denison alumnus, asked, "Why should my child go here? Faculty attention; that's what changed my life. I want it to happen to every student, not just one here and there."

Faculty also are proud of the school's strength in the arts. Its drama department, they point out, has been the starting point for many careers on Broadway. They also brag about how good the departments of dance, music, art, and art history are, not forgetting the cinema major.

Some of the credit should go to the active concern for the art of teaching. There is a brown-bag discussion group in which faculty talk about teaching problems and trade ideas. "We talk about learning all the time," said one, adding, "These are the kinds of kids I like to teach. This is a value-added school for the B student. We are turning them into active learners."

Later, a Sigma Chi senior, who could legitimately be put in the preppy category because he'd gone to Hill School, said, "As a freshman the fraternity gave me a sense of belonging and friends; now I look beyond the fraternity for friends. Also, the college is changing, the administration is more involved in student life now." He said he was more service-oriented than he'd been as a freshman, that he was going to take a year off "to work, and to think things over." He was grateful that Denison, because of its small size, "has given me a chance to get involved, to develop my leadership skills."

He would do it all over again, like everyone else I talked with, who each had his or her own reasons. Several freshman girls were still enamored of the college adventure, three black seniors from South Africa were full of praise for the helpful attitude of faculty members and their acceptance by the college community. A senior from Ethiopia said it had so opened him to new ideas that he was going to graduate school, something he never would have dreamed of otherwise.

The clincher was an African-American freshman from Bloomfield, New Jersey, a hard-nosed consumer. Because he was a good student, several other colleges had been courting him. He said, "I made four all-day visits here to be sure this was the place."

Was he happy with his choice? You bet!

Ten years later, the expressions of love and gratitude are undying. Students and alums continue to say they have gained confidence, become active learners and better persons, and that empathetic professors have helped them discover who they are. And it usually has nothing to do with the original major, or the fact that Denison has enabled them to stop worrying. As an alumna said: "I didn't have a clue about what I was going to do with my life. The answer I know now is, 'it doesn't matter because I can do whatever I want.' You get prepared to do anything." Many chose Denison because "everyone was so friendly; there was an incredible sense of community."

The alum who did the most consumer research, Greg Holden, wrote three enthusiastic pages, single-spaced (and said he could write a lot more), in responding to a survey I'd requested. At each of the many schools he visited, he wore a backpack for anonymity, asked to see the president or an administrator, and was refused or laughed at everywhere but at Denison. Later, as a freshman he asked President Knobel's help in starting a crew and Dr. Knobel found a donor for the crew's first shell. Greg's goal had been broadcast television, but he graduated as a religion major and started his career with an investment-banking firm interested in such things as affordable housing, health care, and senior living.

A triplet was happy he didn't get shortchanged at a university, as his two siblings did. "Denison offered me the opportunity to thrive . . . everyone supports each other. I joined a water polo team and you don't have to be good to feel wanted and to enjoy your experience. I encourage students to come here and change their lives as I have."

Several said their professors would give out their home phone numbers, invite classes home for dinner, or get helpfully involved in a student's life. As one graduate put it, "Because of the kind of mentorship and guidance I received, I have been able to pursue what I now know is my calling, something that would have been impossible had it not been for their support, inspiration, and guidance."

Several alums said their foreign-study terms and internships had opened their minds to different perspectives or had been important to their career goals.

Here are some of the other accolades:

"Denison wants to produce people who will change the world in every walk of life."

"Denison has a commitment to developing the whole person, not just the academic. They push you to excel and then challenge you to do it better."

"It is a community where you are not told no. Anything is possible and encouraged. Denison's alumni are eager to help new grads and students."

After his first year at medical school, an alum said that at another school he might have been intimidated by the competition, but "Denison's attitude was one of passion based on collaboration and teamwork; clusters of students working on similar projects."

A lawyer from the class of 1998 said, "Choosing Denison was the best decision I ever made. Denison is where I learned always to be aware of the marginalized and oppressed. . . . Finally, I thank Denison for my full scholarship to law school, because it was Denison that prepared me to be such a strong candidate."

 Earlham College

Richmond, Indiana

If every college and university sharpened young minds and consciences as effectively as Earlham does, this country would approach utopia. People would tend to live by reason and the Golden Rule, they would vote by their convictions rather than by their pocketbooks, and our capitalist society would be a model. But by itself Earlham has made great contributions and it quietly sets the standard.

The colleges in this book are notable for their sense of community, but none has more concern for others, their rights, their views, and their selves, than Earlham. It is a community governed not just by democratic, majority decisions, but by Quaker consensus. Likewise, the learning environment is cooperative rather than competitive. Over all, the words "warm" and "caring" apply.

For its students, so do the words "earnest, intense, politically aware, and interested in studying." These students have a sense of stewardship about their lives. In fact, if you're not interested in studying, don't come. And if you're not open to exploration, don't come; this is a challenging place. To parents who have wanted their child to go to a college of their religious faith, I have said Earlham would be a better moral and intellectual influence. Since 1920 it ranks number thirteen among all colleges in the percentages of future scientists and scholars it has turned out. Its seniors get accepted in graduate and professional schools at nearly perfect rates. The graduate admissions committees know about Earlham.

All this may sound overblown, but where do other college professors and educators send their own kids? To Ivy schools, Berkeley, Chicago, Stanford, Michigan? No. Fifteen percent of Earlham's students are children of college and university professors and administrators, and half of them are children of educators. Many of these parents are in Ivy League schools and top universities like Stanford and Berkeley. Earlham administrators have reason to believe, from anecdotal evidence, that they have more Ivy League parents than any other institution, though it would be a costly handwork item to isolate them in the database (they're not that interested in bragging). Only the College of Wooster, which draws heavily from Great Lakes Colleges Association faculty families, can boast such hard currency of confidence from its own establishment.

The beautiful Earlham campus of 800 acres is a world apart from the city of Richmond, Indiana. The front campus of 200 acres houses the academic buildings, including a new state-of-the-art athletics and wellness center for all students, and a new $13 million Center for Interdisciplinary Studies and Social Sciences, along with residence halls and playing fields. On the back 600 acres, an equestrian center completed in 2003 has large indoor and outdoor riding arenas, as well as horse stables. It is a natural laboratory for biology classes with its mix of woods, creek, and meadows, and it has paths for jogging or cross-country skiing.

Earlham's endowment of $200 million puts it in the top rank of colleges, so it's not surprising that its facilities range from very good to superb. Its Lilly Library, with more than 400,000 volumes, 90,000 units of microform, 25,000 art slides, 10,000 maps, and 9,150 periodicals and newspapers from all over the world, has for decades been recognized as the foremost undergraduate teaching library in the country. In the information age, that means not only rich resources, all kinds of computer hookups and audio labs and a pleasant place in which to use them, and close collaboration with the faculty, it also means developing the student's ability to find, organize, and use the information.

Earlham's 1,200 students are a diverse lot. Only about 12 percent are Quakers—usually there are more Methodists, Jews, Catholics, or Muslims in the freshman class. About 25 percent come from Indiana and more than half come from more than 500 miles away, from forty-seven states and thirty-four foreign countries. Twelve percent are minorities and they graduate at a slightly higher rate than the Caucasian majority, 60 percent and 56 percent respectively in four years, and 71 percent and 69 percent in five. Almost 90 percent of the freshmen return for the sophomore year. Half of them get financial aid.

Earlham accepts 72 percent of its applicants, nearly two-thirds of whom are in the top quintile of their classes. The middle 50 percent had SAT verbal scores of 580 to 700 and math scores of 550 to 600. But the kind of concerned world citizens Earlham produces cannot be measured by such numbers, and the admissions office looks far beyond such misleading labels to the whole person.

The fact that three quarters of them go on to earn graduate degrees, and that only a dozen colleges are more productive seedbeds of the nation's scientists and scholars offers proof of the pudding.

In national surveys of freshman attitudes, Earlham students are twice as interested as the national average in developing a meaningful philosophy of life, promoting racial understanding, keeping up to date with politics, or helping others in difficulty. They see themselves as well rounded, high-spirited, hardworking, and down-to-earth. Here, there are no fraternities or sororities, and no racial separatism; it is one community.

All first-year students are personally matched with veteran faculty to help them make sound course choices. And if someone needs help, he or she gets it. Supportive services and a learning center are available. But more important is a caring faculty. For example, professors will give students with dyslexia extra time on tests, or let them take exams orally or even tape-record their papers. There is also an August Academic Term for up to twenty-five students who need additional work in writing and critical reading.

For many, orientation begins with a small-group wilderness boating or mountaineering trip led by a faculty member. These expeditions build self-confidence, outdoors skills, and early friendships. It is no wonder Earlham loses few freshmen.

Earlham is on a two-semester calendar and an optional May term for foreign study, special topics, etc. Freshmen have two small, intense seminar courses emphasizing critical thinking, writing, and other skills they'll need.

Everybody takes a four-course humanities sequence. The first three are taken in freshman year, and they operate somewhat differently from other colleges in that the students have to respond in writing to the texts they've been reading before there's any class discussion. Humanities IV may be taken at any time from then on, and it serves to make students apply what they have learned, and to make connections. All four courses stress the disciplined use of logic and imagination in the study of human civilization and its outcomes.

Earlham has emphasized global education for decades, and two-thirds of the students have at least one foreign-study term in one of thirty-eight programs in twenty-five countries. These figures make it one of the top six in the country. Nationally, the average is about 2 percent. And at home, nearly 200 of the college's courses have a global emphasis and many of them are interdisciplinary.

The curriculum reflects both the interrelatedness of world issues, and the fact that international education is not just for the few specializing in international studies, nor just for those studying off-campus, but for all who wish to be educated in the broadest sense for life in the twenty-first century. Hence, each foreign-studies program is tied into the student's program so that one complements the other to make a cohesive whole. In Earlham's nationally recognized peace and global studies program, for example, off-campus programs in Northern Ireland and Jerusalem expose students to the issues of peace and conflict.

Earlham is an excellent place to learn to speak Japanese or to prepare for a career involving Japanese culture. The college has had ties with Japan for more than a century, and for thirty years it has run study programs there. It now has three, which are used by two college consortia. More than a quarter of the faculty have lived and taught in Japan and some use the language in their upper-level courses. Japanese students, scholars, and artists-in-residence spend time at Earlham, and one passes a couple of Japanese gardens en route to the bookstore.

Among the other programs are majors in international studies in which the student works with a team of faculty advisers to ensure a broad coverage. The African/African-American studies program likewise involves courses in many disciplines, as well as study in Africa, and prepares students for graduate school and for a variety of careers.

Students constantly coming and going in these programs give the Earlham community a cosmopolitan awareness and sophistication. The effect is to make one sensitive to the fact that no man is an island, and to the Quaker belief that everyone deserves respect.

To make these things work, everyone is required to become proficient in a foreign language, so there's a Super Languages Program—multiple-hour immersion courses in Japanese, German, Spanish, and French—which enables students to communicate in a relatively short time.

For all students, there are distribution requirements that provide the framework of a liberal education, and there are comprehensive exams in the major, which may be individually designed with the help of an adviser.

What makes Earlham what it is? My view is that any place staffed with the perceptive, caring people I've known at Earlham couldn't help exerting a lot of mental and moral torque. But here is how Dean Len Clark and several faculty members analyzed what happens to their students: "Before they come here, their culture has defined success by the percentile they're in and how much better than somebody else they are.

"From the first day their responsibility to learn from and with other students is stressed. That is a Quaker tenet and a part of the mission of the college. It takes new students by surprise but then liberates them. It takes some practice to listen to and learn from other students, and to build on ideas the other people have. That's a central focus of the humanities program for the first year. They talk about the text and then they talk about one another's analysis of the text. There are lots of exercises throughout the curriculum in doing that, and that's of central importance to making students successful later, because almost nobody works by himself, in the college or in this new world."

All professors agreed that teaching at Earlham was more challenging and that students got more out of learning than at the universities where they had taught, which included Yale, Northwestern, the University of North Carolina, Cornell, Purdue, and Delaware. When asked what Earlham did that Yale didn't, the answer was, "Earlham students work with faculty in a way that is enabling, that produces self-confidence, and that comes at a critical time when it can accelerate their career growth. I did not find that to this degree at Yale." (From what professors elsewhere have told me about minimal student-faculty contact at Yale, Dr. Clark wanted to be gentle.) A philosophy professor added, "It is much more intense here than at Northwestern. Also, status was very important there." One who had taught at Cornell and Purdue said the Earlham students were not only more interested and more challenged, but much more politically aware.

A history professor who had taught at North Carolina said

there was no comparison. "At UNC, kids wouldn't come to the office; I never had anyone show up. They were always out partying. In class here, they are not ashamed to ask questions. This is a real community of learning. It is also dangerous here because they find there are no satisfying, easy, comfortable assumptions they can take refuge in. They have to understand different points of view, that there is no particular argument that is right, and that they have to question, they have to confront."

I had a pretty good idea what the students would say even before I talked to any. Over the years, enough former clients or their parents have written to say how much Earlham had done, that I expected only positive comments, and that was what I got.

Some came because of the atmosphere of acceptance and tolerance, some because they'd heard of the close student-faculty relationships, but whatever their reasons, they wouldn't change schools. A senior honors student, one of the many university faculty members' sons who'd had offers from prestige colleges, said he had made the smartest choice, and other heads nodded in agreement.

Two frequent topics were how Earlham had affected their values and outlooks, and how it had pushed them intellectually. They said such things as:

- I came from a conservative town, and Earlham gave me new ideas, made me think about my own values, and made me change some of them.
- It came as a shock to find out others had differing ideas and it made me think. It's great to intermix and to accept everyone and his or her ideas; it promotes tolerance.
- A lot of different views opened up to me and there was no pressure to believe any one thing. When I go home I see that I've changed a lot compared to my old high school friends.
- On race relations, there are some separate interests, but everybody is ready to accept everybody else. It's some-

thing we're taught. Consensus is acceptance of differences.

I often tell clients that Beloit, Earlham, and Wooster are remarkable, special places by reason of their strong sense of community. Beloit I rate as the happiest campus and Earlham the
most serious. But don't get me wrong; this is not a convent. There
simply is no better place.

Ten years later, Earlham students and alumni express the same
kind of appreciation for making them better people and better
thinkers than they were ten years ago.

A junior said, "In three years I have learned as much about the
concept of thought and how to think about how I think as I have
about specific subject areas. Concepts of community define all
that holds this school together. It is a community that aspires to
utopian principles and attempts to practice them."

A Ph.D. candidate in clinical psychology said, "Not to be arro-
gant, but I was amazed at how well prepared I was compared to
other students."

Two summer courses at the University of California at Santa
Barbara after his freshman year made this junior "realize that
Earlham had already overprepared me for anything I could en-
counter there." And a conversation with a postdoctoral student
made her think he was a Ph.D. candidate. Earlham, he said, "has
prepared me to be successful anywhere."

A senior talked about her four "incredible years" at Earlham
that "helped shape me into who I am today. Your professors see
you as their peer and the interactions of professors and students
are amazing. I left the Southwest Field Studies Program with a
deepened appreciation for, and a new way of looking at, the
world; it was a life-changing experience."

A senior from the Philippines said, "I have developed a third
eye to see beyond the limitations of personal perspective and

I have stretched my ears to hear and accept diversity, and I have developed a strong, passionate voice to speak against injustices."

A 2000 alumna said, "I continue to be who I am and to be challenged and grow in new ways because I went to Earlham. Earlham changes lives."

A 2001 graduate said, "Earlham has set the highest precedent to nurture its students and to foster an environment where seeking truth through critical thought and giving back to your community through service is integrated throughout the entire academic experience."

An alumnus in his thirties said, "It is difficult to express all the ways that attending Earlham has affected my life, I have incorporated so many principles I learned there into my life." Professors truly cared about their students, he added, and had helped him when he needed it.

A National Public Radio congressional reporter said, "It is the focus and attention of the teaching staff and a ruling sense of social responsibility that makes the school truly change lives."

A 1992 graduate encapsulated the thoughts of many others with, "Academics, global travel, local community volunteerism, principled community life on campus, individual student-teacher relationships—it all seemed seamless at Earlham, which is why so many alums refer to our 'Earlham experience,' rather than to our 'Earlham education.'"

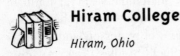

Hiram College

Hiram, Ohio

No college anywhere, and certainly no university, works more good magic on young minds and souls than beautiful Hiram College in a lovely Ohio village of the same name. In short, it is a national asset, and one that deserves recognition of the challenges it asks its students to meet.

Many years ago a curious administrator at Hiram College went through records to find out what had happened to students I had referred there. Of forty he found, two had WDs (withdraws) after their names and two had less-than-C averages. All the rest were in good standing or had stayed to graduation. Only Harvard and Princeton have four-year retention rates as good as that sample's, so it says something about what students find at Hiram and what it does for them.

It also says that I think this attractive college of nearly 1,000—the panoramic view from its campus is stunning—in its pretty village, is excellent. It's a well-kept secret. But in the fraternity it is known; the top honorary society, Phi Beta Kappa, has long had a chapter there. Since 33 percent of its seniors go to graduate or professional school right after graduation, and 60 percent go within five years, something is sparking, inside classroom and out.

On weekends the population jumps to 1,300 because Hiram has a Weekend College for adults that not only offers them a variety of courses, but also provides overnight dorm facilities, not to mention cafeteria food, which I found to be pretty good.

Hiram hasn't been a household name nationally because three quarters of its students are from in state. If quality determined selectivity, it would be mighty tough to get into. But as things are, provincialism is a greater influence on selectivity, and Hiram accepts more than 80 percent of its applicants, which means a lot of Bs and Cs are in those transcripts. Not quite half were in the top 10 percent of their high school classes, and the mean SATs were 580 verbal and 560 math. It has done well in the competition for minority students, who make up 14 percent of the population (9 percent are African American), and all the minority students I talked to thought they had made a smart choice.

Eighty-seven percent get need-based financial aid and 93 percent get some help. That number is high because Ohio gives residents grants for tuition at the state's private colleges. The average total financial aid for 2005 exceeded $19,000.

Whatever their past records, the kids at Hiram, especially the upper-class students, have a proud sense of ownership—a familiar theme in colleges that matter. For their part, faculty members—most of whom have taught at universities or other colleges—take equal pride in their young charges.

The results are good. Hiram has a long history of great success in medical- and graduate-school admission. In a far more competitive area, veterinary school, Hiram tops every college in Ohio State University's multistate region in the number admitted, and by a ratio of three to one.

This is not surprising; a science student at Hiram has such a great wealth of resources beckoning him and such evangelistic teachers, he gets excited and works hard. Students do hands-on learning and research and confront the critical issues in environmental protection at its wonderful Barrow Field Station. This is 360 acres of mature forest, streams, and ponds, a two-mile interpretive nature trail, a lake with a waterfowl observational building with teaching and student-research areas, and a wetlands-ecology teaching laboratory with a solar greenhouse. There is also a system of outdoor habitats for maintaining a collection of captive birds in seminatural habitats. The animals and natural areas are maintained by students under faculty supervision.

The Northwoods Field Station, a camp in the Hiawatha National Forest in the Upper Peninsula of Michigan near Lake Superior, serves as the headquarters for field trips in the spring, summer, and fall. In the summer, Hiram students can take part in a marine-biology program at the Shoals Marine Laboratory off the coast of New Hampshire under an arrangement with Cornell University.

By 2005, Hiram had added several new facilities. One is a comprehensive sports, recreation, and fitness center. Another is a major state-of-the-art science building. There is also a renovated computer-science lab, an expanded lab at the Barrow Field Station, and an all-faith chapel and meeting house.

Whereas elementary- and secondary-school teachers were a drag on the market several years ago, and education majors in the state's other institutions couldn't find jobs, every one of Hiram's applicants was hired before graduation.

As at Beloit, freshmen get an orientation, before the fall term starts, that is much more than how to use the library. In a week-long Freshman Institute, when they have the campus to themselves, they find out what college work is like. In seminar groups of twelve to fifteen guided by a professor who will be their academic adviser, they start to grapple with such topics as the Quest for Justice, the Development of Scientific Ideas, or Studies in Self-Identity. They do readings, discuss them, and write essays about them. They attend and discuss lectures. They may take placement tests if they plan to major in mathematics or language. In the evening they may see a movie, go on a picnic, attend a dance, or have an ice cream social, and in that week they also make new friends.

The bonding continues with the five-credit Freshman Colloquium in the fall term. Not only is there a list of topics to choose from but each is described in detail and includes a brief biographical sketch of the professor teaching that course. They do a lot more of what Freshman Institute foretold: They read about great issues or ideas and then discuss them and write essays about them. Meeting every day in such intimate groups means everyone is encouraged to think straight and to write clearly.

These groups become little families. They may meet in the professor's home for dinner, drive to Cleveland to see a relevant film, or, as one group did, make a trip to Washington to listen to a Senate hearing on a Colloquium topic.

In the winter and spring terms, everyone takes a sequence that provides an introductory experience in western thought and is taught by teams of professors from different disciplines. The class will examine a topic such as freedom, in order to get an overview of the major ideas that have shaped the way we see the world.

Then, in one of the next three years, a Hiram student has to get it all together. He or she must take a collegium—an integrated three-course sequence diving into an issue—that may be molecular biology and its implications, gender and power, decision-making, or some other topic. The purpose is to explore and appreciate the interconnectedness of knowledge. The collegia are interdisciplinary and taught by two or more professors from different fields. Again, there is much discussion in small groups and much writing.

In addition to a major, which can be an individualized one, Hiram also has distribution requirements to ensure exposure to the fine arts, humanities, natural sciences, and social sciences.

For those afraid of language or who have problems with it, a skills requirement can be satisfied with computer science, creative arts, or reasoning and analysis, which means two five-hour courses in philosophy or communications.

What do the students think about all this?

The most euphoric testimonial, from a junior majoring in English and French, also reflected a consensus: "Many catalytical things have happened to me. These are incredible people. They love to teach. We have a mentor relationship; they are always making cross-connections from one area or discipline to another. They are always encouraging, pushing me to do better. There is so much pressure, so many responsibilities, it forces you to keep going. They say, 'This might be a publishable paper.' One would like to come back here to teach—or to one like it." That reminded me of a letter from a client long ago who wrote (much to his amazement), "I've never had to work so hard in my life; this place is great!"

A senior physics major added to the girl's comments that while "it's intensely stimulating intellectually, that doesn't mean you can't have fun." He said he had done research with a professor, as had a psychology major, who added, "It's so easy to get involved in research here."

Over half of Hiram's students have an off-campus experience, foreign or in this country. And, just as they do everywhere else, they think the experiences have changed them. For an African-American girl from the inner city in Cleveland, a junior sociology-anthropology major, it has been the blinding light. "Hiram has expanded my horizons, but my experience in Germany was the wonderful thing. It transformed me, made me a woman of the world and opened my eyes to possibilities that otherwise I wouldn't see."

Other students had these expressions of allegiance:

- It has taught me how to write; there is so much writing and reading. One course was so interesting I changed my major.
- It has taught me time management. I feel indebtedness to Hiram.
- There is a wonderful sense of community. There is a sense of trust. It is very supportive. It is very confidence-building.
- It's our school.
- I look forward to coming here; I couldn't imagine studying in a city.

A faculty member may have put her finger on the key to the Hiram ethos when she said, "We teach students, rather than subjects. That's why we create a comfortable environment." In other words, the professor's concern is a young mind rather than the research that determines whether a university professor will keep his job.

Every faculty member I talked to took an obvious pleasure in teaching and being friends with the students. One observed, "We are sort of surrogate parents."

They preferred the kids at Hiram to those they'd taught elsewhere. At Carleton, said one, more students are from well-to-do families and "they come to college assured of success; they have no worries," whereas at Hiram, some are first-generation college students and many have not traveled widely or known what college is about. The result is that they tend to depend on their own resources and are hard workers.

They also made a point that is important to teenagers who do not feel as sure of themselves as they should. One professor said that the fact that the college is not well known "leads to a nice environment because students can find their own resources; they don't need to worry about keeping up." As a result, most tend to do very well. "They are a joy to work with," said another.

The Hiram faculty I talked to are happy to be there, and they work to improve their teaching on a daily basis: What are you trying to do today? Have you read this book? There are weeklong workshop retreats, and they find team-teaching to be very effective.

One faculty couple's visit to their daughter's graduation at Williams tells a lot about their priorities. At a reception after commencement, the professor under whom their daughter had majored and who was her advisor asked, "What are you going to do next year, Anna?" They were appalled, as they should well have been. The husband said, "I had to hold my wife; I thought she would spring at the woman."

My guess would be that any Hiram faculty member would have reacted as that couple had. Concern for the student's personal, as well as academic, welfare is one of the qualities that makes Hiram such a warm and happy place and such an exceptional college. It is one of the reasons why young people find their power and their confidence burgeoning, and why they talk about realizing potentials they didn't know they had when they came here. More than a wonderful place, Hiram is a national asset.

Ten years later, I got the same fervent superlatives from students and alumni about how the Hiram experience had made them better persons and better thinkers, had given them confidence to become winners, and had made them open-minded, caring world citizens. In fact, just about everyone said the study-abroad program had been a high point and a mind-opening experience. Of the London term, a 2004 graduate said she'd been there before, "but my term in London was my seminal experience at Hiram."

A medical school faculty member, the first in his family to go to college, said, "Hiram professors challenged me intellectually, yet they also showed me that it is so vitally important to know the student as a person."

A 1994 alumna said Hiram gave her, "the experience of a university with its priority to encourage students to learn about other cultures and the unmatched first-year curriculum with its focus on writing, analyzing, and problem solving."

Many of them said the concern professors had for their welfare outside of class was "amazing" or "incredible," that they'd been invited for meals, even that they were on a first-name basis with some. Several said versions of, "My professors have all taken a personal interest in my progress and want me to succeed as much as I do." A senior girl said a professor "once bought me lunch and sat at a table with me for three hours on a Saturday to fuss with my honors thesis." Another senior said, "When I look back on that person I used to be, I'm so incredibly glad that I've been encouraged to grow and mature as much as I have. If I had chosen to go to another school, I might still be that ignorant, closed-minded person I was four years ago, and that would have just been a tragedy." Another said, "Hiram has exposed me to worlds I had originally thought were beyond my ability to experience."

The most pervasive note was how much a caring faculty had done to change young lives. Several called them Hiram's "greatest asset," and a 2004 graduate said, "These professors are underpaid, overworked, and they love the school, they love their students, and they love their work. Hiram is a human-to-human place."

Several had the same desire a junior girl had expressed to me ten years before: They wanted to be, or had become, school teachers or college professors "to pass on to the next generation the same transformative experience" they'd had at Hiram.

A rising senior said, "The amount of community service and care for the world that goes on at this institution is so incredible that it has really inspired me to be a better person." Another junior said, "Hiram taught me how to think and speak for myself, and then Hiram listened to what I had to say. The faculty and staff have an open-door policy not only when students are upset but when we're happy too. I want to get a Ph.D. and teach English at a place like Hiram."

Especially moving was the testimony of a West Virginia girl who'd been "a big fish in a small pond and my high school theater was competitive and combative, and my drama teacher made fun of me because I wanted to be a director and because I am too short and homely to play an ingénue. When I came to Hiram it was with my fists swinging, ready to prove my worth. To my great surprise, everyone at Hiram was laid-back and noncompetitive. 'Alisha,' said one professor, 'why so afraid? No one here is going to eat you.' I was mad at the time but he pinpointed that it was fear, not ambition, that tugged me along. Since then I have learned to be a collaborator rather than a competitor, and to my surprise, for the first time I found myself appreciating someone else's superior skill and wanting to be around her and enjoy the sheer artistry she applied to everything. The theater here has put great faith in me and taught me incredible amounts. I feel entirely prepared for the MFA directing program I will be entering in the fall. Hiram has made me more polished and confident, and also more ready to face the challenges that life will throw at me."

Hope College

Holland, Michigan

Hope College, just a hop, skip, and a jump from Lake Michigan in pleasant Holland, Michigan, raises higher education's moral and intellectual levels. It is a place where parents can send children of a wide range of abilities in the full expectation that their talents will be increased, vision broadened, and ethical acuity sharpened. They will also be actively involved in their own education and be prepared to prosper in a changed world. Those expectations will be fulfilled.

And a decade later, Hope's story is even better. Its campus has grown to 77 acres, it boasts three new buildings, and it has received much well-deserved national recognition.

The new facilities are a $36 million science center, a $22 million fieldhouse/athletic arena, and for 2005, a $12 million academic facility.

There is no other college library in the country as good as Hope's. So says the Association of College and Research Libraries.

The college has been judged by its peers to have one of the top four programs in the country for collaborative research and creative expression opportunities for undergraduates.

In 2005 it had more National Science Foundation summer research grants for undergraduates than any college in the country. Its science and engineering programs received a National Science Foundation grant of nearly $1 million.

Faculty members won one National Science Foundation Fellowship, two National Endowment for the Humanities Fellowships, and one Fulbright Fellowship.

A biology prof was one of sixty-seven nationwide to be elected to the American Association for the Advancement of Science and the only one from a liberal arts college.

A member of the dance faculty won a statewide award for the best work of choreography.

Nearly a third of the faculty had some research, critical, or creative work published. Quite a record.

Its alumni often say Hope made them what they are. In fact, one of its African-American graduates from the inner city of Chicago kept urging me to consider Hope for this book. I already had a high opinion of it, for Hope has long been preeminent in science. It is third and sometimes second in the number of chemistry majors in the state, an amazing figure in the context of Michigan's array of mammoth universities.

Furthermore, Hope's reputation with state industries is so formidable that chemistry and physics interns often have built-in job offers by the time they graduate, if not before. But that is just part of the story. Hope is first-rate across the board, attracting students because of the reputations of its political science and economics departments and because its theater, dance, and music programs are outstanding. In many other schools they'd be bragging points.

Dr. Jacob Nyenhuis, provost emeritus and a classics author and speaker of note, said, "Hope provides a liberal arts education in the context of the Christian faith. We deal with ethical issues. We teach them to ask the right question, to have the right perspective. We nurture, but not in an intrusive way. We give them a sense of rootedness. We are distinctive. We achieve academic excellence; we have freedom of inquiry, a quest without boundaries. We value and will nurture a faith commitment; this means keeping a delicate balance. Service has been a long tradition. We do make a difference."

Founded by Dutch settlers in the mid-1800s, Hope is affiliated with, but independent of the Reformed Church and has students of many religious faiths, including 137 who don't practice at all. It is like St. Olaf in this regard, rather than Wheaton, where one has to be a Christian of some kind in order to be accepted. At Hope, students feel no pressure of any kind to conform to a set of beliefs, and there is no compulsory chapel.

Since the 2000 revision of this book, Hope is attracting well over a third of its 2,700 students from forty states and thirty-nine foreign countries, among them Muslims and youths of other faiths or no faiths, all of them welcomed as part of the Hope family.

Hope says that more than a third of its acceptees were in the top tenth of their high school classes. But don't let that scare you; most of those statistics come from small high schools. The key figures are that it accepts 87 percent of its applicants, and that the middle 50 percent have SAT totals in the 950–1150 range. In other words, not only B students, but C students who are ready to work are likely suspects.

When they come to Hope they'll have to work, but they must

like it, and they must be interested, because they even work on weekends, which doesn't happen at a lot of places. All freshmen take a writing course, as well as a mathematics course. A core curriculum exposes them to their own and other cultures. In addition to a major, courses in the arts, humanities, sciences, social sciences, and religion are also required. And to wrap it up, a senior seminar course encourages them to reflect on their college experience.

There is a wide variety of off-campus programs, partly because Hope is a member of that consortium of excellent programs, the Great Lakes Colleges Association. A large portion of the student body spends at least one term in Africa, Europe, Scotland, Japan, Hong Kong, Russia, Nepal, China, or India. They may also spend a term in the Philadelphia Center in urban studies, or opt for a New York arts semester.

All these riches add to the latitude students have in fashioning their college experiences. In the process they will get all the help and nurture they need. They won't feel driven to compete; students work together, often as teams, and they also work with their teachers. At Hope, learning is a communal enterprise to which all contribute.

Dr. William Mungall, a remarkable chemistry professor, said, "We don't take attendance. We don't grade on a curve; the grading is absolute. I tell every class at the start how it will be, and if they do poorly on one test they can use the final to neutralize it. The students help each other and the teacher helps them."

Student-faculty research projects are common among the colleges in this book, but probably no college has more of this than Hope; the faculty encourages it both to get students involved in their own education and to promote collaborative learning. Chemistry and physics students even get the thrill of working in some of Michigan's major industries—including Parke-Davis pharmaceuticals and Donnelly, a producer of high-tech mirrors—because Dr. Mungall and a couple of colleagues have consulting contracts with them.

Because some of these firms use Hope's lab equipment, students get to work on real-life problems instead of textbook ones. They also get to work in the various companies' labs on some problem or project for a product.

Back at school, it's easy to collaborate on these problems or projects; adjoining each lab is a study room where students can work together, and the faculty offices are right next door. These teachers like to work with students; any who don't are weeded out in the hiring process when they get grilled in interviews with students.

"Here," the chemistry professor said, "we use research as a vehicle to teach. Students participate in it and it makes things more exciting; it gives them an exposure to what science is all about. Research is why we graduate so many chemistry majors."

These professors, who have taught at most of the leading universities, are giving a most important message of assurance that teenagers and their parents would be foolish to miss. They testify emphatically that their senior students are equal in ability and performance to any students anywhere. Here is how some of them at Hope put it:

"I have taught at Stanford and at MIT; the students here are just as good; they're comparable in every way to MIT's. I had the same problem there: Bright students have problems with chemistry because they've never had to work. I have to help them more, especially on study skills. We are getting a lot of kids with underdeveloped study skills. Kids who need encouragement and nurturing get it here. Talented kids blossom here. Hope develops confidence, broadens perspectives, gets them involved."

A religion professor who had taught at Wisconsin and Harvard said: "There is a great diversity of abilities here. They are universally interested and willing to work; they carry a heavy load—five courses—with a lot of assignments. It's a wonderful group and I have tremendous respect for them. They know the faculty is eager for their well-being. I want to treat my students like I want my own kids treated. There are a lot of people achieving things they never thought they could; for example, this kind of nurturing even produced a poet. They are reaching their potential. At Madison

[University of Wisconsin] there are a lot of people with great ability going nowhere."

A communications professor who had taught at the universities of California and Wisconsin said: "Four years at Hope changes a student; there is such an emphasis on writing, speaking, and thinking skills. A Western Michigan graduate I know did not write a paper in four years. Here they achieve; they learn to be critical-minded; they're asked to engage moral issues, and after four years here, they say values are important."

An economics professor, who turns down offers from universities because he thinks what he's doing here is more important, says, "Here students spend time with their profs. They get ready for the new world. They get confidence. At Harvard they're talented when they come in, but what happens to them there? I wouldn't leave Hope to teach at Harvard. The Harvard faculty's principal goal is to get research published. Here I teach and do community service. Most of the faculty could be making more money elsewhere, but they have a commitment to people, and it's not self-serving."

A most important point for anyone trying to decide between a good small college and a mighty university was made by Dr. Robert Ritsema, who heads the music department: "When a prospective student asks why she should come here rather than go to the University of Michigan, I say you'll play in a better orchestra there because they can choose from several performers, but here you'll get more playing time. The remarkable thing here is that we're all performers; we can't teach if we're not. And we're right there all the time, at night too, when the students need us."

What's more, he went on, "the level of inquiry is high here, of inquisitiveness; there's a work ethic here, and they blossom. We really do affect values. The students feel nurtured. The alumni all talk about how Hope shaped them, whenever and wherever I meet them on tours."

The students aren't the only ones affected. One professor after another talked with feeling about the atmosphere of mutual respect among the faculty. Even over issues that may be very divisive they said there are no fights. People like and respect one another, otherwise there couldn't be the sense of common enterprise and collaboration that is one of the virtues of Hope and colleges like it.

Most of the freshmen I talked to had been attracted by Hope's reputation. As one of them said, "I knew this was a first-rate school." Some pointed to its reputation in chemistry, or its 97 percent rate of medical school acceptances, or the fact that its seniors were in the top percentile in the national organic chemistry test. Still others talked about the economics, political, and music departments as their lures.

Students who had been there longer talked about other things. A junior girl from New Jersey said Hope is "a very friendly place, a great sense of community, people are nice, and the profs couldn't be more helpful." The sense of community was a common theme, along with how interested the professors were in students' personal as well as academic welfare. A senior talked about opportunities "I just wouldn't have had anywhere else" to work in a company's laboratory on "a real live industrial problem." Similarly, getting involved in a research project with a professor was something a couple of others had never dreamed of doing.

No one I talked to felt negatively influenced or burdened by the college's Christian commitment. The intellectual caliber of the religion courses is as high as those anywhere, "a quest without boundaries," as Dr. Nyenhuis said. The fact that there's no required chapel (as there once was in church-affiliated colleges) may have been a factor in their answers. Those who didn't go to church felt no pressure to go, and unlike Wheaton's students, many didn't go. They did, however, feel that Hope was a good place with good people. Every time I asked my stock question about having dinner or spending a night at a faculty member's home five years from now the answer often was, "We're doing that now," or "I'd have trouble choosing." And one fellow asked, "Do you include coaches?"

The affection continues beyond commencement. The African-American alumna, who wanted me to see for myself about Hope, credits her experience there with making her a successful newspaperwoman. She is right. I can now, with more informed enthusiasm, tell more people what a great place Hope is for students who want the kind of educational experience that will develop them into people who can be happy with themselves because they lead the examined and productive life.

Ten years after the first edition of this book, the themes that run through student and alumni comments are at least as full of devotion as they were a decade ago. They say that Hope is a warm and friendly place that has changed them for the better in intellect and character and prepared them for the problems they will face in life.

They say their professors are "incredible" people whom they love and admire, people who have strengthened their moral outlook, people who are interested in their personal lives, people who challenge them beyond what they think they're capable of, and then give them the confidence to achieve.

A first-year medical school student said Hope not only had prepared him well "but I was encouraged to learn about ethical dilemmas, moral issues, and the virtue of compassion. I believe all of these teachings will serve me well in my career as a physician." Two premed juniors said the help of their professors had gotten them through organic chemistry, "two words that scare most sophomore science majors."

A senior said, "Rhoda doesn't ask too much of her students; rather she lets us see how little we ask of ourselves and challenges us never to do it again." Also, "She can turn modern English grammar into a scintillating subject. Grammar! When I leave her class I can actually feel my brain growing."

A 2004 graduate from the state of Washington was lyrical in her praise of the professors as "real people" who always have time to chat and who want to know "what I am thinking about and what books I am reading, or e-mailing me in the summers, and who have wonderful classes of eight where you build relationships. If I knew as a freshman what I am like now I would not have believed myself. Hope is changing me in positive, lifelong ways. Graduation is going to be very sad."

A liberal freshman girl from Chicago thought Hope was very friendly but too religious. She "loved downtown Holland, it's cute and quaint and pretty and all the citizens smile at you." For college shoppers she had this advice: "If a student is looking for a school that is very intimate, caring, the students are a great group of people, the professors are very open to meet with you, and the campus is very open and spacious, my advice is to come to Hope College."

Another city girl, from Minneapolis, had a somewhat different view. "My first year at Hope has been incredible. Hope has provided a nurturing spiritual environment where many opportunities are given to grow spiritually, and serve, but nothing is required. The cool thing is that chapel is always FULL with people who want to be there, not because they're required to. Even though I'm going to school in a place that's smaller than where I'm from, I feel like my world is so much bigger. Inside and outside the classroom, I have come to realize how many opportunities are out there. Students have a strong interest in serving. Each spring break, over 450 students participate in mission trips all over the U.S. and the world."

Another freshman said, "Hope has offered me awesome opportunities to grow in my faith without forcing religion on me. Only at Hope can you start up a conversation with one of the maintenance workers and have that man encourage you to live like a man of God and not conform to the world around you."

One who'd been a top student in high school said, "After being a year at Hope I have had to adjust to how intense the classes are here."

These are the kinds of paeans a remarkable college evokes.

Kalamazoo College

Kalamazoo, Michigan

Kalamazoo is more than a distinctive college; it is unique. Other colleges offer some of its features but none provides the same combination of a career development internship term, two foreign-study terms, and a senior individualized project, which they call the K Plan.

The sense of community is strong because everybody lives on campus and everybody eats together in the big dining hall, often with faculty members. This means the entire community is able to gather to celebrate joyous occasions or to offer comfort in times of sorrow. Every Friday a voluntary ecumenical chapel planned by students and faculty brings in guests from a variety of religious backgrounds and affiliations. The Liberal Arts Colloquium, also operated by a student-faculty committee, brings in about 100 educational and cultural events each year to enhance the educational experience. A student must attend at least twenty-five of these events as part of the degree requirements. At no Ivy institution are the students so deeply engaged, so broadly prepared, or so heavily invested in a sense of community as at Kalamazoo. In short, no Ivy school is likely to have as much impact on a youth's development. Two faculty members who went to Harvard said they wished they'd gone to Kalamazoo.

Years ago, the psychology department chairman at a very selective college spent a day checking out Kalamazoo when I recommended it for his son and came back with the verdict, "That's a good place!" His own school lost a good kid.

Kalamazoo's program appeals to the inquiring mind and adventurous spirit, and the timid learn by example to become risk-takers. In that regard it has the appeal of Antioch, Hampshire, or Marlboro. It is a happy campus where the kids are excited about what they're doing. The atmosphere is one of trust in a student-run honor system. In sports, the Kalamazoo tennis team is the only one ever to win three national championships.

On an overnight visit, my second in a dozen years, the reports of a half-dozen foreign-term returnees made for a rousing dinner hour, and not just for the students. I saw faculty, administrators, and staff scattered throughout the hall. The students who'd been in Paris had complained about such things as a leaky john, while those in Senegal had been euphoric about their hardship-induced adventures. An African-American girl back from Sierra Leone was so excited about her experience, her words gushed out in a torrent. All were enthusiastically testifying to what a watershed experience it had been; how their eyes and minds had been opened; how they had grown in self-understanding.

For its part, the sophisticated and attractive city of Kalamazoo, population 200,000, is also special. It was the first city in the nation to have a pedestrian mall. It supports a symphony, a chamber-music society, an art institute, a professional hockey team, men's and women's professional soccer teams, a nature center, and several live theaters, among other things. It is also in a class by itself for distinguished residential architecture. There are many homes by Frank Lloyd Wright, Alden Dow, and Norman Carver in an area nature endowed with wooded hills and lakes.

The college's 60-acre campus on a hill has the charm of a grassy quadrangle shaded by great trees, some of which seem to date from the college's founding in 1833. The buildings even seem to have sprung from the earth here; even the big state-of-the-art Dow Science Center fits in comfortably. Like Allegheny's it was planned by the science faculty and boasts study and lounge areas scattered among the labs and offices for the very accessible faculty.

A more important feature I've not seen elsewhere—and that no Ivy institution can boast of—is another scattering of small labs for student-faculty research. Indeed, research is a way of teaching at Kalamazoo.

The 1,350 students come from forty-one states and a dozen

foreign countries, half of them from the top 10 percent of their classes and nearly half with SAT verbal scores of more than 600 and 70 percent with math scores of more than 600. But because it accepts nearly 75 percent of its applicants, it takes B students. Like other colleges in this book, it then makes grade-A adults of them. More than half get need-based financial aid and nearly half get merit scholarships that average $7,000 a year.

Like St. Olaf, Kalamazoo is preparing its students to prosper in a one-world economy by giving them a global perspective with its two foreign-study terms. A leader in the field for fifty years, Kalamazoo has study centers at almost thirty locations around the world. As a member of the Great Lakes Colleges Association, it also offers the consortium's many programs. These terms become an integral part of the course work because one's experiences often lend relevance to a class discussion, whether it be economics, sociology, or philosophy.

The career-development internships offer 2,000 different jobs in thirty-five states and a dozen foreign countries. They include publications at major corporations and publications such as *The New York Times,* and all manner of overseas opportunities. So it is no wonder that 85 percent of Kalamazoo's students spend one or two terms studying abroad, and that 80 percent of them complete at least one internship.

Kalamazoo's first-year program of weaving together hands-on involvement, experiential learning, mentorship, and a rigorous academic life has won kudos from the John Templeton Foundation as a national leader, was named one of thirteen "Institutions of Excellence in the First College Year" by the National Policy Center on the First Year in College, and is featured in a book, *Portraits of First-Year Excellence in American Colleges and Universities.*

Every student takes a freshman seminar where one's writing has to pass muster to get a passing grade. The major may be a conventional one or self-designed in consultation with a faculty adviser, and everyone does a Senior Individualized Project, also designed in conjunction with the adviser and which occupies most of the senior year. The completed project must be defended in an open forum of peers and faculty.

The school year is divided into three terms, and a freshman normally spends fall, winter, and spring on campus, and takes a summer vacation. Internships are typically scheduled during the summer following the sophomore year. Two foreign-study terms usually come in the junior year.

This the K Plan. Testimony to its appeal is that its three terms off campus enhance, rather than dilute, the sense of community. Thirty years ago, Beloit students had to have a field term off campus in midcareer but it was abandoned partly because students complained it broke up friendships. At Kalamazoo, as the dinner hour hinted, there is a sense of excitement and cross-fertilization when the kids come back and share the experiences others will soon have, or have had. They come back to classes with a broader outlook and a greater sensitivity and receptiveness. The faculty, who might be expected to deplore the interruptions, find their students born again, full of a new interest and zest; their courses have become relevant.

A former provost and chemistry professor who went to Michigan and got his doctorate at Princeton is another of those who wishes he'd had the Kalamazoo experience. "At Michigan I got into chemistry by accident," he said. "Otherwise my experience there would have been disastrous. In my third year, a graduate student needed a research assistant. For the next two years, working closely with him, I gained more knowledge, insight, and enthusiasm than courses alone could ever have imparted. That experience had such a powerful impact on me that I decided I wanted to teach at a place where close student-professor contact was the norm rather than the exception. K College is just such a place. Here, what happened to me would have been by design rather than by accident."

Students at Kalamazoo, he went on, tend to be more first-generation college, while at Princeton they may be fourth generation. Kalamazoo's students have more motivation, more humility, and more sense of purpose than Princeton's, he said, where many sons and daughters of well-known parents "don't quite know why they're there."

He responded to the question "What does Kalamazoo do?"

"We produce creative people. They change more in four years than in conventional programs. The freshman seminar, the foreign study, and the Senior Individualized Project all contribute to a progression in responsibility. After the foreign experiences, they come back more analytical, more comfortable with complexities and uncertainties, more understanding of the views of other countries, and more tolerant. They have more self-awareness and more self-confidence.

"The K Plan is complex to administer. It creates a campus community. Everyone has an Outward-Bound experience or two, and there is a great bonding within a class. It is a developmental model in undergraduate education."

Kalamazoo seniors get into all the best graduate schools. Eighty-five to ninety-five percent of its medical and law school applicants are accepted, and in that much more competitive area—veterinary school—ninety-nine percent are accepted.

Further proof is the kind of achieving adults the college produces. As a seedbed of the nation's scientists and scholars, Kalamazoo ranks seventeenth among all 2,000 colleges and universities in the country. It is fifth in biology, life sciences, and foreign languages, eighth in chemistry, tenth in psychology, and eleventh in science and engineering.

Testifying to the strength of its international studies and economics programs is the fact that at least four Kalamazoo alumni are economists at the World Bank, three are with the International Monetary Fund, and two have served on the staff of the president's Council of Economic Advisers. It is unlikely that another college can match that record.

The faculty members I talked with were no less enthusiastic than the provost. Whether it was in art or in English or in science, they all said Kalamazoo's preparation was far superior to that of the professional school or the university, the kinds of places where they'd been trained. An art professor said, "At the professional art schools, they're technicians who don't have a whole lot to say. They're concentrating on copying this or doing that traditional thing. In any art, it is essential to have something to say. Here we're helping them express themselves aesthetically."

An English professor said that teaching classes of seventy-five or more at UCLA and Vanderbilt had kept things pretty impersonal. "Here, I am much more involved with students. We have collaborative learning. Students are teachers of others on campus, and tutors off campus. It is interactive, sharing, one of the ways we prepare them to go out into the world."

A chemistry professor underscored a point others had made. "University professors consumed with research aren't good teachers."

As if there's some ESP at work, these teachers echoed what their peers at other colleges often said, that "It's not the top student who's most changed; it's the next group."

Or, "Alums often say, 'bet you didn't think I could do it.' Yes, I did; you didn't. Those are the kids who go out and stomp on the accelerator. They're the ones who come back and tell us. It comes down to having someone believing in them."

Or, "The difference about K students is a manic dynamism. We attract adventurous and we attract those around the edge who want to jump in." And they do jump in. She told of a painfully shy girl who had her first foreign term in Scotland where there'd be no language barrier. This gave her enough confidence to go to Senegal on her next one, and the two terms gave her a new maturity and self-confidence.

Every student I talked to would do it again, emphatically. One senior said it had shaken her Catholic faith, and—as several others said—made her examine herself. She had changed her major four times and was unsure whether she'd go to seminary or graduate school. Another senior, who had come because of the K Plan, already had a job with a major counseling firm. Another, who'd been worried about getting into at least one graduate school, had been told by her adviser, "Don't worry, you'll get into all of them." And she did.

An African-American junior from New York City who'd come because of the K Plan said that a term in South Korea "transformed me. Now I really appreciate the U.S." She added: "I would want my own children to have this experience."

A strikingly handsome African-American junior from Detroit said he'd planned to go to the University of Michigan until he visited Kalamazoo. He was amazed to see faculty members playing with students in a basketball game. He said, "A sweaty guy, a prof, came over and shook my hand and said, 'Hi. I'm Dave Winch.' Right then I thought, I've got to come here." Much as he was taken with Dave Winch, the young man did not follow him into physics. He's a biology and music major, with a minor in German as a result of a foreign-study term. "Speaking in another language," he said, "makes you think more about your own."

Others said such things as:

- Four years here have given me a new life plan. They have forced me to be an aware person and to think more clearly.
- I am going to seminary. It has changed my faith. The foreign programs have helped me to develop more as a person; they've given me self-confidence. It was quite a challenge to live in a different culture.
- The discontinuity here forces you to make new friends. It increases the sense of community.
- It helped me find my capabilities. It did a great deal for my self-awareness. When you find yourself in a foreign environment, finding your way around develops you. I had worried about my independence in going to a small college; that's why I was thinking about Michigan. But I find I've gained independence. The curriculum, the Career Development programs, the foreign study, all were

important contributions to my development. Also, the teachers are wonderful. The short terms (ten weeks) make it intense, and I had to learn to manage my time.

The most dramatic testimony came from an English professor who had gone to Northwestern and the University of Virginia. She said: "I guess the best thing I can say about Kalamazoo is that I went to two excellent universities and I really wish I'd gone to school here. I'm constantly struck by the amazing changes Kalamazoo College is able to bring about in young people and I wonder what might have happened to me at this place. Partially it is the workings of the famous and unique K Plan. As I watch my students rise to the challenges posed by the Plan, becoming surer of themselves, their abilities, their choices, their goals, and accumulating an array of experiences that were beyond my imagination as an undergraduate, I find myself deeply envious."

Kalamazoo's students share her enthusiasm. It is one of those rare places where everyone is excited about what he is doing and in love with the community of which he is a part. It rubs off on a visitor and it becomes a part of the participant's being and improves the quality of his life. Those who choose it have made a choice they could not improve upon.

What Kalamazoo students and alumni have to say ten years later has a different emphasis than that of other colleges. A pervasive theme is that they have learned the importance of involvement, not only on campus and their community, but as world citizens in their two foreign-study terms and the career-development term.

A senior summed up the reactions of several to their study-abroad terms as "one of those college experiences that changed my life. It was a very liberating and independent experience. After six months in a foreign place I came back to Kalamazoo with a new view on life and my existence in it. What is amazing though is that 150 other students returned to campus with stories different from my own. It was enlightening and I felt enriched by those around me; to be able to have experiences so different but to have a common ground on which to share those experiences allowed me to grow even more."

Student after student testified that Kalamazoo had changed their lives in "countless" or "numerous" ways, or "in every way possible," and gave much credit to the K Plan. One senior, looking into her crystal ball, said Kalamazoo and the K Plan, "have forever influenced the individual I am today and I am saddened to leave in three weeks' time; for me it's like leaving a second home."

They also were grateful that the college encourages involvement in campus activities. A senior said Kalamazoo "creates a community in which one feels safe to grow as a person, as well as academically." A 2000 alumna said she'd started a student-run dance company that was still going strong. A sophomore said "The environment here is very conducive to trying new things. Every day, a new event, interaction or activity contributes to this influence. Just yesterday a professor stopped me walking back from class and recommended a book she'd been reading that reminded her of me. Tomorrow I'm going to have lunch with her to discuss topics from the book and talk with her about possible research projects at the Biodiversity Station in Ecuador, where I will be working as part of my study-abroad experience. The professors are your friends here. I have a class with four students and we sit down and talk with the professor as equals. It's a collaborative learning experience that can't be beat."

They had plenty to say about how great the professors were. One said she had planned to major in international studies but, unlike in high school, "I found that math was absolutely fascinating; the professors were so excited about the material it made me excited too. They brought life to what can be a very dry subject." A couple of others said their original career plans had been changed by foreign-study terms, their classes, internship opportunities, "and advising by distinguished faculty members." They also said the opportunities "to get involved locally, nationally, and globally are far greater than I could have found at a larger school."

Another said she was "a better, more broad-minded person,

more whole, more connected, and well-rounded person for having gone to Kalamazoo College." She hoped to find a grad school that had Kalamazoo's virtues, but that will not happen; grad schools are vocational schools and don't care about such things.

A 2000 graduate said Kalamazoo had so well "paved the way for an easy transition to graduate school I now know I'll be going for my Ph.D. in psychology." She also had been "surprised" to find that "I have lifelong friendships with the professors and staff members" as well as with classmates. The other "amazing thing" she's discovered is that "there is a deep connection among K graduates due to the deeply enriching, interconnected experiences people gain at K that spans generations." She recommended "K" to anyone who is "looking to challenge themselves in ways they never imagined."

And finally, a few years ago a client sent me a commencement invitation with this message on the envelope:

"Loren. Kalamazoo really did change my life."

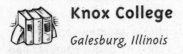

Knox College
Galesburg, Illinois

On my first visit to Knox in Galesburg, Illinois, twenty years ago I thought, "What a wonderful, charming place to spend four such important years of a young person's life." I was impressed by the faculty, the students, and the cloistered tranquility of a campus of large lawns and great trees. The centerpiece is Old Main, an architectural gem. It is where Abraham Lincoln had to crawl through a window to get to his debate with Stephen Douglas because the speaker's stand had been built too close to the door. He then announced he had been through college.

Another jewel among Knox's many buildings is an oak-paneled library of such charm and grace that one student said it was a major factor in her decision to come to Knox. Except for a large reading room that looks as if it had come straight out of Oxford or Cambridge, the ceilings are low, and the rare-book room, which houses the Finley collection of every important source on the history of the Midwest printed since 1820, is a cozy place that brings to mind art historian Kenneth Clark's comment that "no great thought was ever conceived in an enormous room." (John Huston Finley, who was president of Knox around the turn of the century, was later editor of *The New York Times*.)

This look of cloistered tranquility is deceptive; Knox has been very active. First off, it has a new curriculum; the student now plans his own education. Moreover, he has to meet a new kind of graduation requirement: He must be able to work effectively, as well as communicate, with people from a wide range of backgrounds. The plan, which surely will influence those of other colleges, was developed with the aid of a $200,000 Mellon Foundation grant.

The college has received a $1 million grant from the Howard Hughes Medical Institute to start a new major in neuroscience as well as a new faculty position, laboratory expansion, and new science programs for junior high school girls.

Grants from the National Science Foundation and the National Institutes of Health are adding to its strengths in science. Grants from the Caterpillar Foundation and the Merck Company Foundation support the development of creative projects and experimental learning programs needed in the new curriculum.

It has invested heavily in renovating and upgrading facilities for the fine arts, the Lincoln Studies Center, the science and mathematics center, and the Black Studies Center. New residential facilities and a new field house have been built.

There are also new centers to expand and support its programs in global study, advanced study and research, career and preprofessional development, teaching and learning, and intercultural life.

In designing his educational plan, the student must include a broad foundation in the liberal arts and some experiential learning such as off-campus study, independent research, or major creative projects. He must also be able to speak and write clearly and persuasively, understand and use mathematical concepts, have a working knowledge of a second language, and use information technology effectively. The new stipulation says the student "must function effectively with persons from a wide range of backgrounds." This requirement will surely boom off-campus and foreign study. Over half of the students now have at least one foreign-study term.

While the speaking requirement is new, there has always been a great emphasis on writing at Knox. Its literary magazine, *Catch,* offers some proof of its quality. In 2003 it won two top national prizes. One was the Pacemaker Award from the Associated Collegiate Press, and the other was the Association of Writers & Writing Program Directors' prize for content for undergraduate literary magazines.

In the same year, ten faculty published books, a notable number for a college that puts its emphasis on teaching.

At the time of my first visit, African-American students elsewhere were segregating themselves, even at egalitarian Oberlin, but at Knox they told me they were part of one happy family. This is not surprising; Knox was founded in 1836 by abolitionist Congregationalists and Presbyterians and was a station on the Underground Railroad by which slaves fled to freedom. In 1870, the first black in Illinois to get a college degree, Barnabas Root, was a Knox graduate, as was the first black senator from Illinois, Hiram Revels. Knox not only offers a major in Black Studies but is a founding member and hosts the national headquarters of the Association of Black Culture Centers, which leads academic discussion on black culture through its journal.

Knox also has a higher percentage of African-American faculty members—10 percent—than any other college or university.

It also has a program funded by a grant from the U.S. Department of Education to prepare underrepresented groups for academic careers. Each year, ten freshmen are chosen for whom special career-focused programs and summer research support are provided.

Knox has always admitted blacks and women, and today its 1,200 students come from forty-six states and fifty countries. Fourteen percent are American minorities and 9 percent are international students. Grinnell in Iowa is the only other good college so far from a major city able to boast of such diversity.

When I made my recent second visit, it became clear that of the many powerful attractions of Knox, one is that there is no better college in the country for developing a young mind and character; another is that no college offers better entrées to top professional schools, whether for architecture, art, business, engineering, environmental management, forestry, law, medicine, nursing, or social work.

For the budding scientist or scholar, acceptance at graduate school is just as certain, for Knox is in the top 2 percent of all institutions in the production of men and women who achieve Ph.D.s, and it ranks number eleven in mathematics and the sciences. That too is not surprising; 65 percent of Knox graduates do postgraduate study within five years.

Knox offers so much aid, both need- and merit-based, that fewer than 10 percent pay the full tab. Seventy-three percent of them got need-based aid ranging from $5,000 to $30,000 and another 10 percent got scholarships ranging from $1,000 to $10,000 a year in 2005.

Knox also awards scholarships to outstanding mathematics and chemistry students; to National Merit Scholars; to students with special abilities in the creative arts of writing, music, theater, and visual art; to junior-college graduates; and—courtesy of Colorado alumni—to residents of Colorado.

In addition, twenty juniors each year are chosen as Ford Foundation Research Fellows and get support for independent research projects. Knox was one of only sixteen colleges in the country chosen for this program to develop future college professors. The program has been so successful that the college has expanded it so that as many as sixty-five juniors now can undertake summer research projects with a faculty mentor.

In fact, there are so many opportunities and so much support that 85 percent of the seniors have produced a creative or research project by the time they graduate.

What makes Knox such a desirable place is very much what makes other colleges in this book the best preparation. This college is educating—not training—people who can think clearly and independently, who have moral compasses, and who can live fully and courageously.

It does this in many ways. First, a sense of high mission is palpable. It is a family in which the teachers acting as parents encourage, push, and support their children.

They told stories of a black student from the inner city who became a campus leader and is now a sociologist, and of a small-town boy who is now getting his Ph.D., but who probably would have fallen through the cracks at a university. Dr. Brenda Fineberg, author of a praised classics text, said that her going to graduate school after graduating from the University of Chicago had been accidental but, "at Knox, it wouldn't have been accidental."

There is equal concern at the other end of the performance spectrum. Failure is not the end. A student cannot fade into the woodwork because he or she has to be involved.

One faculty member who had taught at Trinity in Connecticut said there is much more discussion at Knox because "there's a better mix here. The minorities are not at the bottom here as they were at Trinity. At Trinity there was no discussion because of the social differences. The students are much more involved in their own education here. At Knox there is no room for pretense, either academically or socially."

A sure test of what faculty and administrators are saying about their college is what the students say, and at Knox they're saying the same things. I talked with students from Spain, Mexico, and China, and with black and white students from diverse backgrounds, and while it may tax credulity, I didn't hear a single discouraging word about the college they had chosen. They all regarded their teachers as their friends and responded with such certainties as "of course!" when I asked if they might have dinner or spend a night at a faculty member's home if they came back in five or ten years. A black student said "the professors have an interest in you, and they don't at Morgan State (an all-black institution in Maryland), where some of my friends go."

Knox also affected their values. A black girl from Chicago said "it broadened my views; the diversity here gave me an appreciation of others." The girl from Mexico called it "a melting-pot experience that makes me more aware and more tolerant." A junior from St. Paul who had one of the research stipends said, "I was so closed-minded when I came, but the experience here and the foreign-study programs have changed all that." A senior history major said of the learning environment, "I look back four years and I can't believe what happened." A sophomore from an all-black high school in a Maryland suburb near Washington, D.C., who plans to go to law school, said he'd had a hard time realizing that there could be so much diversity and so much warmth and acceptance.

The fact that Knox operates under an honor code seemed to these students a most natural thing. How could it be otherwise?

The foreign students dwelt on how different Knox was from their universities. The sophomore girl from Mexico nodded as the boy from Barcelona, a senior majoring in international relations, said; "Here you are challenged and you can excel. At the University of Barcelona you're just a number and all you do is memorize. Here you grow intellectually a lot; you have to do critical thinking; you get a well-rounded view of what the world is like." To which the Mexican girl added that the one-on-one relationships with faculty members is unknown at home, and that there the emphasis is on technology rather than on getting an education.

A Chinese-American senior from Chicago, a chemistry and art history major, said he had picked Knox in the first place because of its strong sense of community—"and I had to feel I was part of the community"—the interaction among students and between students and faculty, and the fact that unlike the universities he visited, Knox would let him have full use of all the scientific equipment. "Knox," he says, "is very conducive to allowing students to pick and choose. You are responsible for what you do and liable for what you don't."

Aside from the preceptorials and the distribution requirements, there is much latitude for students to design their own majors, with faculty guidance, to do independent study, or to do honors work that requires producing a major piece of research or creative work. Currently, 20 percent of the senior class is doing honors work and the college plans to expand it greatly. Honors students get financial help for summer work on their projects.

More than thirty off-campus programs are available to Knox students in Asia, Southeast Asia, Europe, and South America; in this country there are programs that cover just about every student interest, whether in the humanities, the arts, classics, environment, science, or politics (in a Washington seminar). More than half of Knox students spend from a term to a year in one or more of these projects.

Closer to home, twenty miles from the campus, Knox has something few colleges do: a 760-acre biological field station where the Illinois prairie has been restored to its original state. Slender buffalo grass six feet tall lets in so much sun that near the ground there's a whole lower tier of flowers and other plants up to a foot high. It makes believable the western historians' accounts of riders having to stand up in their stirrups to see across the sea of grass.

How the college is using this expanse of prairie it has brought back to life is another example of its intellectual metabolism. It has developed an off-campus residential study term in which professors from several disciplines will study with students the ecological, historical, and aesthetic qualities of the landscape. The students will live in a refurbished structure that also has laboratories and classrooms. And they will be their own cooks and housemaids as well as stewards of the field station.

That look of cloistered tranquility the campus gives truly is deceptive, for it cloaks a vibrant, endlessly searching community, one that will open new worlds and change you.

Ten years later, seniors were still saying that their experiences at Knox had changed their lives whether they had expected it or not, and it made them sad to leave.

One, a first-generation college student, spoke for several others with his testimony: "I did not come to college expecting it to change my life. I simply wanted to earn a degree that would help me find a career I would enjoy later in life. I chose Knox because the brochures were pretty, the people were nice and it was 2000 miles away from home. But as I sat in commencement last year, looking back on my previous three years while looking forward to my last, tears came to my eyes. I realized then that Knox transformed me.

"The change you make at Knox is slow, thought out, and personalized. Each day you are finding out something new about you or those around you. You learn to work with those who have similar beliefs and those who contradict your entire life philosophy, whether they are in India, New Mexico, or St. Louis. You are an equal with upperclassmen, your professors, administrators, and even the president of the college. I find it is just as hard to say good-bye to those professors who have been my mentors as it is to say good-bye to my closest friends. I am excited as I leave Knox because I know my experiences here will be carried with me for the rest of my life."

A senior girl from Chicago said, "I came here thinking that I already was the person I wanted to be and am graduating knowing that I am the person I always wanted to know. I can now reach outside my comfort zone and examine the world and its problems, critically and analytically. At Knox, students are educated to be the people who make a difference in the world, not the ones who watch people make a difference."

Of all those who talked about Knox's diversity and sense of

community, a gay senior's homage and his thanks were by far the most eloquent. He said, "Simply put, I began college a terrified closet case, and am graduating a proud gay man. Knox provides a comfortable, nurturing environment for GLBT students to find themselves, just as it does for every person who grows here. Some publications tout Knox diversity, but they tend to neglect what makes Knox, in my opinion, a truly diverse community. Every student comes from a unique background, has a different story to tell. It is this wealth of exposure that nourishes students hungry to learn, to step outside their comfort zones."

Lawrence University

Appleton, Wisconsin

I f an omniscient being were to describe the vital difference between Lawrence University in Appleton, Wisconsin, and one of the Ivies in New England, she or he would say that Lawrence is a growth hormone that raises kids' trajectories and instills the power to soar. The Ivies take in fast-track kids and turn out fast-track graduates who are not much changed.

A former Japanese ambassador to the United States said of his experience at Lawrence that it "remains in my heart as the most rewarding. It made a deep and lasting imprint on my life. . . . It shaped my outlook. . . . Without it I would not be where I am today. I am very grateful for the education I received at Lawrence; it is one of the best colleges in the United States." He had also spent a year at Amherst. Grammy Award–winning opera star Dale Duesing said Lawrence "transformed my life." Another alumnus said, "Lawrence cared about my education even when I didn't."

If people weren't provincial and if they were concerned only with quality, Lawrence would be as sought after as any college in the country. But since it's not on the East Coast, it's a jewel you can have.

The educational establishment is not so provincial. Three of Lawrence's presidents have subsequently been presidents of Harvard, Brown, and Duke. One of them, Nathan Pusey, developed Lawrence's powerful and much acclaimed Freshman Studies sequence before Harvard snatched him.

Dr. Richard Warch, a former Yale dean and that rare college president with a sense of mission, retired in 2004 after twenty-five years. His successor, Dr. Jill Beck, is a true Renaissance woman. She had been dean of the school of arts at the University of California, Irvine, where she was also a professor of dance. She is a much-published scholar, and has been a dancer, choreographer, and ballet director. She founded two organizations to promote arts education and has won the American Red Cross's Clara Barton Award for humanitarian service in the arts.

Lawrence has had seven Rhodes Scholars and it ranks in the top twenty colleges in turning out future Ph.D.s in the humanities and in all other nonscience fields. It is a first-rate entrée into graduate and professional schools. Back in the mid-nineties, President Warch said, "Lawrence kids are better than they think. Yale kids think they're better than they are. Lawrence kids are less broad at first but broader at the finish. It is less competitive here than at Yale and there is more joy."

Lawrence is called a university because it has a music conservatory—a superb one that is most unusual. It is not only music for the nonmusic majors, but the music majors are ensured a liberal education. Furthermore, if someone wants to do a double major, say in government and music, as one fellow was doing when I visited, it's no problem. The music department would love to have everyone exposed to music courses or doing double majors.

"Here everyone participates," a piano teacher said. "Students are coddled; I go to hear every student's recital. At Oberlin nobody on the faculty came to hear mine. We have music for all. We work so hard for them. A course a girl wanted wasn't offered so I did it one-on-one."

Lawrence's 1,300 students come from forty-nine states with

the Midwest most heavily represented. Its percentage of minorities has climbed to 14 percent, partly because of a program of internships with major corporations in the area, such as Kimberly Clark, which often lead to good jobs for these students after graduation. Eleven percent are international students from forty-five countries. Lawrence accepts three-fourths of its applicants, about half of them in the top tenth of their high school classes. But here again, many of those were small rural schools. The average SAT scores were 630 verbal and 630 math. In other words, there are plenty of B, B-, and maybe C admittees, but they have shown that they mean business.

About two-thirds of the students get financial aid, which in 2000 averaged $18,700 a year for the need-based recipients, and about $8,000 for the aid given on a merit basis.

In the perspective of a young British art professor, Lawrence is "a conservative college where kids work. Its location increases student-faculty contact because they are thrown together, unlike in a big city [he went to University College London]. They are very friendly. There is a lot of volunteer work."

Lawrence's faculty, the equal of any in the country, has few peers as mentors and as friends who motivate young people and equip them to cope in a new kind of world. It is cosmopolitan, liberal, and active professionally. In one year alone, nearly a third of them published books, articles, or reviews; presented papers; or were panelists at professional meetings. The National Institutes of Health picked a psychology professor to serve on the peer review board that votes yes or no on its grants. The faculty of the music conservatory was equally active in composing, performing, and music scholarship.

The Lawrence freshmen are mainstream teenagers unlikely to have considered either conservative religious schools like Wheaton or very liberal, do-it-yourself places like Antioch, Hampshire, Marlboro, or New College. But four years later, they would not be recognized as the same people. They have become critically thinking do-it-yourselfers with the confidence to achieve goals they hadn't even thought of as freshmen. They also have a far broader view of the world thanks to Lawrence's emphasis on off-campus and foreign-study terms, and firm value systems.

The accolades of students and graduates section at the end of this chapter indicate why over half of the alumni contribute financially, one of the highest percentages in the country.

The attractive campus is on a bluff overlooking the Fox River, so Lawrence has crew as well as a full lineup of other intercollegiate sports. The location also provides the site for a posh new residential hall, set into the bank, which the kids have named the Ritz-Carlton.

Lawrence also has an $18 million state-of-the-art science building that opened in 2000 and was designed to intertwine teaching and research. In 1997, Briggs Hall was opened to house several departments. A beautiful, 405-acre wooded estate in famous Door County on Lake Michigan is used for small group retreats, and the college hopes to make such experiences available to all students.

The centerpiece of the Lawrence experience, the two-term Freshman Studies course, was designed by President Pusey as a kind of intellectual culture shock to introduce students to the fundamental character of liberal learning. They read, discuss, grapple with, and write about questions of abiding concern: Why am I here? How should I conduct my life? What things are worth knowing? But that is not all; works of Bach, Beethoven, Mozart, and Stravinsky are on the syllabus, as well as those of Miles Davis and Frank Lloyd Wright.

Faculty from all departments teach the classes. To give different perspectives, instructors are changed in the middle of a term. It is often a collaborative learning experience. A chemistry or a biology professor leading the discussion on Plato's *Republic* and grading the papers may be struggling and learning right along with the students.

A freshman may write five or more papers each term, often for different instructors who don't do or see things the same way. But help is provided. For one thing, the staff meets at lunch once a week to compare notes on interpretation of their texts and teaching methods, and just to try to keep everybody on the same track. This is possible because all are discussing the same topics at the same time.

For another, Lawrence provides a magical little booklet every college ought to emulate. *The Freshmen Studies Book* explains what the system is trying to do and how to beat it. It tells how to "use" your instructors, making the points that not only are they good sources of information, both practical and scholarly, but also that they too may be struggling with the text, and furthermore, that they will enjoy the chance to chat about problems.

A section that students everywhere should read, "What Your Instructor Wants," says that what he wants is for students to "stop asking what your instructor wants and to start asking some more fruitful and self-liberating questions. . . . He wants you to think more deeply and more clearly, to examine and test your ideas, and to express them more lucidly and completely."

There are excellent sections on how to study the readings, how to be effective in discussion, and how to write a paper—with good and bad examples, plus tips on good usage. It even has some sample quiz questions. Any freshman who uses this sixty-page booklet will have it made, and not just in the Freshman Studies course.

The Freshman Studies courses do indeed engage students in their own education. By the time they're seniors, 90 percent of the students are doing some independent study and half of them have had a foreign-study term abroad. All of the science students get involved in undergraduate research. One professor said, "Kids blossom here. My students have produced a dozen articles in six years. They develop critical thinking skills." In history, students have coauthored two papers this year, and one student is lead author on another.

Lawrence students are much better off than those at Wisconsin or Brown, said professors who had taught in those places. At

Lawrence they have many more opportunities in the way of independent research, and they get better recommendations. "We give good recommendations," said a biology professor, "because we know them. I know what my students' aspirations are. We find them summer internships, which they don't do in universities, and parents aren't aware of this. Faculty members here are in academia because they want to teach. At Brown they're not interested in teaching."

The academic dean, who had taught at Princeton before coming to Lawrence in 1993, took a longer view. "This kind of place is the cutting edge of higher education. I didn't think so when I was at a research university. We're teaching them to think for coping in a fast-changing world. Now the Ivies are emulating us."

The students will buy that, and then some. A senior had heads nodding when he said, "I have gained a lot of self-confidence; I've been recognized for what I've done. My professors are all from the best schools. They're interested in trying to help you find your way. I feel I've gotten a lot of individual attention, one-on-one, with professors. You can make it what you want to make it, which you can't at a university, and it's kind of a good feeling to be a big fish in a small pond. Everyone here is concerned about academics but it's not an atmosphere in which you're racking your brains worrying about competing."

Another chimed in with, "Lawrence's Honor Code opens a lot of opportunities. I took a test at home. It's great; you can take a test wherever you want to take it. The professor puts the test on the board and walks out. They really treat you like adults. I think everyone obeys the Honor Code; people can leave their backpacks when they go into the cafeteria."

Other very prominent themes were that they had learned to analyze, to read and think critically, to question things; and emphatically, they were better writers. They said there was much discussion out of class about what went on in class: "It's something all of us do." The Freshman Studies course got much credit here.

"In high school," a senior added, "I could avoid thinking about things that are really important, analyzing what my life was about. College gave me an opportunity to consider who I really am. My head would be burning about things we'll never find the answers to. Lawrence gave me the opportunity to grow intellectually. It encouraged me with all the personal attention. The music department is incredible. I wanted a course but couldn't fit into my schedule, so the prof gave it to me as a tutorial."

Several seniors headed for graduate or professional schools thought they had a decided edge because of research opportunities, independent study, or the quality of learning. One of the aspiring lawyers said, "I did quite a bit better on my LSATs than those from the University [of Wisconsin]." A future geologist said, "Here we have small classes and we get to use the equipment. I really like it; it seems like home."

However, Lawrence has a good deal more diversity than home. There were so many international students on campus that many felt it was "a microcosm of the United States and the world." Also, as already noted, half of the students take at least one of the college's array of foreign programs.

But what was consistent was the enthusiasm for their school. A number of nonmusic majors used terms like "phenomenal" or "incredible" to describe the conservatory and the performances it brings to the campus. They also praised the overall quality of imported attractions such as plays and lectures: Several athletes were glad that they had been able to compete successfully at a smaller school like Lawrence, and be at least some kind of visible fish in the pond. Even more unusual was the number of students who volunteered that Lawrence was generous with financial aid. (About two-thirds get aid.)

The sophomore with a double major in government and music had been accepted by a couple of Ivies but chose Lawrence after spending a day at each. His verdict was, "Here it felt like home; there were more options; it was more laid-back and relaxed, not competitive. At Yale you have the feeling you're lucky to be there; here they thanked me for coming. Here you can do graduate-level research. You can go as far and as fast as you want. Faculty, staff, and administration are all here to help you."

Alumna and successful novelist Susan Engberg had been an art major who loved words and took a creative writing course. She wrote in the alumni magazine: "If the course description had had a secret text, visible only to me, it would have read, 'Dive in Susan, do the work with your whole heart, let the pleasure of working do its work on you, trust the teacher, and by midwinter you will emerge with the seed of your future in mind." She did, and she was hooked on writing. What had happened? "These are the people who help us turn into ourselves."

If the undergraduates were as skilled with words as Susan Engberg, they would be saying much the same thing. Lawrence is a place that helps young people find themselves and then make the best of what they find.

Ten years later, students and alumni were saying the same things, that Lawrence had changed their lives; it had opened their minds, made them critical thinkers and better persons, but that wasn't all; it was "a home away from home." And most of them had warm words to say about the "amazing" faculty who wanted to help them.

Some who had breezed through high school as straight-A students were shocked to discover that Lawrence was a tougher ball game; it was intellectual and demanding. As one of them said, "Lawrence has made me use my mind, not just my brain."

A lawyer and two college professors echoed what the Japanese ambassador had told me in 1994: "I would not be where I am today if I had not attended Lawrence." Two said the intellectual rigor had helped make them successful, and that they still had friendships with professors. One who'd been a hot-shot student in high school said Lawrence "was a milestone in my life that forever changed my perception of the world. At Lawrence I delved into the world of ideas and critically analyzed subjects I had never even thought about before. Lawrence prepared me well for law school and my career as a civil attorney. While some of my fellow attorneys struggle with legal issues, I am able to get at the heart of my cases swiftly. . . . Some of my professors have kept in touch with me over the past thirty years. I wouldn't trade my Lawrence education for anything in the world. It was a defining experience in my life."

One professor said, "I have opportunity every day to appreciate how my emotional and intellectual development during that period provided an exceptional foundation for personal and professional success." Lawrence, he added, "inspires an enduring sense of devotion."

The other professor, a 1992 graduate, said, "It would be difficult to overstate the influence that my years at Lawrence have had on the shaping of my life. The impact extends to my academic, professional, and personal development to the person I am today. The academic rigor taught me persistence, critical thinking, and love of knowledge. I developed relationships with faculty that continue today."

Another 1992 graduate credited Lawrence with enabling him to become his own man. He said that while Lawrence had given him the skills to "forge ahead in my career, I credit Lawrence with giving me something more. I was empowered to confidently reflect on what it is that mattered most to me. And it is this self-awareness that allowed me to pursue a life of my own choosing rather than something prescribed by societal pressures."

A 2001 graduate teaching in Japan said that a professor he'd had for only one course had set such high standards that "You have been an enormous influence on my young career."

A football player of the class of 2000 said, "The coaches weren't simply concerned with my abilities on the field, but genuinely cared about me as a person. The team supported me and fostered my growth, not just as a player but as a human being."

A 2004 graduate from war-torn Sierra Leone had not intended to go to Lawrence, but his two sisters eventually followed him. His father sent him to live with an uncle in Texas, where he became a high school football star recruited by Lawrence and others. He wanted to go to the University of South Dakota, his father's alma mater, but as an alien, he couldn't get the promised athletic scholarship. So Lawrence got him, Lawrence became his ideal of a college, and he persuaded his sisters to come. Of Lawrence he said, "I can't imagine being anywhere else," because of the academic rigor and because the people are so wonderful.

Ohio Wesleyan University

Delaware, Ohio

On many counts, Ohio Wesleyan is one of the best academic bargains in the country. A chemistry professor voiced a prevailing faculty attitude when he said, "Regardless of where a kid comes from, we can take him somewhere."

And the testimonials in the "Ten Years Later" section at the end of this chapter prove it especially, but by no means exclusively, in science. Ohio Wesleyan is one of the top fifty producers of the nation's future scientists. It also is one of the few that has a 3–2 engineering program with Cal-Tech.

The college is providing new and better facilities to stay in the elite group with a $35 million comprehensive science center completed in time for the 2005 school year.

The first-rate Fine Arts Department has new state-of-the-art multimedia design space. There is also a building for 3-D arts, and an art museum was dedicated in 2002. An extensive expansion and improvement of athletic facilities is in the works.

As every college and university did before the college-going rush after World War II, Ohio Wesleyan accepts a wide range of students, from C to A. It makes a special effort to help those with

learning disabilities, and it has honors programs for the very talented or the very motivated.

Ohio Wesleyan is likely to be a financial as well as an academic bargain, for over 90 percent of its students get some type of financial aid and about 70 percent get some form of merit aid. The average SAT score is in the 1,200s and the average GPA of enrolled freshman was 3.25, about a quarter of whom get into the honors program. The school accepts just over 80 percent of its applicants, most of whom come from outside of Ohio. It is a diversified group, from forty-two other states and sixty countries.

An important morale consideration is that 70 percent of the students accepted considered Ohio Wesleyan their first choice; another 20 percent listed it as their second choice. That bespeaks "a happy-band-of-brothers" esprit that may have something to do with why, across the board, it has a long history of helping them become achievers. A young client who'd been the despair of his parents in high school has done so well at Ohio Wesleyan that as a junior he won a summer internship with CNN news. Another, who'd wanted to drop out of high school, now has a doctorate in geology. Like Denison, Ohio Wesleyan is not the same place it was twenty-five or even fifteen years ago, thanks in large measure to the efforts of its recently resigned president, Dr. David Warren. There has been, in the words of one longtime professor, "a massive change in the student body and in the college." A $100 million fund-raising campaign is enabling it to hire the best faculty available, offer more merit scholarships to good students, and complete a student center that rivals a shopping mall for attractions. The recruiting of honors students has been most effective in changing more than just the profile of the student body in ten years. It has changed the retention rate and the level of enthusiasm in the classroom.

Today, the professor said, "there is much one-on-one with eager students," an assessment others not only agreed with but enlarged on with such comments about their departments as:

- Half our history majors are converts after taking a freshman course.
- Our new Latin-American studies program is strong and many go on to graduate school.
- Our fine arts program is unique and it is tops. It is strong throughout. We are one of the few to offer both the bachelor of fine arts and the bachelor of arts degrees. We have the widest offerings of any of the twelve in the Great Lakes Colleges Association (GLCA) and one of the widest in the country. We are less career-oriented; we require writing in the art program as part of a liberal education.
- We have the most comprehensive teacher-education program of any GLCA college, and one of the most comprehensive in the country, and we require a 2.6 average to get into the program.
- Psychology majors have coauthored eleven research papers in the last few years. Another fifteen are doing independent research, and five have apprenticeships.
- Our faculty's research citations in scholarly publications rank number two among the top colleges.
- Several chemistry majors have coauthored papers given at professional meetings, and we want to get more and more students engaged in research with faculty.
- The honors program has a special curriculum and tutorials.

They kept saying things like "we nurture students; they are being taught how to think; there's writing across the curriculum—even in art. They are more eager students; they are more service-oriented."

In fact, every faculty member I talked to had the same kind of lively interest in his or her students I found at other campuses reviewed for this book. Some of it may have rubbed off from the chemistry professor, who was as passionate about getting students involved as any teacher I've ever talked to. He said he'd originally been headed for a seminary and the ministry. I told him he was still in religion.

There is, at other colleges, a new interest in public affairs and in public service. A professor said, "There's something about this institution that does attract students interested in global and public issues and we can claim to be distinctive in that area." For ten years, Ohio Wesleyan has put on a major lecture-discussion series called The Sagan National Colloquium to explore some public issue. The program brings in noted speakers for talks on various aspects of a given issue. They are followed by workshops and discussion groups with the speaker, and for students wishing to get academic credit, there is more intensive work. The colloquia are heavily promoted; they are discussed in classes, and it would be difficult to avoid a poster or a reminder of the next event in the popular campus center. They draw large turnouts, unlike some places such as the University of Richmond, where faculty have to give credit to get students to listen to such stars as the famed paleontologist and geologist Stephen Jay Gould.

The Colloquiums continue to have a major impact. In 2004, a freshman girl said, "There are two elements to Ohio Wesleyan that have helped me become the person I am after only a year. The first is OWU's faculty and students; I have witnessed incredible dedication and cooperation between the two. The second element is [Colloquium] guests from the outside world. It is through them that I have been nothing less than inspired."

Every bit as important is what Ohio Wesleyan is doing to give a hand to those with learning problems. Thousands of college students have learning problems, but their schools give them no help. Freshmen with the lowest academic credentials often need a helping hand, too. Many institutions list services for them, but most are on paper only, especially in universities. Ohio Wesleyan delivers with orchestrated help.

A student's academic adviser is the first, and confidential, source of help. The adviser will arrange any accommodations needed, such as choice of courses. A counseling center gives workshops on test anxiety, time management, or psychological counseling. A writing center helps those with problems in that area. A psychologist advises those with learning disabilities and offers strategies for dealing with them. Teachers, advisers, and the resource people all work together to meet the student's needs. They may even waive the foreign-language requirement for graduation or permit a reduced course load. This is a far cry from the experience a student would have at a big university. The best help is still a caring faculty.

Kids at these colleges feel they're getting a better deal than their friends who went to prestige schools. Ohio Wesleyan students say they have to work hard, that the demands are great, and the level of expectation is high. They say the professors are first-rate and they count them as friends interested in their success, and that they often have dinner, dessert, or coffee at faculty homes. Those going to graduate or professional school are looking forward to getting recommendations that not only will be good but that will mean something, because the professor knows them well and can be specific about their virtues.

Several of them confirmed the faculty claim that they were having to learn to think. One fellow responded, when asked if the college had affected his values, that he wasn't sure whether that was the input of his home life or the college but that he and his friends thought they were much more reasoned in their attitudes and beliefs now.

Several upper-class students said they were able to get much more involved and have more satisfying and important roles in their schools than did their friends at universities. A California girl, a top student who had come on a merit scholarship, said that after a visit she would have come without a scholarship, even though several other schools were bidding for her with big grants.

An obvious change at Ohio Wesleyan, as at Denison, is the diminished importance of fraternities and sororities. A senior girl said she dropped out of her sorority because they're not necessary for campus involvement, there's such a strong sense of community at the school. There's also a great deal of social-service work now, and (perhaps as a consequence?) a lot less drinking. A senior boy said his fraternity was heavily involved in service projects, something that was rare a decade ago.

Eight percent of Ohio Wesleyan's 1,900 students are African-American, and 12 percent of the freshmen in 2000 were international students. As was the case when I visited there a dozen or so years ago, the ones I talked to all said they felt they belonged, that it was one community and not a lot of separate groups.

I've already mentioned one of the things that helps the sense of cohesion. It is one of the most stunning campus centers anywhere. A very large and imposing $12 million building, it is a good deal more than a student union. In addition to the usual facilities for student activities are counseling, advising, and career placement centers; a variety of snack shops, dining nooks and terraces; a full scale—and very popular—bakery; meeting rooms; private dining rooms; and of course, other shops. Just one of the publications is a four-page daily bulletin that tells everything that is, or soon will be, going on. When I was there it seemed like the busiest place on the campus.

Since its founding in 1842, Ohio Wesleyan has had a distinguished history, albeit with some ups and downs. Now it is clearly a very effective force that is helping students of a wide range of academic abilities and home backgrounds. A first-rate faculty and administration share an enthusiastic commitment to making good on the boast of the chemistry professor that "regardless of where the kid comes from, we can take him somewhere."

Ten years later, at Ohio Wesleyan, as at other colleges in this book, there were repeated testimonials that the profs were the smartest, most challenging, and helpful persons ever, and how loved they were. One girl called them "inspiring." For the freshmen, OWU had opened a world to them they hadn't conceived of.

Next in frequency were declarations about foreign study experiences that some called "incredible." They all testified in one way or another that the experience had opened their eyes to the views and the worth of other cultures and made them more understanding. And some cited the similar value of OWU's diversity. A freshman girl said, "OWU's large international and minority population brings such different dynamics and perspectives to the school. I have become friends with students from Thailand, India, Great Britain, Jamaica—the list goes on. It is not necessary to sit in a classroom to learn about other cultures. I can simply go to the dorm room next door."

Another freshman, a fellow who'd gone to a "99 percent Caucasian high school" said "OWU is such a rewarding and diverse change for me, I can honestly say that being around such a blend of individuals has shaped my character into one of passion, tolerance, and understanding." He also thought "the atmosphere of academic excellence has pushed me to be a better student and a better person," and the professors "who really push you and help you every step of the way to reach that next level are really life-changing. They take students under their protective wings and guide them to reach for the sky."

Several said the National Colloquium was one of the two "main elements" of OWU, the other the impression made by the close relationship of students and faculty and their "dedication." One girl said the late Senator Simon of Illinois had given her the best advice she'd ever had: "Don't expect perfection; you'll always be disappointed."

A junior from Oregon echoed the views of several others when she said "the warmth of the student body and faculty decided me in favor of OWU over other colleges I visited." She enlarged on that with this: "There is something about the students at OWU that sets them apart from the student bodies of the other small liberal arts colleges I visited. I think there is more emphasis on real human values, and while it is difficult to put a finger on, it has a strong impact on the atmosphere. The kids are down-to-earth and genuinely friendly across the board."

Practically everyone had sentimental words for how challenging the professors were, but how much encouragement and help they gave. "They bring out the best in their students and helped me gain the confidence I needed," said a senior headed to law school.

A girl from New Hampshire said OWU "has made me a completely new person. Inspiring professors have made me rethink my future. I want to be able to touch lives like my professors have for me. I would love to be a professor at a school that is similar to Ohio Wesleyan. The school has done so much for her that she became "an enthusiastic volunteer in the admissions office" to be able to persuade others. A sophomore also worked in the admissions office because her experience was so good she wanted to push OWU.

A freshman paraphrased the poem of a Colloquium speaker, poet Seamus Heaney, to express her feelings: "Ohio Wesleyan has caught my heart off guard and has blown it open."

St. Olaf College
Northfield, Minnesota

What strikes visitors as they drive around and up the curving hill of the St. Olaf campus is the beauty of the place, with its impressive light-gray limestone-and-glass buildings, grassy expanses, emphatic shrubbery, and stately trees. The architecture might be called Norwegian modern, as could the mostly blond- and brown-haired students, looking as attractive as the buildings. Aesthetically and academically, it is Camelot. If it were on the East Coast it would be as selective as any Ivy. But it will just have to be satisfied with being better.

As a matter of fact, St. Olaf puts Camelot in the shade, it has few equals. Here are some of the ways in which it excels:

- It has had six Rhodes Scholars, fourteen Fulbrights, and seventeen Goldwaters as of 2004.
- It ranks fifth among colleges since 1990 in the number of graduates who go on to get doctorates. It is first in mathematics and religion, fifth in chemistry, and sixth in life sciences.
- It is in the top ten colleges having graduates going into the Peace Corps.
- Its music department is one of the finest in the country and one-third of the student body participates in its performances.
- Over 90 percent of the freshmen return for the sophomore year.
- Two of its baseball players were signed by the Los Angeles Dodgers in 2003.

Its campus and facilities make the life-changing four years there very pleasant. Its new $29 million Buntrock Commons has been called "the model for student unions for the twenty-first century." It has a soaring dining hall of light wood and much glass that makes for happy mealtimes; it has student offices, a coffee shop, a student-run nightclub, and perhaps the only college post office where the mailboxes have no locks. That's because the students, as they do in everything else, had a say in what went into the building.

A magnificent new health center has state-of-the-art fitness equipment, a six-lane, 200-meter track, several basketball and tennis courts, a raised walking and jogging ring, and a forty-eight-foot climbing wall.

The old student center, a striking glass structure, has been renovated to become the new art and dance building. St. Olaf is one of the few colleges in the country to offer majors in all four areas of the fine arts.

For the growing Muslim population, a prayer room has been added in the old arts building, along with space for a newly formed African-culture group, which in 2004 took first place in an African Dance competition at Carleton College. The college has added a Dean of Diversity and Community Life.

It is a place that inspires powerful devotion. The graduating class of 2004 challenged 1954's to a giving contest. A phenomenal 82 percent of 2004's contributed but lost to 1954's 87 percent. Few colleges can boast half of either percentage. Also, at few colleges would a senior say the cafeteria food was good.

It looks clean and wholesome and that's exactly what it is, through and through. An anxious father can send his daughter here knowing she'll be safer than at any other college that is not a fundamentalist detention center. St. Olaf is one of the few mainstream colleges with a religious commitment and a commitment to the life of the mind. Not many other colleges have the same sense of common purpose. President Mark U. Edwards says, "St. Olaf is committed to helping students discover their calling. We firmly believe that our mission as a liberal arts college of the church is to help students develop lives of worth and service."

St. Olaf is a place of friendliness and trust as well as of high expectations. Not only are there are no locks on the mailboxes, but most of them sit open, and at strategic walkway crossings lie bags, briefcases, jackets, and other possessions waiting for their owners to pick them up after class. Not one, I was told, has ever been missing.

The college is Lutheran but its commitment is to character, not to denomination or creed. And it is a place that has an impact. Random interviews the college conducts with seniors reveal that their values have changed. They are more interested in service and less interested in wealth, and they emphasized, among other things, the effect of worship services and the international programs. On my first visit to St. Olaf twenty years ago, I went to church on Sunday out of curiosity and found at least 1,000 of the college's 3,000 students were there.

St. Olaf bans cars for any students living within 250 miles, as well as alcohol, and visitation in the coed dorms after midnight

(1:00 a.m. on weekends), but if many kids had complaints, they weren't very vocal.

Indeed, a 2004 graduate wanted to be sure I had the right picture of her community with this testimony: "Some might think St. Olaf is a pretty conservative place because we're affiliated with the church and have a dry-campus policy. But we're really not. This is a place where you can truly be yourself. On campus, there are all kinds of things going on and Northfield has two colleges (Carleton is the other), so the downtown area is fairly hip. It's always fun to hang out there. Good restaurants, bars, and pubs. If you get bored with that scene, though, St. Olaf has a bus that goes to the Twin Cities on the weekends."

The student body is a healthy mix, and the administration is trying to increase the diversity. A little more than 40 percent are Lutherans, nearly 20 percent are Catholics, with Methodists and Presbyterians trailing. Nearly 50 percent are from Minnesota but 49 other states are represented. About 10 percent are Asian, Asian American, European, or African American. I asked a junior from Jamaica how she liked the Minnesota weather and she said, "By now I like it, and I have a job with 3M lined up in Minneapolis when I graduate."

St. Olaf accepts about three-fourths of its applicants, over 90 percent of whom are in the top half of their high school classes, so plenty of B students and a few strong Cs are in the mix. The median SAT scores are 630 verbal and 630 math. The median ACT score is 27. Forty-three percent of the acceptees enroll. And they like it; a phenomenal 91 percent return for the sophomore year and 80 percent graduate in four years. Three-fourths of them have college-educated parents; two-thirds are on financial aid. In addition, to attract more outstanding students, the college offers 300 merit scholarships.

The college meets 100 percent of demonstrated family need, and in addition is "committed to making St. Olaf affordable for anyone who is accepted."

St. Olaf is best known for its famous orchestra and choir. Both have performed in all the major U.S. cities. The choir sang at the 1988 Summer Olympics and is the only college choir ever to sing in the Sistine Chapel in the Vatican.

It is equally respected in the academic world. It has always been a prolific producer of the country's scholars and scientists, out of all proportion to its size or selectivity. Its faculty is superb across the board and works closely with their students. The student-faculty ratio is 12:1. An average of forty-five chemistry majors a year puts it at the top of colleges, and its nonpareil math department attracts seventy majors or more each year. Only biology, with seventy to ninety majors, and English, with eighty to one hundred a year, have more.

There is a core curriculum to ensure that everyone shares a common understanding of the western heritage in science, humanities, the arts, religion, and languages, as well as some non-western cultures or minority cultures of North America. But, with faculty help, students may fashion this experience in their own way. Students may take regular course sequences and distributions, or they may develop their own programs in consultation with an adviser. They may also have all the freedom they could possibly conceive of in the way of individualized majors. The Center for Integrated Studies, a new initiative, provides support for students who want to pursue individualized majors that are interdisciplinary or that combine diverse methods, learning styles, experiences, off-campus resources—you name it.

St. Olaf operates on a 4-1-4 program augmented by two summer sessions. A student takes four courses during each fourteen-week semester (fall and spring) and one intensive course in a January term. He may use the summer sessions to graduate in three years or to go further and deeper in four years. The January term is a no-goof-off period: A student is expected to work forty hours a week between class time and studying.

The opportunities for independent study, off-campus internships, or study almost anywhere around the globe are very nearly without limit. There are 120 programs, and some include study at several different locations. The Global Semester, for instance, takes students to Hong Kong to study the arts of China; to Cairo for themes in ancient Greco-Roman and Islamic-Egyptian history; to Bangalore for Indian political economy; and to Kyoto for the religions of Japan. I don't know of another college that has such a wealth of foreign programs, and nearly 80 percent take advantage of them.

In conjunction with the other thirteen members of the Associated Colleges of the Midwest, St. Olaf also has a rich variety of programs in this country in the arts, urban studies, science, the environment, and humanities. Just about any interest a student has can be served, and some new ones might be discovered.

Whatever their fields, the faculty members I talked to both on my recent visit and twenty years ago thought the years at St. Olaf affected students' values. Some are attracted to St. Olaf, said an English professor who had gone to Holy Cross and then to Harvard for his doctorate, by religion, but everyone feels welcome, and there is a strong sense of community. Also, the college is carrying forward its plans for more diversity. "The kids here are wholesome; they're a delight to teach. They're capable and committed; overachievers." Asked if relations with the students were close, he spoke for many other professors when he said, "That's easy; the faculty here are committed to the undergraduates. The whole system undergirds that. The faculty are active scholars, but to get tenure or to be promoted, St. Olaf has a different philosophy: A decision about tenure is promise, a decision about promotion is performance." In other words, a professor doesn't have to have a long list of books and articles to get tenure, but he has to be a stimulating and caring teacher as well as an active scholar in order to be promoted. One professor has won a national teaching award and a math department professor has been a national leader in shaping college math curriculums and has been president of the national professional association of mathematicians.

Several faculty members emphasized what one called, "a tremendous feeling that people ought to do things of service" that runs through the place. "There is a moral element here, no question," said one. "Students have the chance to be confronted with their values, but there are no religious requirements and we expect them to be comfortable in talking about religious views." Like at other schools in this book, every faculty member I talked with at St. Olaf believes that college has an impact on the development of values as well as giving students a broad outlook as a result of the Global Perspective element in the curriculum. After the foreign experiences, the kids come back "changed," which is just what faculty members have said at every college that has an active foreign-study program.

As at the other colleges in this book, the students and faculty have a mutual admiration. Comments I heard often were, "The teachers know me; the attention I get is wonderful," "I'm very close to my adviser," "When the profs write recommendations, they know me," "These teachers are my good friends," "The sense of respect is very strong." My sampling did not find a single malcontent in this area.

The president of the student council said, "There's a kind of energy here that's not found elsewhere. St. Olaf is inclusive, friendly, and is becoming more diverse politically. It is definitely a place of people who care. It builds a strong sense of community." And in a comment that may surprise teenagers, she added, "No cars is a help." Incidentally, I did not get a single gripe from any student about not having a car. One reason is that if you want to do something there's always a way.

A girl who had already paid her deposit at the University of Chicago when she visited St. Olaf was so enamored of the way it allows the student to participate in her own education, unlike the university, that she switched.

St. Olaf is lovingly regarded as a place, as one boy said, like Outward Bound: It challenges and tests you, supports you, and pushes your bounds outward and upward.

Whether the rest of the country rediscovers values in the next twenty years or not, St. Olaf will continue to offer unequalled preparation for a full life and for being a winner and a contributor in a new world. It is enlightened, forward-looking, and innovative; the teachers are caring human beings, and the welfare of the student takes priority. Whether you're Muslim, Jew, Unitarian, agnostic, or atheist, at St. Olaf you will not only be comfortable, you will be respected, and people will be interested in your views and beliefs.

Ten years later, the students and graduates could hardly be more enthusiastic about what St. Olaf had done to open their eyes and minds; to make better thinkers and persons who want to serve others.

A 2004 graduate voiced the mind-changing surprise that college had been. She said, "I came ready to impress as I had been expected to in high school," but found that at St. Olaf, such things didn't matter. "Instead," she said, "St. Olaf has challenged me in much better ways. It has provided an atmosphere that made it okay to question faith in a community so strong and loving that its bonds have forced me to question my values, morals, and basic beliefs. I am stronger, yet more vulnerable because I have let people into my heart. I have lost so much of what I was, only to become more of myself. I desperately want to stay on this campus for more than four years." Another found it "a very special place," as her high school counselor had told her.

They, and almost all of the others, testified to the mind-opening foreign-study programs. A junior said his values had been "challenged and shaped by peers from around the world." Another theme was their "lifelong" affection for professors, staff, and custodians.

A 2004 graduate who hadn't wanted to go the same college her parents had, or to "a college of the church," was one of the most committed at the end. She talked about "the terrific relationship" faculty and staff have with the students, and how students "spend time with everyone from the custodians to the secretaries." She called her five-month Global Semester in which she'd studied in eight countries around the world "an amazing experience." She'd also had January term in Costa Rica, Greece, Turkey, and Rome, the latter three as a religion comajor.

Several talked about having their religious faith forcefully challenged but winding up feeling secure because, in the words of one, St. Olaf is a community that "took both my faith and my skepticism seriously and didn't have answers to questions of faith I felt were impossible to come by. My faith has deepened and so have my doubts. Both are more and more informed. I am better to live a life of worth and service. Life-changing stuff, no?"

A self-described overachiever who graduated in 2004 said she had been changed from being a driven perfectionist to a person wanting to serve and ready to "work to live, not live to work." A classmate said that four years at St. Olaf "will allow me to succeed in whatever occupation I choose."

St. Olaf's Student Support Service (SSS), which has a Summer Bridge Program to raise the sights of inner-city kids to get them to college, got a testimonial from a 2003 alumna. She grew up in a single-parent home, "surrounded by drugs and violence." She was the first in her family even to finish high school, and only went because her friends did. College was not something she had even considered, but SSS got her interested, taught her how to study, provided tutoring and help in applying. The very idea of college, she said, "terrified me." She said that "even though I was a low-income student, I had the opportunity to go abroad. I also had the opportunity to hold many leadership positions. After working with SSS as a student, I became interested in serving low-income, disadvantaged youth much like myself. The SSS program prepared me for St. Olaf and St. Olaf's programs prepared me for life."

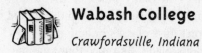

Wabash College
Crawfordsville, Indiana

Wabash is a happy band of 850 brothers, fraternity brothers, mostly. But it is a place like no other. Not only do these young men take pride in working hard, their fraternities see to it that they do. Students are proud of their faculty and faculty take pride in the students. All are proud of their school. Wabash has no church connection, but its religion department draws even skeptics as majors. On this lovely campus forty-five miles from Indianapolis, Wabash comes first.

This is a clan with élan. Not a single student I talked to would be anywhere else. Wabash was their first choice, and one reason was that they'd been told, "It won't be easy, but it will be worth it." And if as a teenager long ago I'd known the luxury of comparison shopping, I'd have been one of them.

Not surprising, it is a place that turns young males with great, medium, and even mediocre high school records into clear-thinking men who lead the life of the mind and who have the confidence to take risks. And they go on to become high achievers and contributors to society at a rate that puts very selective and famous colleges to shame.

Winston Churchill might have credited the buildings in which they work and live for some of the potent Wabash influence. "First we shape our buildings," he said, "then our buildings shape us." And this campus breathes a quiet commitment. It is architecturally coherent. Every building is lovely Georgian, including the new $33 million science building, the $20 million athletics and recreation center, the $2 million new home for the Malcolm X Institute for Black Studies, and the newly renovated fraternity houses.

The facilities they provide and the programs most of them house are unsurpassed. And beyond them are a rich array of off-campus "immersion learning" experiences in many parts of the world. Some are scheduled in the summer or during breaks in the school calendar so that participants don't miss classes or activities.

This is an academically serious place. As more than one faculty member pointed out, "There is a lust for learning" for learning's sake, and, "The quality of conversation here is as good as any place I've been. We discuss big issues." Or from an alumnus, "I read as much here as in graduate school." It is rigorous but not overly intellectual. Everyone takes pride in working hard. It is competitive for achieving excellence, but the competition is with oneself."

The goal of every fraternity house and dorm is to have the highest grade point average on campus. "They push each other," explained a former Greek, now on the faculty. "Peer pressure will bug him to get his work done."

Professors took pride in boasting, "Our students almost never miss class." Or, "Even when they bring their girlfriends to campus, they don't cut class; they bring their dates." And girls are not in short supply. DePauw, with 1,300, and Purdue with 13,000 are only thirty miles away. A bit farther is the cluster of universities in Indianapolis with thousands more. President Andrew Ford says that when prexies of former men's colleges ask him why Wabash is still single-sex, his answer is, "You're asking the wrong question. The question is, why did you go coed?" And everybody on his campus feels the same way.

Unlike any other college I know of, this is a collaborative community of learning because of the fraternity, not in spite of it. It is a distinctive thing about the Greek system at Wabash. Indeed, so far as I know, it's unique. The sense of community is so palpable, it's as much a part of the atmosphere as the great trees and lawns or the New England feel of its lovely quadrangle. I can't remember ever having been at a place where I heard "we" so frequently, even more than "I" (except perhaps at Agnes Scott).

Where else would a fraternity man say, "I have a hundred times more pride being a Wabash Beta (Beta Theta Pi) than in being a Beta. We have a concern for each other and for the school. When high school visitors come to the campus, you talk about Wabash first and the fraternity second."

A Delta Tau Delta added, "At the Delt conferences, other chapters don't understand what we do. Each house has pride. No other Delt chapter has the pride in its school that we do. In our Greek system we work together for the good of the school."

As befits surrogate parents, the teachers are no less committed. A young professor of English, Dr. Joy Castro said, "I have two classes of twelve each. If one of them misses a class, I inquire. If one fails to make eye contact, I inquire."

Historian Dr. Peter Frederick added, "I have sixty in one class, and if someone misses he'll be embarrassed, because at some point during the day we'll meet."

Another young professor, economist Dr. Kealoha Widdows, summed it up with, "They can't get away from us," and then proudly pointed out that unlike the eastern school where she'd previously taught, "Here they don't become business majors; they're economics majors."

There is no doubt about how pervasive the attitude of "It-won't-be-easy-but-it-will-be-worth-it" is when that's what the head football coach talks about. In our chat he never once mentioned won-lost records or outstanding athletes. He said, "It's a joy to watch these kids blossom and become self-starters, and to have them leave here with a real confidence. A special young man wants to come here who knows the value of a difficult, tough row."

That kind of concern is not lost. Later in the day, a football player who'd been recruited by other schools explained, "The way the football coach talked about the school, you could feel the pride and tradition. It has far surpassed my expectations. As for jobs, the networking of Wabash alumni opens doors."

Two other distinctive things about this community are its freedom and the responsibility that goes with it. Wabash has only one rule, The Gentlemen's Rule. It says, "The student shall live both on and off campus as a gentlemen and a responsible citizen."

A Wabash man has the freedom, as one professor put it, "to be who you are. You are free to slump and recover. You accept the consequences. You can't hide." He can even fail and pick himself up and start over. He won't get kicked out. Dealing with such responsibility is important to a young person's development. As in other colleges in this book, cheating is virtually unknown.

Several students expressed variants on, "Coming to school here makes you a man." A black senior said, "I decided to go here to be a better man. Wabash could take me somewhere. Tradition and pride go into being a Wabash man. The other schools I looked at, they weren't that good."

Even those who were second- or third-generation Wabash men had their own definite reasons, such as the rapport between students and faculty, "the integrity of the school," or "Wabash overshadowed all the other schools I looked at. The camaraderie here is just great; it's wonderful! It's a good place to study, and the involvement is really important."

Among the many notes of pride in the faculty, one senior said, "Wabash's religion department is unparalleled in the U.S., but I didn't come here to be a religion major." It is so good, he said, that students who have no interest in the ministry, even skeptics, major in religion. They have a wide range of choices: Jewish, Muslim, Christian, or one of the Asian faiths, an area of particular strength.

A senior psychology major warned that Wabash is not for everybody. He'd been drawn to the school by the quality of its faculty and its liberal arts curriculum. "Wabash," he said, "is not the kind of place you can push on people."

The frequency with which it was mentioned made it clear that the Wabash men believe a vital part of their experience is involvement, and they are heavily involved. Athletics are important. Over 40 percent are on one of the many varsity athletic squads and 90 percent are on intramural teams. And the teams are good. Long ago they earned the nickname "Little Giants" for knocking off opponents from much larger schools. And they have beautiful athletic facilities that are extensive, expensive, and state-of-the-art.

As I was reading the campus paper at lunch, one of the fellows I'd been talking to earlier passed by and said, "We all work for it." Furthermore, faculty members and their spouses are also involved. Three had roles in that evening's production of *The Grapes of Wrath*.

At many of the other colleges in this book, faculty members exulted in the wonderful spirit of collegiality they had found at their colleges. At Wabash, they went further. As one put it: "This is an involved faculty. We are getting the best. If someone publishes a paper or a book, we are proud of each other's success. There is an attitude of mutual support, with no sense of competition. There is an esprit de corps."

Even when offers from other schools are made, he added, they usually choose to stay. Joy Castro had received several other offers, but chose Wabash, she said, because "I was treated most professionally here."

It's not surprising that what Wabash produces is remarkable:

- Thirteen percent of its alumni have Ph.D.s, a higher figure than most of the Ivies.
- An amazing 12 percent of alumni hold the title "president" or "chairman." One recent chairman was AT&T's Robert Allen.
- Only two Ivies have a higher percentage of alumni in *Who's Who*.
- At only four of the eleven Ivies and Little Ivies do the seniors perform as well or better on the Medical College Admission Test.
- Three-fourths of its graduates go on to graduate or professional school within five years.

In the Revised Edition five years ago, I wrote, "In short, Wabash is a continuing repudiation of the idolatry of selectivity. It does an outstanding job of developing productive citizens . . . while accepting nearly 70 percent of its applicants. Fewer than half had SAT verbal scores over 600, and only a third were in the top tenth of their high school classes, many of them small and rural." Today all of that is true except the 70 percent acceptance figure, which President Andrew Ford would like to keep. He wants it to be inclusive.

In 2004, for the first time, Wabash accepted fewer than half of its applicants. It wasn't high GPAs or SATs that got them in; it was what kind of human beings they were, "who will benefit most from a Wabash education and contribute most to the Wabash experience." In short, essays, interviews, or both, elicit the qualities Wabash has always sought.

And it has always chosen well. Only eighteen institutions in the country can boast of greater alumni loyalty in giving, and Wabash counts anyone who's been there only a year as an alum.

As President Ford observed, "With quality now equated in the public mind with selectivity, many colleges work to see how many students' dreams they can break. Colleges encourage students to apply, then reject them."

Wabash is spending its money to help those who need help, whether they have learning disabilities or come from schools where their preparation was not adequate for such a rigorous program. As President Ford noted, "We can't assume students will have similar preparation and skills."

Equally important, Wabash gives more financial aid per capita than any other school, largely thanks to the generosity of Mr. Eli Lilly. About 95 percent get substantial help; a lot of this is merit scholarships. Each year it gives ten full-tuition Lilly scholarships to outstanding leaders. Every student automatically gets all the need-based aid his family qualifies for; he doesn't have to ask for it. Indeed, Wabash, for most, is cheaper than a public institution. For many families it is the best financial bargain in the college world.

This financial aid bounty enables Wabash to have a 20 percent minority population. Each year it gives ten Lilly scholarships of full tuition to outstanding minority applicants.

The Wabash student gets a truly liberal education. He has to be proficient in his own and in a foreign language. He has to take at least three courses in science or mathematics, and he has to become familiar with other cultures and traditions. He has to examine and discuss his values. As at many other colleges, he is introduced to the academic way in a small freshman seminar examining a topic of the instructor's choice. He has to have a major and a minor and take comprehensive exams. And there is writing in every course, even mathematics.

But the magic of this or any other place is not in what they do; it's in how they do it. Every college in this book achieves its goals by different methods. Here, the "how" is the pride the whole community takes in its commitment to learning for its own sake. It is the common enterprise.

Long before the end of my overnight visit, I was wishing I'd gone here instead of to its coed rival, DePauw.

Ten years later, Wabash students and alumni are a clan with élan and fierce loyalty. They say the same sorts of things I heard years ago, sometimes in the same words. So far as they are concerned, Wabash produces a kind of religious bond.

Typical was a 1997 graduate's "Wabash students display a rabid pride in their college. And they are quick to include you in their club. As a freshman you immediately become immersed in a feeling of brotherhood, an all-for-one, one-for-all mentality. An extraordinarily deep bond forms between the men of Wabash. The studies are rigorous, and if you meet those challenges you will reap the rewards. But Wabash has something else to offer its students: family.

"Wabash taught me anything you want to do you can do it. I graduated with a major in English and a minor in theater. Today I am a software developer for a global clinical company. I had no formal college training in software and programming. Wabash, with its tough academic program, gave me the skills and the self-discipline to meet my goals."

An inner city sophomore from St. Louis, and a reluctant

prospect whose friends had to drag him to a Colleges That Change Lives fair was "amazed at how accessible the faculty is, and how great the peer-to-peer student support is. Wabash is not just another competitive environment; it is a place where everyone helps everyone else succeed. I have gotten to know my professors on a personal basis and eaten dinner at some of their houses. I have become a brother of Lambda Chi Alpha and am involved in the Fellowship of Christian Athletes and the Malcolm X Institute. I hope to go on to medical school. Thank you, Mr. Pope, for giving me the opportunity to get the education of a lifetime."

A hearing-impaired member of the 2001 class said he wanted and found a college "that would afford me the ability to succeed at anything." He did. At Wabash he won a scholarship for students with disabilities, and later, for his work helping people with disabilities, he was appointed to Indiana's Hearing Aid Advisory Committee. He said, "My disability was never an obstacle. When I hear the name 'Wabash College,' pride immediately comes to surface."

One of the several in medical school said, "The Wabash alumni body is a fraternity in and of itself. Five Wabash men will be in my wedding."

Many talked about Wabash's rigor with the same fervor of one who said, "It made me a man," or in another's words, that "it seemed overwhelming at first," or that the profs were "hard but fair, and always willing to help." Almost everyone spoke of "the sense of family" and later of belonging to a band of brothers.

The 2004 valedictorian chose Wabash over Harvard. He'd been a Latin and Writing Center tutor, fraternity president, and tour guide. In high school he'd been a hot-shot quarterback, but at Wabash he'd spent four years as a backup to an All-American. He would tell prospects he chose Wabash "because of the unbelievable alumni loyalty and support Wabash men show for their school." He was won over by the zeal and persistence with which several alums kept persuading him of Wabash's special virtues.

A 2002 graduate in law school said he'd had several job opportunities from alums "willing to give me a chance simply because I'm a fellow Wabash man. It shows how much faith they have in the institution."

A 2003 graduate in medical school voices a frequent comment that "Wabash is an amazing place. It takes young men and transforms them into thinking, responsible, well-mannered individuals. Further, Wabash men are challenged in every aspect of their lives, and that has served me well ever since graduation." He, like others, said that Wabash had shown him that "accountability, honesty and hard work are the most important values one can have. It changed my life by making me realize and accept what my gifts were, and that I am obligated to share those gifts with others in making this world a better place the best way I can contribute."

Wheaton College

Wheaton, Illinois

An hour's drive west of Chicago, is attractive Wheaton College, a place where both students and faculty enjoy themselves, where most of them work hard, and where the friendly atmosphere would impress even a curmudgeonly atheist. Now the students at this Christian college are even happier. The original ban on dancing has finally been lifted. But alcohol, of course, is a no-no.

Wheaton will not admit you unless you're a Christian. The college's stated beliefs include the parenthood of Adam and Eve and the divinity of Christ. Its stated mission is to "address the needs of the world and to provide leadership for the work of the church."

Within that context it is a community that embraces at least thirty different stripes of Christianity, from liberal Episcopalians to literal fundamentalists. It is also a place that produces many highly respected scientists and scholars. Indeed, over a seventy-year period it ranks twelfth among all the undergraduate colleges as a source of future Ph.D.s. And just for good measure, it ranks twenty-fifth among all four-year institutions in the percentage of alumni listed in *Who's Who in America*. The presidents of forty-three colleges went to Wheaton.

How is the teaching of geology, which deals in eons, or biology and the theory of evolution, reconciled with the biblical story of creation?

A biologist put it this way: "In natural sciences, for instance, when 'issues of origin' are taught, the faculty do not try to indoctrinate. They attempt to discover and lead students through discovery processes that discern truth through revelations of God in Scripture and nature. Students are challenged to discern and act upon truth as revealed by God and to do so within a Christian context. Students are given an education designed to help them appreciate the Creator, beauty, and order in God's creation and human creativity in the arts and sciences, and to apply those insights in the pursuit of righteousness in the life of both the individual and society."

A geology professor said, "We have an attitude of humble uncertainty," observing that science is not a place for dogmatism. A professor of Christian thought added that there are different forms of revelation and that "the scientists are not sweating over trying to fit together the principles of organic chemistry and Genesis."

Wheaton is often called the Harvard of the evangelicals, but that moniker does not do it justice because it is head, shoulders, and heart above Harvard in its concern with good moral compasses and strong value systems, as well as in the percentage of future Ph.D.s it has turned out.

Financially, Wheaton is a bargain. Not quite half (48 percent) the students got need-based financial aid averaging about $13,000 a year in 2005, and another 37 percent got merit aid averaging about $1,000 a year.

Its impressive record of producing contributors to society puts it in this book, even though a B student has to have credentials other than grades to get in. Wheaton accepts over half of its applicants. The middle 50 percent of acceptees have SAT scores of 1,250 to 1,400 and their grade point average is 3.6, but one-third of those high averages are from rural high schools. All must have been involved in "quality service to others, not necessarily in church."

They come from all fifty states and from forty foreign countries. There are two groups of applicants; one applies only to Christian colleges, the other applies also to the Ivies, especially Princeton and Yale, and to Virginia, North Carolina, Michigan, Northwestern, and William & Mary. Ten percent are minority. An Ivy-like 94 percent return as sophomores, and 77 percent graduate in four years.

The admissions director said, "We want students willing to think through issues. Wheaton provides an atmosphere that honors the individual. They come here with a set of beliefs but they make their own choices. They spend semesters in youth hostels with atheists and those of many other persuasions. We hope students will leave Wheaton having thought through issues of life and developed a theology of their own. We are not stuck in the nineteenth century. I rejected one applicant whose well-meaning high school counselor had written that she saw everything in black and white.

"We hope they will learn how their commitment relates to living and learning and are open to discover truth. We are confronting the world with deep moral issues and we have a lab with Chicago right here. Nearly half the student body [of 2,200] is involved in helping roles of several kinds: in jails, shelters, social work, tutoring."

The ban on dancing was lifted when the college adopted a new Community Covenant in 2003. On my visit a decade ago, a dean said dancing was "a nonissue," but students I talked to several minutes later in the dining room felt otherwise. One girl who had said, "I hope they have dancing when my daughter comes here," must surely be relieved.

Also new are two majors: one in environmental studies and

the other in international relations. The college has doubled its full-time minority faculty to 10 percent; 4 percent; African American, 4 percent Asian and 2 percent Hispanic.

It also has a sports and recreation complex completed in 2000, a fancy new student center designed to be the hub of activity on campus, and a research center housing the books and papers of seven prominent British authors who also had an impact on Christian thought. They are Owen Barfield, G. K. Chesterton, C. S. Lewis, George MacDonald, Dorothy Sayers, J. R. R. Tolkien, and Charles Williams.

It is a pleasant place; as I walked across the campus on a sodden gray day, everyone, students and professors, smiled and said, "Hi." It is also very Republican and those who said they wanted to work in think tanks or political action groups all had the conservative variety in mind. Everyone was enthusiastic about Wheaton and involved not only in their own education but in any one of an array of social, musical, theatrical, athletic, literary, or other activities. There is a wealth of lectures by people famous in their fields, concerts, and other cultural events.

There is a strong sense of community, partly because one of Wheaton's main attractions is as a Christian school. The thrice-weekly chapel, one senior said, helps create a sense of being one. A girl added, "We have such a wide range of beliefs here but the common denominator is Christ."

Its other principal drawing cards are its reputation for academic excellence and its friendliness. Several had decided Wheaton was as good or better academically than such schools as Northwestern or Princeton, and that its Christian commitment gave it the edge.

A black girl from Chicago was one of those who said that when she visited, everybody seemed so welcoming and so sincere. Or, as another put it, she was disappointed in other Christian schools but when she came here she knew this was it, there was genuine welcoming acceptance. All of the African-American students I spoke with said they felt they were an integral part of the community.

When students were asked what kind of person would be happy at Wheaton, the most common answer was that he or she should be motivated and disciplined, interested in learning, and willing to be involved. They were assuming of course that the person was a Christian. For the most part, they offered the same descriptions as did the faculty: The person should not only be serious about education but also have an interest in how Christianity affects life and learning.

But all don't fit that pattern; there are also, one senior said, "nonorganized, go-with-the-flow, free-thinkers, objective, open, so there are almost two groups here." Another senior interjected that quiet, reader types are also happy at Wheaton, and that "we have a mix of A, B, and C students, but mostly A."

They study hard. An academician there for a weekend conference asked after going to the library, "What kind of students do you have here? The library is full on Saturday morning!"

These students also have to make up their own minds. As a freshman, said another senior, she was frustrated when a professor didn't take a stand on an issue and made the class decide on its own answers. And there is much discussion in the dorms about questions raised in class. She gave a description of the school echoed by others when she said: "I think a unique part of school is integrating values into academic studies. And I think Wheaton is unique among Christian schools in that we're not only to learn what we believe, but also what other philosophies are so that you have a full understanding of what you believe. If you know only your own fundamentals, you can't relate to other people's perspectives, and you see that because of the different backgrounds here. Our beliefs have to prove themselves in the marketplace."

To a visitor, several other things are apparent. One is the students' conservatism; three seniors planning to go into public relations all wanted to work for conservative political groups that deal with issues important to the family, such as the Heritage Foundation. One didn't want to work for a Christian organization because "I don't think we should have all the people with morals in one group."

Another is the commitment to service; many go into teaching or ministries. A premed senior said he wants to practice in some underprivileged rural area. Great numbers do volunteer work and enroll in a program that prepares them for helping careers in Third World countries.

And the students come across as likable, clean-cut, all-American kids who very much know who they are, and judging from most of those I talked to, why they are here: to improve things, not by evangelizing but by helping.

The faculty of this Christian school could be switched with that of almost any other school in this book and no one would be able to tell the difference in regard to their affection for their students, their scholarly standards, or their sense of humor. "Nurture" was a word heard as often here as on any other campus, and as elsewhere, professors said in effect that they were in surrogate parent roles. Not only did they frequently have students to their homes for dinner or dessert, go on hikes or picnics with them, or provide help in the evening, but they made it clear that the reason they were here was because "I love these kids."

There is much student-faculty research, and a good many resulting papers are presented at professional meetings. There is— as elsewhere—much collaborative learning because they've found that a person learns more by working in a group than in isolation. The school is changing tactics to take advantage of this new wisdom, even though there's always the problem, as Dean Kriegbaum noted, of some pulling harder than others.

To hold his job, a faculty member must be a teacher first. Before he or she even gets a job, the prospect has to pass muster in an interview with students at lunch. But to get tenure, he needs to get recognition beyond the campus in his or her scholarly field.

Professors from a dozen disciplines were at pains to say there was no indoctrination, that they were trying to prepare people for a new world of job mobility and where "they will have to understand where the other guy is coming from."

Although ethics is emphasized across the curriculum, what

they called the single most important thing in the curriculum was not religious studies at all, but an innovative new program in Third World issues called Human Needs and Global Resources. After fourteen to eighteen hours of course work, there's a six-month internship in Third World clinics and schools. The object is to learn about the local culture so as to be able to give help intelligently within that cultural context. This program equips graduates to work in the Third World with missions, development groups, governments, or international organizations, or for a variety of graduate studies. As faculty at other colleges have testified about theirs, Wheaton's students come back "transformed" by the foreign experiences, which fully a third of the students have.

Another imaginative program run by the chair of the music conservatory is a concentration in arts management. A collaborative enterprise of the music, theater, business, and economics departments, it prepares graduates for careers in the burgeoning field of managing orchestras, ballets, theatrical, or other cultural enterprises.

Of long standing is the Christian Sports Ministry, which originated at Wheaton in the 1940s, with track coach and alumnus Gil Dodd, the world's greatest miler of his time, and by Billy Graham, a fellow graduate. The object is not to create a distinction between sports and ministry but, as elsewhere, to affect its values.

Wheaton assumes a set of beliefs in the youths it accepts, but thenceforward it sees its role as nurturing both moral and intellectual growth and development. And each person is to arrive at his or her own judgments and answers. As Dean Kriegbaum said, "We hope they'll be lifelong learners. What they're learning will change, but what they do with their philosophy will be important."

Ten years after my visit, students and alumni continue to testify that they can better serve God and change the world because of their four years at Wheaton. They often say both they and their Christian faith have been challenged, stretched, and strengthened.

A 2002 alumna said, "I loved that my classes taught me to wrestle with the subject matter at hand, but also with my faith. I learned to worship with people from all ethnic backgrounds in Chapel Choir, and when we raised our voices in Chapel I felt as if I'd tasted a spoonful of Heaven. And I love that God got bigger while I was there. And I love that He's gotten bigger to me every year since. Wheaton is a fabulous place to me."

A classmate said she'd chosen Wheaton because "I just felt that that was where I was called to be." Only after she graduated, she continued, did she realize "what a rarity it is to find an entire community made up of people who, by and large, are excited about learning and are passionately hopeful at the prospects of changing the world around them." And she came to believe it was more important to alleviate "the suffering in our own American cities" than do missionary work abroad, as her evangelical upbringing had taught her.

A sophomore who had been home schooled and was determined not to go to a Christian college changed her mind after a visit to Wheaton that answered her two objections. She found "at this evangelical school students' beliefs could still be challenged. I also found there was a plethora of ministry opportunities offered to students, both nearby in Chicago, and around the world." She also found it was a place for spiritual growth. She said, "Living and studying with so many other Christians in one place has been an experience I will not likely have the opportunity to repeat later in life. If I were to describe my experience using one word it would be 'stretching.' In all areas of my life I have been challenged and stretched. At times it has been painful but at others it has been exhilarating! I have had an amazing two years so far! I have learned more about who my Father is, and in turn who I am because of Him."

A Californian who graduated in 2002 said she thought she wouldn't be able to live through the grueling eighteen-day hiking, mountain climbing, and camping "High Road" experience before the freshman year began. "My body never hurt so much." But now she looks back on it as "one of the best experiences of my life. The tough mental, physical, and emotional challenges taught me true dependence on God."

The hardest part of her experience was "doubts and confusion prompted by the number of questions I was forced to ask myself." Ultimately, she said she had "a peaceful discovery: Christians can have different views on the nonessentials and we can still all be Christians. Wheaton will take you in, stir everything up and then allow things to settle in place before releasing you to the world. Wheaton is a hard place but it's a good place. It stretched me farther than I wanted to stretch, and at the very end it said, 'See? Look how much you've grown.'"

College of Wooster

Wooster, Ohio

The College of Wooster is my original best-kept secret in higher education; for thirty years I've been telling clients that. As I have gotten to know what it accomplishes, I can testify that there is no better college in the country. Its record is unmatched in turning out scientists, scholars, and other kinds of achievers and contributors to society by multiplying the talents of B and C as well as A students.

Its 320-acre spread, forty miles south of Cleveland, complete with golf and cross-country-skiing courses, looks like it was built by and for millionaires; it is a quintessential college campus. I was struck by its charm on my first visit in the '70s, and even more impressed twenty years later by its expanded grounds, new facilities, and what it has done to protect the area of that attractive town near the campus.

In the new millennium a Wooster program is giving Youngstown inner-city kids a college education. In 2004, it gave diplomas to three of the first cohorts of its Early Intervention Program and twenty-three started college, ten of them at Wooster. Starting in the ninth grade, promising students spend two weeks in July each year on campus. They take English, math, and anthropology courses, get counseling, make visits to three other colleges, and get letters of recommendation. One of the grateful 2004 seniors, eager to help others, asked me to tell her story. It's in the "Ten Years Later" section at the end of this chapter.

That is only part of what Wooster has done since the 2000 edition of this book. The campus is even more attractive and several handsome new facilities have been added to an already-well-equipped physical plant. There is a lush new dorm, a wellness center, a new science library, a new academic building, a new addition to the library, a new admissions building (where all visitors get red carpet treatment) and a major renovation of the chemistry building.

Each year there's a $100,000 increase in alumni giving, and a $122 million capital campaign was completed in 2005. It will go for such important things as faculty salary increases; an unmatched, fifth-year, full-pay sabbatical plan to improve teaching; and scholarships, among other things. Remarkably, 94 percent of Wooster's students are on financial aid and the average aid package (for 2005) is $15,400. Furthermore, 75 percent have merit scholarships averaging over $10,700.

Perhaps three hundred or more of my young friends have gone there. Not only do virtually all of them graduate, but I get such comments from their parents as, "Wooster turned Tania's life around, and she still has ties there," or "Wooster is one school I'm giving money to; our other two daughters didn't have such a good experience at Sarah Lawrence or the University of Virginia." A transfer from Davidson wrote me at the end of his first term, "I have noticed quite a difference between Wooster and Davidson. I feel as if there is a much better social life here and I have already made many friends. Academically, the work is just as challenging as at Davidson. Also, there doesn't seem to be the rift between the faculty and students that existed at Davidson. The professors here are more personable and seem more motivated. My grades, of course, were affected positively and I earned a 3.4 average. I am impressed by the [baseball] coach just as I am impressed by all of the people at Wooster."

Things like this happen because Wooster is that unusual college with a sense of mission: to produce educated—not trained—people. "Our goal," said Dr. Henry Copeland, a tennis buff and that rare college president with an educational vision, "is a reflective life" and the development in each student of "the sense of self-possession and critical distance which permits an individual to resist involuntary servitude to the intellectual fashions of the day." Besides that, he will have a powerful ability to achieve his goals.

Dr. Copeland rounded out twenty-five years as president in June 1995 and, unlike so many upwardly mobile college presidents looking for prestige jobs, went back to teaching history. At commencement, the senior class of 365 gave him a tennis racquet and one by one tossed 364 tennis balls into a large basket on the platform.

Wooster has been producing achievers for a long time; it's a college that has never been particularly selective, often accepting 80 percent to 90 percent of its applicants, yet it ranks number eleven among all the 914 colleges in the country in the percentage of graduates who go on to get Ph.D.s. And it has done this for three-quarters of a century, ever since the National Academy of Sciences started keeping tabs in 1920. In percentage of chemistry Ph.D.s it is third in the nation. It also ranks in the top half of 550 colleges whose graduates become executives in leading corporations. Its graduates have been presidents of MIT, Washington University, and the University of Washington, among others, and one was a Nobel Laureate.

Just one of the reasons for Wooster graduates' achievements lies in its senior-year requirement: an original project and a 100-page thesis. It may be scientific research, or a play, or any good idea in between. The entire college experience culminates in this, for the faculty as well as for the students.

This project fosters creativity, resourcefulness, and self-reliance, all attributes students will need in this new world. They have much control over their educational experiences; they can design their courses or even their major. They have access to a wide variety of internships in government or major companies, as well as foreign-study programs, some of which are provided by the college and others by the Great Lakes Colleges Association.

Something important is said about the Wooster experience when more professors and administrators in the Great Lakes Colleges Association send their children to Wooster than to any of the other twelve colleges in that very good consortium.

Wooster is looking for people with potential. They may have had mediocre high school records, as some of my clients have had, but if there is promise of performance, Wooster will take a careful look. It will say no if the prognosis isn't promising; some years it has accepted only 60 percent of its applicants, but often it accepts 80 percent.

Although Wooster has always been innovative and a pacesetter, it did not try to make itself known until the college-going rush was well under way a few decades ago. Its faculty members haven't had to get into the federal competition for research grants because Wooster has the most generous sabbatical and research-funding program in the world. Not even Harvard matches it. Not surprisingly, Wooster's faculty does more research than most others, including prestigious Oberlin's.

In Wooster's program, more than 10 percent of its faculty is on leave every year. Every fifth year a professor can submit a proposal to a faculty committee for a year of study with full pay. Usually there are sixteen or seventeen proposals, of which fifteen will be approved. And if he or she wants to spend a year in Moscow, or study Eastern European countries' transition from Communism, for example, a rich endowment fund will provide the several thousand dollars needed for travel.

The program is also unique in that its purpose is to enable professors to get all juiced up to work with seniors on their independent study projects. It is not designed to create new knowledge;

"we're underwriting no patents in chemistry," said Dr. Copeland. "It's to help them do a better job. After a year in Moscow, you can imagine how excited a professor would be to work with a student whose independent study project is on Russia."

Right from the start, in 1870, Wooster considered the education of women and blacks to be as important as that of white males. Back then, coeducation was a controversial topic and its early doom was widely predicted. A dozen years later Wooster, then a university, not only awarded the first Ph.D. ever given to a woman but was turning out women graduates who made careers for themselves in foreign missions, founding colleges, administering hospitals, and managing print firms, often doing abroad what they could not do in this country. And female graduates still have groundbreaking careers in business, higher education, and diplomacy.

Wooster also has the distinction of being the only institution in the country to have deliberately chosen to change its status from a university to a college, and to have considered that a step forward. By the time of World War I, the college of arts and sciences was a minor part of a medical school and seven other divisions. But its faculty had a vision, and, bucking the wisdom of the day, started a long fight to make it purely an undergraduate liberal arts college.

Today, with more and more colleges becoming vocational training or preprofessional institutions like the universities, Wooster is one of fewer than sixty colleges that gives at least 90 percent of its degrees in the liberal arts.

Dr. Copeland says about his college: "You need A students; they are essential to the mix. And Wooster, like many others, offers merit scholarships to get them. As a result, Wooster has a range of students, in ability as well as economic, cultural, and geographic backgrounds. The Woosters and the Hirams of the world have students who are just as bright as any in the world and who would have gone to Harvard, Yale, or Princeton. And we have faculty members who can deal with such a mix of students. We want faculty members who can deal successfully with the best students and inspire them, and we also want faculty members who are capable of inspiring and developing the underachievers.

"Wooster can take the kids with native intelligence, who, for some reason, have never developed, and turn them on. What Wooster does differently is independent study; each student needs to learn to make up his own mind. Our message is articulated so clearly. We are successful with a certain kind. All of the colleges in this band [of selectivity] are offering something that's a treasure; we can do some things for you here that Yale can't do. What we do for your kids is a liberal education. We give students standing ground, intellectual self-possession; you can make up your own mind, be critical and analytical. We do a better job than Yale," where his own son had "a miserable education."

Stanton Hales, the president, an Olympic badminton player who had taught at Pomona (the Amherst of California) for twenty-three years, said Wooster is every bit as impressive in what it does for students. The range of ability is broader at Wooster and "there's an intangible spirit of 'hey, let's try that.' They don't squelch ideas and are open to new ones. Students know they're going to be called upon to be creative. They have to show something and they grow up in the process. This is a place of high expectations."

The smorgasbord of testimonies of a dozen faculty members who had taught at many place, including Stanford, Pomona, Illinois, Emory, Chicago, New York University, Carleton, and the University of North Carolina, gives some insights into why Wooster is a place that doubles talents and changes lives. I wish every high schooler picking a college could read what the people who have taught at the prestige colleges and universities have to say:

- The Pomona students' approach to the professors was different; they had a sense of entitlement; "I've paid so much to come here I don't deserve a C in this class." You don't get that here. You have to work harder here but the rewards are greater when the students finally get it; their sense of appreciation is so much more.

- There's a lack of pretension here. There are some who come to be credentialed but they all have to take responsibility for meeting a challenge with a major piece of work that's going to take an entire year, in which they deal with a significant question, marshal the arguments, and present the evidence. If they go on to graduate school it's a leg up. And if they don't, if somebody asks "What did you get out of college?" he can hold up this. The challenge is there for everyone.

- We have a phrase in our college culture: "the Wooster success story." My favorite is a student who's practically flunking German but who is working so hard and he's coming to me, and if he's willing to give it the time, I am too. It's about students who are not particularly gifted but who make it. The faculty is here to give that kind of encouragement.

- People in the Midwest come to college for somewhat different reasons than in the coastal culture of the East. In the East going to college assures your success. My friends in high school who went to the Ivies weren't bright; they were wealthy.

- A former student of mine, now a university department head, said that going to Wooster exposed him to a quite different range of people in ability, background, and attitudes than had he gone to an Ivy League school. At Wooster, students are naïve enough that they feel comfortable in asking questions; they don't have the same inhibitions. They're more open.

- Students here are engaged in the process of their own education. There's no such thing as a foolish question. If you've done your homework and it's a question to you, it bothers somebody else. And when a prof is teaching out of his field in a freshman seminar it's a case of "we're all learning together." That brings a kind of humility to the shared joys of this new enterprise.

- The great satisfaction here is in the act of learning and understanding it and being able to apply it, not just learning it and stuffing it away. One of my majors last year who got honors is another Wooster success story. In his first year, he was one of the worst students, but he got excited about a problem, was allowed to use creativity to approach it, and he did a fantastic job.
- These students are having a cracking good time; there's something very playful about the best of our students, and that is what helps keep us on our toes. They challenge our positions and I reserve the right to be wrong. And there's an atmosphere here that encourages that. We're constantly being surprised; I love to encourage half-baked ideas and I love being argued out of my position. It's sort of liberating; it's a lot of fun teaching here. It's depressing when people are trying to guess your position.

Even a coach doesn't have to have a winning record. "If the morale is good and the players are having fun, the coach doesn't have to have a good win-lose record," was how Dr. Copeland put it. What happened in a basketball game several years ago is illustrative. The opposing team was playing so dirty the Wooster coach called time out and said to the players, "Gentlemen, I have nothing to say about basketball just now. I want to say if you remember nothing more from your four years at Wooster and playing basketball here, I want you to remember this is a class institution and we want to be a class basketball team. Now go out there and show those guys how class people play basketball." They won the game.

In over thirty years just one client of mine has wanted to transfer from Wooster. During the Thanksgiving holiday she complained that the social life was inadequate. I told her to send me her transcript and we'd discuss options at Christmastime. I never heard from her again; she got a boyfriend. Now she's a

Wooster alumna. Usually my clients visit several colleges and report, "Wooster's a *good* school!" Parents without exception feel
they've been warmly received and well-cared-for by admissions
people as interested in helping their child as in talking about their
college.

The differences between the reactions of students and faculty
members were largely governed by youthful enthusiasm. One boy
expressed the consensus of many others with, "The professors all
know you by name. It's a good place! It's exactly what I was looking for!"

They all spoke of how Wooster had made them examine their
values, broaden their views and accept those of others, and realize how important people are to each other. One transfer from the
University of California at Berkeley said, when I asked him what
Wooster had done for him, "So much I want to stay. I'm leaving
now for graduate school but I want to come back. I wasn't a geology major to begin with but I was turned on by a class."

Among those who had been made aware of interests they
didn't know they had was a lovely, lively African American. A top
student in her Atlanta prep school who had been voted most
likely to succeed and was wooed by many colleges, she had come
to Wooster planning to be a lawyer. But a freshman art history
class was so fascinating, that became her major instead of political science.

A young man from Virginia found Wooster "everything it said
it was; everything I envisioned, as contrasted with conservative
Washington and Lee where everybody is exactly the same." A
young woman from India was bringing her sister the following fall
because the school had done so much for her.

They all valued Wooster for what it had done to give them new
powers and new confidence, to help them think critically, to live
the reflective, responsible life, to learn how to change and adapt
no matter what, and to land on their feet.

.   .   .

Ten years later, students and alumni are saying the same things their predecessors said many decades ago: that Wooster is wonderful, the senior thesis (Independent Study) was the hardest job they'd ever sweat through but was "the most memorable experience of my life." They say "the faculty is there to push you, but they don't push you without holding out their arms to catch you if you fall."

Sarah Pritchard, the Youngstown Early Intervention Program senior, said, "There are so many young adults out there with so much potential and so little hope, simply because of a lack of faith, and of knowledge of the aid that is out there, I really want to be able to touch some of them with my story. I started out as a student at the College of Wooster who had little faith in her future and limited perspective on the possibilities of life at Wooster. I am now a senior and have just returned from studying abroad in Florence, Italy, where I have had the opportunity to explore the world and develop myself as an individual, via Wooster. Never in my life would I have imagined that an inner-city girl would be able to study halfway around the world. My professors, peers, and experiences have challenged and developed me in ways I never imagined and that has resulted in a renewed confidence. I have learned not to limit myself based on where I come from or my economic or social class. I am now applying to graduate school and continuing the exploration process with a hope of finding a future where I can make a difference because of the life experiences that Wooster has been able to provide for me."

A junior from Michigan whose father made her apply to Wooster, the last college on her list, had a quick conversion. On her visit, even on a cold, rainy March day, she said, "I knew this was where I belonged." To her surprise, the financial aid package made Wooster cheaper than Michigan State and that sealed the deal. Now, heavily involved in campus activities and two jobs, and "even with the stress of the Junior Independent Study I can say I would never have gotten this kind of challenging education anywhere else. More important, I never would have been this happy anywhere else. I am among intelligent people with common goals and equal ambition, and at times I don't think all the money in the world can buy that kind of contentment." For other college seekers she said, "I would at least challenge them to take a look. I know, we wear kilts and play bagpipes and have an unhealthy addiction to plaid, but that's what makes us fun and unique, and we wouldn't have it any other way. Go Scots!"

A sophomore from Massachusetts summarized the reactions of several underclassmen when she called Wooster her home away from home and said it had made her feel that "I can accomplish anything I want to, including IS" (the much-feared Independent Study). And like almost everyone else, she said that the faculty kept pushing her to do ever better work and was always ready to help her.

A senior said that, as a college shopper, she brushed off all the talk that "college would be the four best years of my life." But now, "Looking back at my time at Wooster brings tears to my eyes because it was the most memorable experience of my life. It was an incredible journey."

Austin College

Sherman, Texas

In the early nineties, I wrote: "The word that best describes the lovely sixty-acre enclave of Austin College in Sherman, Texas, is 'exemplar,' which means 'ideal,' 'model,' 'pattern.'"

A visit in 2003 revealed a campus a dozen acres larger and several handsome new buildings, a stadium, a large student and reception center, and a thriving college community. There is more on these things in the "Ten Years Later" section at the end of this chapter.

I would still say, as I did then, that if I were advising a high school senior trying to decide whether to go to Austin College or to Brown, Cornell, Harvard, Penn, Yale, or some other name school, I would tell them this:

This 160-year old community of learning, with its 1,350 students, will excite you, stretch you, expand your world, and make you believe in yourself. This college does marvelous things to multiply talents and to develop character, something of no particular concern to the name brands.

Someday, if reality should dispel myth, people will know that Austin—and colleges like it—has a special magic the prestige ones don't. You will find the work is harder than at the Ivies, and so is the grading. More is expected of you; you can't hire somebody to take notes for you. Austin will do more to give you a successful and satisfactory life.

What a high school senior, especially one with an SAT verbal of 500 and a B average, simply cannot imagine is that by the time a diligent student is an Austin senior, his work will be as good as, or maybe better than, an Ivy senior's who had a 700 or 750 verbal and an A average. Here's some evidence:

The professor in charge of international programs had been curious to find out how Austin students stacked up against those of the highly selective Eastern colleges. She was told by the director of the London program of the Institute of European Studies that Austin students' work was better than that of Haverford or Williams students. It was partly because the Austin students weren't as impressed with themselves, and partly because they had been encouraged to think and to look around a little bit rather than to try to finish the paper that afternoon.

An obviously tough German professor who had taught at Texas and at Williams said the Williams students "were very aggressive, very well prepared, worked very hard [the Texans were laid-back]. When I compare them with the students here, there's a wider range of ability, so it includes people who are very good and some who aren't so good academically. But at the end, in the quality of the research paper that's done, I can see very little difference."

"What does this say about our SAT system," the first professor asked, "when you also consider how the graduates of colleges like Austin are more productive or contribute more?" The conclusion is obvious. What it says about SATs as a measure of a person's potential is pretty devastating. It's a phony, one-dimensional measure that serves as a competitive, status industry.

At Austin you will have great teachers; they will want to stretch you, and they will want to be your friends. They got their doctorates from, and now could be teaching at, those other places. They just think what they're doing here is more important.

At Austin you will not be cheated, as you will at any of the others, by trying to understand instructors who can barely speak English, by being second-class citizens who get only teaching assistants, by being caught in a competition for grades, or by being unable to have any kind of conversation with a professor.

Nor will you spend four years passively taking notes at lectures. You will be actively involved in your own education, which is the only way, no ifs, ands, or buts. At Austin, in the fall, you will take a freshman seminar with thirteen others on some contemporary issue to develop writing, speaking, and research skills. The instructor becomes the mentor for that group, the person with whom you plan your program and to whom you must report at least once each semester.

The other requirements are three terms of Western Heritage, and distribution requirements that will expose you to the arts, sciences, social sciences, and philosophy or religion. There is much freedom of choice, and beyond these you may plan your own major, do one-on-one directed or independent study projects you plan yourself, and you may even get into a collaborative research project with one of your professors.

A January term offers all kinds of exciting off-campus, as well as on-campus, opportunities to go to exotic places or to try something completely different. Austin offers a rich variety of foreign-study programs in the fall and spring terms in England, France, Germany, Austria, Spain, Japan, and Singapore.

Also very important is the fact that students cooperate and collaborate. A faculty member said, "We like to encourage the idea that education is not a competitive activity." They've succeeded. As others nodded, a senior girl said, "You hear a lot about cutthroat competition for grades at other schools where you have 400 in a class graded on a bell curve; here we're helping each other get into medical school." In some courses, a junior girl said, you can't make it through unless you have a study group. There is also an honor code, which students said is observed.

If you should ever need help it will be there in full measure, but the chances are the Austin professor will have anticipated your needs. Why? In class he doesn't need to call roll; he knows you're there; he calls you by your first name. He may have guessed your need when he and his wife had you and a couple of others over for dinner or dessert or a cook-out. Students told me that most teachers will come back after hours to help you study, or come in on weekends to help you, "even at ten o'clock at night, and they give you their home phone numbers."

After graduation, when you come back to campus you may have to decide at which professor's home you might have dinner or spend the night. If anything like this were ever to happen at the big name places, or the University of Texas, you could account it a miracle.

Austin College accepts about 80 percent of its applicants, most of whom are from Texas and the West or Southwest. Twenty-five percent are minorities. If more people knew about it, over half the enrollment would be out of state, it is such an outstanding academic as well as financial bargain. Seventy percent get need-based aid, with the packages averaging $20,000, and 90 percent get aid when merit scholarships are included.

What kind of person would be happy here? Any student planning to go to a mainstream college would find happiness here, whether from the Northeast, Southeast, Midwest, or far West. This was as friendly, open, and accepting a community as I've seen anywhere, and far more so than most. The kids simply are very nice people.

It ought to be clear that this kind of college isn't for the person who has to have the football weekend extravaganza; he won't be satisfied just watching students play for the fun of it.

This school is for those whose priorities are in order. The only ones who wouldn't be happy here, students agreed, would be those who wouldn't be happy at most of the other good small colleges in this book. Those who don't want to get involved, those who live off campus and want to go home on weekends, or who can't relate to other people—who aren't involved in the life of the community—are not affected by the college experience. They are the ones who feel negative, or drop out, or fail. The satisfied students are always the ones who participate, who make it their life.

Two exceptional juniors, a Latino boy who plans to help other Latinos get a leg up, and an African-American girl, said Austin had changed their lives. The girl said, "Coming here was a big change. It was a white majority but everyone is so accepting I feel like I'm in a majority. When other blacks asked me why I didn't go to a black school, I said I wanted the best education, so I came here because I'm going to be competing in a white world. My roommate feels the same way."

This sense of family was one of the big attractions for several others. Two seniors who'd been marked for the University of Texas because their parents had gone there were converted when they visited. As one said, "I could just feel the sense of community; second, it was one of the few schools with an international-relations program, and it was easy to get involved here. You can start a group with two people."

The other, a football player, said there wouldn't be so many college transfers or dropouts if teenagers were smarter consumers and looked at themselves and then visited colleges. Then they'd go to places like Austin College, he said, "but instead they go where their friends are going and wind up going to three or four schools or dropping out."

Many of the faculty—as at other colleges in this group—had planned to stay a few years and then move on to a university, but got hooked by the place and the people. They talked with obvious pride and pleasure about their students. One said, "We enjoy our students. I like the contact here. There's hardly a week goes by I don't hear, by phone, mail, by office visit from someone who graduated last year, five years ago, ten years ago, fifteen years ago. And the continuing interest that I have is finding ways to open doors for our students that their life experience up to this point just hasn't opened."

A chemistry professor who thirty years ago had planned to stay a couple of years and then go to the West Coast, his home area, said, "We are particularly effective in polishing up what you might call these diamonds in the rough. They may come from high schools that weren't particularly demanding and suddenly the level of expectation is high. We've been effective partly because of our accessibility and partly because the freshman seminar gets them off to a good start and gives them a real adrenaline rush because they realize there's a level of expectation they've never had to contend with. Then they're off and running. I told my freshman class they were going to give up memorizing and learn to think. At evaluation at the end of the term, at least a third thanked me and said they had begun to think."

An English professor said the story of one of her students illustrates how a college like Austin works its magic. "At some competitive place—she was like a tightwire anyway—she would have become more and more aggressive in trying to beat it. But here it is not competitive, it is collaborative and cooperative, and what has happened is that she has learned to open her mind, relax a little bit, and trust herself."

Students I talked with, most of whom were juniors and seniors, echoed all the good things their teachers had said. Every one said emphatically that they would attend if they had it to do over again. They reported they had learned to trust their own minds, to take a chance, and that they had been broadened by the general education requirements and by the enthusiasm of their teachers in ways they wouldn't have been at a university. The foreign-study terms, the international-relations program, and even the service experiences evoked especially good testimonials.

One senior said, "Austin has affected me because I've gotten interested in history and psychology, and I hated history in high school. Working in Habitat for Humanity also affected me; I wouldn't have done that anywhere else. I tried to explain to my parents how contact with other peoples and other conditions was necessary today."

Several said the ease of getting involved had not only given them a lot of pleasure but also had developed their abilities to work with people and improved their leadership skills. Uniformly they felt they had powers they hadn't had a few years ago. And whether prompted or not, they talked about their teachers. One girl said, "I'll be in touch with faculty members over the next few years while I'm working, and when I want recommendations they will remember me and be able to give me good ones." Another boasted, "One of my profs is going to be in my wedding."

For many years I had been aware that Austin College was a first-rate school, but until I spent a day there, I hadn't been able to know how very special a community it was. It is one of those that is doing the essential work of producing the enlightened, responsible, creative people with moral compasses who make democracy work. We need many more colleges like it.

A visit ten years later more than confirmed what a great place Austin College is. Students voiced the same kind of superlatives, professors bragged just as much about their students, and the administrators had the same pride in what the college was doing for its students.

Physically, the campus seemed to have grown up. It was a dozen acres larger, with new buildings including a stadium that seats 2,500, and a landscaped look of formal garden, trees, and greenery.

Most impressive of the new buildings is the big multipurpose center, the campus hub. It has a soaring two-story living room for functions and student study or socializing. Surrounding it are the campus dining room, a snack bar, a post office, a convenience store, and the bookstore. The second floor has facilities for student organizations, the Leadership Institute Suite, banquet and meeting rooms, and a lecture hall for college and community gatherings.

New residential facilities include a language-learning house with wings for French, German, Japanese, and Spanish. Native speakers in each language provide support and cultural insights.

Juniors get priority and seniors get the next shot at new 1,200-square-foot suites completed in 2003.

A newly renovated technology center enables faculty to try out new technology for their classes and provides for a variety of computer-related functions. An elaborate athletic/recreation complex completed in 2001 provides athletic and recreational facilities for all students, whatever their exercise wants.

The college has added a major program in southwestern and Mexican studies, and has expanded an environmental-studies program begun in the nineties.

The students ten years later talked not only about caring and wonderful teachers who had helped them find out who they really were, but also about their foreign- or community-service experiences. Both experiences had opened their eyes, they said, to other peoples' views, and made them more tolerant and understanding. Some felt the need to help and gained the confidence to do it. As one of them said, "I learned I can make a difference."

 ## St. John's College

Santa Fe, New Mexico (also Annapolis, Maryland)

St. John's is one of the four most intellectual (and indispensable) colleges in the country. The others are Marlboro, New, and Reed. It has no majors or electives, it has one mission, one catalog, two campuses, two presidents, two faculties, and two student bodies that may freely move from one campus to the other.

This unusual duality is the result of the expansionist mood of the '60s when education was a booming industry and the college heads in Annapolis, Maryland, decided to install a clone in a Santa Fe, New Mexico, mountain.

It is a hard-working Shangri-La for the life-of-the-mind teenager who may hate or is bored by high school or is disgusted with education's stupid SAT system. St. John's has the courage to reject all that stuff; it's what you are and what you want out of college that count. Dr. Eva Brann, a tutor and former dean at Annapolis, said, "We are about as selective as a pickup baseball team." But every one of that pickup team has something to say in his or her essays.

For this edition I asked for reactions to their experiences from current students and recent graduates. In the "Ten Years Later" section of this chapter you'll find two. One, a 2004 freshman girl, gives you in fascinating detail a fellow teenager's assessment. The other, a 2004 graduate, gives her perspective of four years with the Great Books and the community that reads, discusses, and evaluates what they have to say. I hope they (and a visit) will help you make up your mind.

Many years ago, as education editor of *The New York Times,* I went to Annapolis to do a Sunday article on the coming-of-age of the St. John's Great Books program in which everyone confronted the greatest minds of western civilization by discussing 100 great books. They also took four years each of science, mathematics, and language, and two of music. Grades were neither issued nor discussed, only recorded for graduate school purposes, and they depended on total performance, emphasizing contribution in class discussions rather than exams. The most important form of evaluation was the Don Rag, in which each student met with all his tutors at the end of each semester for a no-holds-barred discussion of him and his work.

St. John's, founded in 1696 as King's School, became a different kind of college in 1937 with the introduction of this radically classical program. There were no choices and no one could transfer in. All students had to start at the beginning. Even so, nearly a third of the student body were—and are today—transfers who found the ideal college, some after spending three years at another. There are no faculty ranks, and there is no need to publish; their role is to stimulate. All are tutors who may lead discussion in a Greek or literature class this year and in a Ptolemyic geometry class a few years hence. It is a true community of learning, one of only 450 students.

My newspaper story was calmly descriptive but I came away a zealot. This was the kind of education Jefferson had in mind as the sine qua non for American democracy. As democracy's problems grow more complex this kind of education grows more necessary.

As an educational adviser, whenever possible I have persuaded young friends to go to St. John's. One year there were a mathematically improbable eight, two of whom were deep into specialties, one in French literature, and the other in the study of butterflies. They were able to pursue their special interests later and, like their lives, more effectively. At the end of that season, the admissions director said, "Amazing! That's 10 percent of my freshman class!"

St. John's charming tidewater Colonial campus in Annapolis, with its ancient trees and mix of historic and modern buildings, is on a Severn River tributary. Next door is quite a different place: the Naval Academy. On as dramatically beautiful a campus as any in the country, nestling on the shoulders of Monte Sol in the southeast corner of Santa Fe, New Mexico, a student body of like size is wrestling with the same questions of the human condition.

Intellectually demanding and intense, as it is, St. John's is not selective; it is selected. It accepts 80 to 85 percent of its applicants, who demonstrate whether they belong there by writing as many as six to ten pages about themselves; sometime more. Most years a modest 20 to 30 percent of their applicants will be in the top 10 percent of their high school classes, compared with Harvard's 95 percent. More than half the applicants will have verbal SAT scores of more than 600, sometimes nearly three-quarters will.

But scores are not essential. The St. John's criteria are radically basic. What is essential is "desire more than brilliance." A tutor who served as admissions director several years ago insisted that St. John's was as valuable and as necessary for the person with a 500 verbal score as for one with a 600 or 700. Dr. Brann adds, "It is, in fact, a rare tragedy that a person wants to learn here and is unequal to the program on some respectable level. Weaker students may, for example, ask the most useful questions. More-over, our communal style of learning is antithetical to competition—to competition, not to distinction."

Presidents or deans at most colleges would about as soon admit to taking syphilitics as B students, but when Dr. Brann was asked what kind of students they wanted, she said, "All we want is people who read and can do a little mathematics."

St. John's has no need of Establishment pretensions, for it produces future scientists and scholars, winners of such things as the major graduate fellowship awards and Rhodes Scholars, at a rate higher than any Ivy school. It turns out writers because good writing is 80 percent good thinking, and it produces a disproportionately large number of future math Ph.D.s, even though there is no math major.

It should be clear that this is a place only for those who read and who are interested in ideas and fundamental questions. The interested person can find out for certain whether St. John's is for him or her by going through the most sensible college-visiting program in the country. In a two-day period the visitor goes through the whole regimen, classes, and a formal Great Books lecture-discussion. For the latter he gets the reading assignment in advance but may not take part in the discussion. If he gets hooked, he can have an admissions interview and probably be admitted; if not, he should look elsewhere because there is no middle ground; it's excitement or misery.

The students come from every state and nine other countries, and aside from a common interest in ideas, they are as diverse as any group. Although there are no intercollegiate sports, there are as many kinds of intramural and club teams as there are people interested in playing them. Boating and water sports are popular in Annapolis, and one can even build a boat while there. Santa Fe has, naturally, a great outdoors program, with hiking, skiing, climbing, and so on.

Well over half the students get need-based aid averaging more than $23,500 a year.

I recently made my third visit to Annapolis, and my first to

Santa Fe, but thought the word would be heard more clearly if it came from someone under thirty. She's a former client, Mrs. Virginia Beck, a freelance editor who lives and works in Austin, Texas. She said to me, "I simply couldn't produce an impersonal report of this school, especially not when I spent my whole two days there trying to figure out how I could manage to go there myself . . .

"I first visited St. John's on a clear spring Sunday. The campus was quiet and my visit was brief, but two things impressed me. The license plates in the student parking lot came from all over North America, indicating an eclectic mix of students who had traveled far specifically to study at St. John's. The second thing was the atmosphere. St. John's Santa Fe campus is at an altitude of 8,000 feet. The clean, thin air acts as a magnifying glass; pine needles and shadows are distinct from hundreds of feet away. Such clear vision can't help making you feel smarter, more aware, and it was inspiring. Studying at St. John's would be like climbing the mountain to study with Socrates.

"I later went back for a real visit. I spent two days on campus, observing classes and a Friday night seminar and talking to students. I was there just before finals, and while the stress level was high, all the students I met were enthusiastic about their studies and happy to explain what it was like to attend such an unusual school.

"I can testify to many problems with being an undergraduate at a big-name university. My main problem was so big I never recognized it while I was there, and it came from not knowing as much as I thought I did. In graduate school and later, out in the working world, I realized that despite all the classes on all the topics that had interested me so much, I had very little idea of the Big Picture. I had read and learned little pieces of history, literature, science, and philosophy, but I had no way of fitting those pieces into any larger order.

"The Big Picture means 'everything.' It's what the great modern physicist Stephen Hawking said we would understand if, impossibly, we could comprehend every bit of information in the universe for even a second. The Big Picture shows the connection between, say, mathematical logic, Pablo Picasso, and World War I. No one has ever drawn or been able to describe the Big Picture, but for 2,000 years Western civilization has evolved because certain people needed to know more about it. Those great thinkers have investigated the Big Picture from a million angles and have discovered a lot of new territory. You can follow any of those angles at almost any college or university in the country, but only St. John's will give you a guided tour.

"St. John's students are self-selected. It would be hard to convince most high school seniors that four years of college could be fun without frat parties or varsity sports when attendance is required at Friday night seminars and everyone has to do things like study (and even write) classical music. St. John's is a school for the intellectual explorer, the student who likes math because it makes sense or who reads Dickens because he's a good writer.

"For those students, it's important to emphasize the value of a St. John's education. After four years here, you need not find yourself in a fabled position of the Ph.D. washing dishes for a living. The unusual curriculum, with its complete lack of electives and its seemingly outdated reliance on the 100 Great Books, is designed as a tool for each student to use in his own self-development. Simply put, at the end of your four years you should know what you like and what you're good at. Without seeing the whole thing, you should be able to find your place in the Big Picture, should know how to conduct your own explorations.

"The experience of my student guides illustrates the success of St. John's in helping its students figure themselves out. My guides were twin sisters who had started college at the same time, one at St. John's in Santa Fe and one at MIT. The difference in their freshman-year experiences was huge. During my first day's tour, the original St. John's sister told me how she had convinced her MIT twin to transfer, 'just in talking on the phone about the discussions we were having in class and about the kinds of things I was starting to think about.' Those telephone calls often became long-distance debates and discussions themselves, and the MIT sister finally decided she wanted to experience them for herself.

"On my second day, I asked the MIT transfer twin whether she missed MIT. She had gone there to study science but found, she said, that her classes taught her certain facts but didn't help her understand why those facts were true. At St. John's she was learning the same facts, but here the facts were by-products of understanding the concepts. Plus, she said, she was always amazed at how much the classes that at MIT would be labeled the 'liberal arts' helped her understand science. (Pythagoras would not have been surprised; he was as much a philosopher as a mathematician.)

"Even with a year's credit from MIT, the transfer twin had to start at St. John's as a freshman. All St. John's graduates study the same four-year program, thus ensuring everyone not only a quality education but the opportunity to talk to almost anyone on campus about almost anything. St. John's is a true intellectual community. As a sophomore, the original St. John's sister found that she and her freshman twin had plenty to talk about and teach each other. 'It was illuminating for both of us. She was taking classes I had already taken, but it was never like I knew more than she did. She was thinking new things, and since I was a year further along, I could help point out where those concepts and ideas were going to be important. We had a really great year.'

"St. John's is proud to point out, especially I think to parents, that 80 percent of its graduates go on to graduate school or to study medicine or law. I'm interested in knowing about the other 20 percent. This is a school that inspires self-confidence, that makes its students believe they can do anything. While that one student in five may look like an underachiever, I'm willing to bet that's the one who has chosen not to follow even the road less taken but is exploring a new angle, a new way to glimpse the Big Picture. Those are the thinkers who will boost us past our fuel, pollution, population, and financial crises into the next millennium; you might be one of them."

Mrs. Beck would have seen and heard the same kinds of things had she visited Annapolis. The testimony of the MIT twins recalls one of my favorite comments from an Annapolis student of about ten years ago. At lunch at a table with eight students, I asked two transfers from Berkeley if it didn't bug them that they couldn't have a course in psychology under someone like the late Eric Erickson at Harvard, then at his peak of fame. "Oh no," they said simultaneously, "we can go to the library and read all that." The others at the table agreed; they made it clear they were engaged in a more important search.

Here is a 2004 freshman girl's account:

"I spent high school working to get into a 'good college.' To get into a 'good college,' I was told, you needed to have perfect grades, and to totally devote your life to one thing in which you would excel, preferably at the national level. Even then, I was told, it is nearly impossible to get into the really, really good schools, and so I should steel myself for rejection. Having tried my hardest at such endeavors and still feeling my application lacking, I was not looking forward to applying to colleges. In the moments when I stopped considering whether or not I would get into the colleges that I was looking at, all the many possibilities captured my imagination and the experience was exciting. I began to consider all the things that I could accomplish in life. Yet, the fear of rejection still lingered.

"When I found St. John's College, my first reaction was total excitement. Here was an entire community of people that loved to learn as I did. All the things that I had someday wanted to learn, all the books I had someday wanted to read, were all here and required. I laugh at the term 'required.' Even though the curriculum is required, it doesn't feel that way. Some people when first considering St. John's are a little apprehensive about not being able to pick their classes. What I'm discovering, however, is that the texts that I am least excited about actually teach me the most. Every text is on the big list for a reason and deserves its own unbiased consideration.

"My second reaction to St. John's was frustration. Here I had spent four years working as hard as I could to show colleges that I was worth accepting by quantitative means (i.e., SATs, grades, etc.), grumbling to myself all the way about the stupidity of the system. Then I find St. John's, actually interested in seeing whether or not a student should come by qualitative means. 'What!?' I asked. 'You want me to write three to four essays and send two teacher recommendations? You don't want my list of extracurricular activities? But that's cheap. It makes sense, it is the right way to do it but it is cheap! Why have I spent so much time prepping for the SATs?' Don't get me wrong, St. John's looks at that stuff too, but in the end you get in or not on your essays.

"Another concern that I had was getting a liberal arts degree. What on Earth would I do with a liberal arts degree? I was considering going into science or medicine, would I be able to get into graduate school? For that question, I was given an entire pamphlet titled 'But What Do They Do?' I found that graduate schools love St. John's graduates. Graduates are teachers, lawyers, doctors, scientists, computer professionals—you name it you can do it. I can't even list all the opportunities for graduates here, but I would like to invite anyone with questions to request a pamphlet. Also, for those less sure about what they want to do there is a full-time career counselor available for not only current students, but also alumni.

"Coming here is an amazingly awesome experience. Everyone who comes wants to be here and everyone here is just interesting to know. I have met the coolest people here that I have met in my entire life. All the students who actually cared about their classes are here because St. John's only wants the students who want to be here. I would say the hardest thing about being here is that there are not enough hours in the day. I actually want to do my homework here. I know that I will get something out of my work outside of class every time I sit down to do it. The Program here is usually referred to with a capital P, and for good reason. This is not easy. Before I came here I had the mistaken impression we would read a little and talk a little and that everything would happen at a more relaxed pace. This is not the case. We read and we discuss but the sheer amount of reading and discussing paired with what we have to read and discuss makes the Program very hard. But it is important to point out that it is not unaccomplishable. True, sometimes in Greek I feel like I'm drowning, but I found a study group to help with that. Everyone here has at least one class that they just get, and are willing to help others. This isn't a competition, this is a learning experience. The goal of your classes is not to be the best but the best you can be. It doesn't matter if you are the best in your class and so many brilliant people come here you probably won't be. While this fact paired with the text is very humbling, it also inspires confidence. You are a part of the class as much as they and as much as your teacher. That is why professors are called tutors at St. John's, because they are the most experienced student in the class. In a nutshell: Don't come here because you think it is going to be easy. Come here because you want to.

"Santa Fe itself is beautiful. The campus sits on a mountain, poking out from the trees. It borders a National Park. If you like to hike, there are many trails that actually start on campus. One of my favorite sunset spots is only one minute from campus and overlooks all of Santa Fe. Not a country person? Santa Fe itself has excellent food, more art galleries than I have ever seen in one place, movie theaters, shopping, and so many opportunities that I cannot even claim to know them all yet.

"Student life is what you make of it. I have friends that completely devote themselves to the Program; friends that are working and doing six extracurricular activities (although I would not recommend it, I don't think that person gets much sleep); and friends that just party. The awesome thing about St. John's is that there is no pressure to participate in anything you don't want to outside of the Program. You make your own way here, as much as in colleges where you pick your own classes. The extracurricular activities here are so varied and exciting in and of themselves, you don't have to feel like you're being swallowed by the Program.

Want to learn a martial art? We have at least three. Want to learn how to dance? Waltz or swing or tango or . . . you get the idea. And if we don't have it, start your own club. The administration makes it easy and is sure to give you support. They're here because they care about the students and the Program.

"As far as how the college has changed my life so far? I have been humbled and I have been uplifted. I have begun to learn why I think the way I do, and what assumptions are built into my thinking process. What was science like before Darwin and why did they think that way? What is mathematics without numbers? These things may seem important to a prospective student. Well, math has numbers now, doesn't it? Why is learning what it was important? This college is based on the theory that every new perspective has some value and teaches you how to think so that you can determine for yourself how much value you want to place in that perspective. Without the knowledge you are at the mercy of popular thought. What if popular thought is wrong? People seem to forget that for a very long time we thought the Earth was flat and it was only the ability to consider new ideas that taught us differently. I want to explore the past, the evolution of thought, so that someday I am able to add to the future of thought.

"In the end, each reason that makes people want to come here is unique and what people get out of the Program is unique, but they all want to be here and they all get something out of the Program."

And here is the view of a 2004 graduate:

"I graduated valedictorian of my [high school] class, but I also left feeling like I hadn't actually learned anything in the last four years of my life. So much of the classes were based on simply learning the facts, that I was never given the chance to figure out the reasons behind them. I didn't now how to explore subjects for myself, or what questions to even ask to begin such a process. St. John's appealed to me because it offered more than the what; it offered the how and the why and the what-this-means.

"My goal in life is to be a writer, (I'm interested primarily in fiction) so I figured the best way to improve myself in that department would not be to take a bunch of classes that would teach me mechanics and devices I already knew, but rather to read *a lot*. That's what first caught my attention about SJC. I read over the booklist and realized to my dismay that these writers lauded as the best western civilization has produced were largely unknown to me—not just that I hadn't read them, but that I actually hadn't heard of a lot of them.

"My father, of course, asked, "Why should I pay that much money to send you to a school to read stuff you could read on your own?" But as I told him then, and as I have reaffirmed time and again over the course of my four years here, it isn't just reading the books that's important; it's talking about them and getting those other perspectives that really open the world of the text up to us all. Without that, I really wouldn't come away from most of these readings with very much insight or inspiration.

"And as I also told him, I have to be honest with myself; if left to my own devices, I would *not* read a lot of the works on the list, especially the science and math. The philosophy, the literature I would probably pick up at some point, but I can't imagine actually waking up one morning and thinking, 'Gee, maybe I'll tackle Newton's *Principia* today.' And yet, those things I would have shied away from are the things that have most influenced me over the years, have most opened up my world. Granted, I'm probably not going to have to perform calculus or quantum physics equations in the course of my novel-writing, but having that knowledge of what the science is, how it came to be, what it accomplishes, and where it might go in the future gives me an edge that a lot of literature-minded people don't have. I can talk about that math and science with a fair amount of understanding, just as easily as I can talk about Eliot or Austen or Tolstoy.

"Moreover, my experience at St. John's has provided a lot more than what I can get from the books or classes themselves. I've learned important communication skills and, even more amazing for me, how to accept what someone says without judging them on it. I've learned to evaluate an argument from every possible point of view and make my decisions based on reasons as well as

belief, hearing others do the same and coming away with a satisfaction that it's okay to disagree, as long as we understand why—
why we don't come to the same conclusions as well as why we
each come to the one we do.

"In many ways, this school has helped me articulate the fun-
daments of my own being. I'm not a different person than the student who stepped onto the campus four years ago, but I'm a
much better version of who I've always been. I feel like I can go
into the world and hold my own in any environment, something
the eighteen-year-old from a small West Virginia town may not
have been able to do as well as she thought. Because, after all,
when all else fails, if I find myself in an intimidating situation, I
can always throw out something like, 'Well, according to Kant,
that's merely an a priori condition of the soul that arises from the
categorical imperative,' etc., and watch them scratch their heads
in confusion. And then laugh to myself when I realize they
wouldn't even know what I meant if I accused myself of being a
sophist. Some people accuse Johnnies of being pretentious; I
won't deny that some are. But most of us have just learned to take
education seriously without losing our senses of humor, and
though our jokes might not make a lot of sense to those who
haven't 'suffered through' the same curriculum, we've also man-
aged to identify ourselves in the huge and rich context of this culture we live in; how many colleges can claim that?"

 ## Southwestern University
Georgetown, Texas

Southwestern University, which encompasses 700 acres of pleasant Georgetown, Texas, a half-hour drive from Austin, is the
story of an exciting transformation. Chartered as the state's first
university in 1840, until the 1970s it was doing the conventional

thing, providing the B.A. union card for its graduates' first jobs. Then, with the catalysts of the new president's vision and the generosity of three Texas foundations, it was born again as a place to prepare for the twenty-first century.

The vision was that of Dr. Roy B. Shilling, who retired in 1999. But making a top-drawer liberal arts college takes a lot of money. Luckily the Brown Foundation wanted to stimulate giving from Texas college alumni, which had been uniformly low. The Houston Endowment and the Cullen Educational Trust were also interested in Southwestern's rebirth. A matching-grant fund drive doubled and redoubled the foundations' gifts. The striving for excellence also brought in a $6.5 million grant from the Olin Foundation. The result, as of 2004, is that Southwestern has an endowment of $280 million, one of the highest per student in the nation.

With the new flow of funds, Dr. Shilling brought in a first-rate young faculty, created a new liberal arts curriculum, foreign-study programs, and built eye-popping new facilities. There was a state-of-the-art academic building with electronic classrooms, a new campus center, an enormous new physical education plant, new residence halls and new apartment-style housing. Since then the fine arts building has been expanded and new athletic fields have been added.

In 2000, Southwestern got its first alumni president in sixty years, Dr. Jake B. Schrum. And since then, more new facilities and programs have been added.

The most dramatic innovation is what might be called a distinctive honors college, the Paideia Program. It was made possible by an $8.5 million grant from the Priddy Charitable Trust that enabled the college to hire ten new faculty members. That freed ten senior professors to work with cohorts of ten students each through their sophomore, junior, and senior years. They apply as freshmen.

The program offers opportunities to compare, contrast, and integrate various knowledges and skills. They also get $1,000 stipends as juniors or seniors to use toward one of their outside experiences in service, leadership, collaborative/creative, or inter-cultural projects.

The college has also instituted new programs for service in Mexico, research, and creative works.

To cap all this, in 1994, Phi Beta Kappa, the scholastic hon-orary society, gave Southwestern the academic stamp of approval by installing a chapter there. Now it is one of the few jewels of the Southwest whose mission is to prepare a new generation to con-tribute to a changing society, and to prosper in their jobs, what-ever and wherever in the world they may be.

Dean James W. Hunt explained, "We are well underway with an ambitious master planning process looking toward 2010 that will focus on preparing a new generation of leaders whose actions and values encourage contributions toward the welfare of hu-manity. Southwestern will eventually be recognized as a model for undergraduate liberal arts education."

The conviction on campus is, naturally, that the day has al-ready arrived. Students wax enthusiastic about how close their re-lations are with their teachers and how strong is the sense of community. They use such phrases as "a new dynamism," and "a changing school." Faculty members talk about what good and in-terested kids their students are, about "the contagion here," and "the sheltering environment." When I asked the professor who had used that phrase if she would send her own daughter here, she said, "You bet! This is a safe place to be a college student. No sex problems here!"

Ninety percent of the freshmen return, and 70 percent of students graduate in four years. The retention rate for minority students is even higher than that for whites. The director of insti-tutional research said proudly, "We are providing the Hispanic leaders of the future."

The college has also seen new alumni interest and involve-ment. Not only has alumni giving tripled since the '70s, with many substantial gifts, but large numbers are coming back as volunteers. To meet the demand, the college started a "days of service" program, but the trouble has been too many volunteers and too few jobs for them.

For now, but probably not for long, Southwestern accepts two-thirds of its applicants, so there's plenty of room for B students. Over 60 percent rank in the top 10 percent of their high school classes—many of which are small and rural—and over half have SAT verbal scores of more than 600.

Ninety percent of the 1,200 students come from Texas, a statistic that fails to reflect the student body's actual diversity. Twenty percent are Latino and other minorities. A small percentage of students hail from thirty-six states and several foreign countries. In a conversation that included a half-dozen students, a Vietnamese senior said his only complaint about "a great school" was a lack of diversity, yet in that group were two Latinos, one African American, and two whites. At any rate, the college is working to attract students from other parts of the country, and it does.

For out-of-staters, Southwestern is indeed a bargain, and 60 percent of the students get need-based financial aid averaging a little more than $18,000 a year, with another 25 percent receiving merit scholarships averaging $6,630 a year.

Why is all this happening? Vice president William B. Jones, who doubles as institutional research director, noted, "We have a sheltering environment, plenty of resources, and a spirit of harmony. We change the perspectives of students. They may not come here with the same vision of doing good as the kids at Millsaps [in Mississippi where he had taught] but here they are awakened. International studies is now one of the top five majors, and 50 percent of the students have an overseas experience."

It is not only a sheltering but an uplifting environment in which students are given encouragement at every turn, so their self-confidence is reinforced by teachers who want to help. By contrast, said one professor, "at the University of Texas, if a student goes to a professor for help the reaction is likely to be, 'What? You don't know?'"

One prof spoke for several when he said, "We can address values here—unlike a university. There's a hunger and a thirst for it. There's much discussion of issues in class, which is a requisite. Southwestern is a changing school. There's a contagion here!"

Furthermore, he went on, as students develop, they may change majors or shift from premed to graduate school and a research or teaching career. Such things happen because their horizons are being widened and their aspirations raised by an energetic young faculty that most other colleges would envy. They are teacher-scholars good enough to be courted by research universities, which was where most of them had been planning to wind up. But something happened when they came to Southwestern, and fourteen out of fifteen have decided to stay. These young profs hadn't expected that which changed their minds. After having had to lecture to apathetic classes as graduate assistants, they were confronted by eager, questioning learners. For a real teacher this is a wonderful but rare experience.

From the Southwestern students came emphatic confirmation of the feeling of family. Individual students I encountered crossing the campus and groups in formal discussion agreed that "the strongest feature of this place" and its great virtue is its ability to foster close bonds between students and their teachers. They mentioned being able to work on research projects with faculty members, having dinner at a professor's home, and valuing them as mentors and as friends. Others said their minds had been opened or that a professor's passion for his subject had struck a spark or changed a major.

Several made a point of expressing gratitude to the taskmasters who had inspired and pressured them to make their thinking and writing clear. Others volunteered that Southwestern had caused them to examine and become concerned about their value systems. Southwestern, they said, is "dynamic, open-minded, and there is much sense of community," due in part, no doubt, to the broader view of the world instilled by the new foreign programs.

Students have a role in choosing faculty. Every prospect has to teach a class, and the students' reaction is critical, for they not only serve on the search committees but they also vote in the hiring decisions. If the prospect is not the genuine teaching article, he's wasting his time coming to Southwestern.

It's not surprising that every professor I talked to thought highly of his or her students. Southwestern, they say, has been getting a different type of student and his goals are being affected; he tends to choose a graduate rather than a professional school. One prof said, "They are bright and capable; they are also southern and conservative and it takes longer to bring them out of their shells, but then they're on par with the best mainstream liberal arts college kids. They are also very nice kids and very good achievers, really good kids."

Another added, "The value-added factor here is turning passive learners into active learners. So many of our graduates are successful. The percentage going to graduate school has about doubled."

Southwestern has done a near heretical thing in Texas by turning its athletic program upside down, ending athletic scholarships, and playing only genuine students on the varsity team. Now, 92 percent of the students are on intercollegiate or intramural teams, a vast change that has contributed greatly to the sense of community.

The curriculum has also changed. There are strong general education requirements, beginning with a freshman symposium that develops critical and analytical thinking and requires frequent paper writing. Along the way, students must develop some familiarity with mathematics, the great ideas of western civilization, and those of at least one other culture. They must take courses in science, the social sciences, and the arts—an area the college is especially proud of—as well as a values-analysis course. Every senior must fashion a capstone experience for himself, a major project for the year, but there is great latitude. Depending on the department, it might be a research project or a creative work—an art work, a play, or a novel—but it must be a significant effort that brings together and applies what he has learned in his years there.

What faculty members said is true; the students are indeed very nice, very friendly kids. That is why a senior girl who'd been accepted by three very selective schools chose Southwestern. She made three visits and every time "everyone was so friendly. I was really impressed that they would remember just a high school senior. The people here were attractive; the campus was attractive; I can't think of anything negative." After working for a year, she planned to go to medical school, which had already accepted her. Another said that on her visit, a philosophy professor took nearly two hours "to talk to a high school nobody from New Mexico. Now he's my adviser and I talk to him all the time."

Whether African American, Asian American, Latino, or white, all said it was a place that had helped them grow, given them self-confidence, and broadened their horizons and their view of the world. It had also made them realize the importance of friendship and of working in their community.

One result has been a surge in community service. In a student-initiated project, half the student body worked with residents of Georgetown to build a city park that has graphic displays on the history and heritage of the region and provides three hours of child care daily. Students also tutor in the public schools and repair homes of low-income residents. After Hurricane Andrew, two busloads of students, faculty, administrators, and staff went to help repair the damage, another student-inspired project.

Southwestern is a warm and friendly place that evokes in its teenagers and in its teachers a pride in belonging, and for good reason. It will do the same for those who come from the North, the Midwest, the West Coast, or the Northwest. True, they might as freshmen find their classmates a tad more conservative than themselves, but also probably kinder, more tolerant, and more considerate. Four years later, as seniors, they'll probably have found some common ground, and those from afar may have acquired some of the warm virtues of their Southwestern friends, as well as an exceptional four years of growth.

. . .

Ten years later, an alumna lawyer whose son graduated in 2004 gave one of the most eloquent testimonials I've had from any college. It is a conversation about "our Southwestern educations," yesterday, today, and tomorrow.

The son said, "My education at Southwestern taught me to look at all sides of an issue before I take a stand. I know I must be able to support it. This is true in intellectual arguments and in practical decisions I make about my life."

The mother said, "We did not stop with this evaluation of a liberal arts education. The Southwestern experience is much broader than academics. Recognizing the dignity and worth of individuals and working toward justice and common good are the real focus of the Southwestern community. My son and I saw it in the classroom, in the focus of campus organizations, and just in the way students treated each other. I held on to the focus as I went through law school and then practiced law. Sometimes I felt like I held on to it for dear life. I could easily have slipped into a decision-making process that involved only the consideration of the bottom line, but my process had to include considerations of what was just; what was right; what was fair. I hope that I succeeded.

"Southwestern earnestly commissions its graduates to maintain this focus. Pick up any issue of Southwestern's alumni magazine and you will be blown away by the stories of alumni who have done so much for so many different communities. I am amazed by the number of alumni who have been creators of programs to promote justice, healing, and understanding."

She added that three generations of her family have been affected by the values of colleges that change lives. Her father is a Hendrix alumnus, and her younger son will graduate from Millsaps in 2008.

A 1995 alumnus from New York said "Southwestern taught me that I could accomplish anything. The community encourages risk-taking and experimentation at the most fundamental levels, both inside and outside the classroom. The entire campus is a laboratory for leadership. Students test their own assumptions, stretch their own boundaries, and while doing so are given the enviable opportunity to fail and learn. I developed a tough-minded belief that I could do anything I wanted, which I carry with me today. I would put the Southwestern education on a par with the best and most competitive colleges in the country." (Actually Southwestern is far better; the elite colleges aren't much interested in the kind of community or values that made a difference in his life; grades are what they live by.)

A member of the class of 2004 said the small class sizes and interaction with the faculty "resulted in a curriculum vitae strong enough to catapult me into one of the top research institutes in the country. Just as important, I have been forced to confront and evaluate critically many issues of divisiveness in America. The result is a better understanding of myself and my relation to the world, and a knowledge of why I chose where I choose to stand. This provides me with the tools necessary to develop throughout my life."

Another 2004 graduate who suffered an acute case of sophomore slump said she wouldn't have made it except that "to my amazement, almost every one of my professors was helpful and supportive (although I can't say as much for the registrar's office). The faculty at Southwestern are nothing short of spectacular people whose interests and compassion know no borders. Every class is a good class."

The Evergreen State College

Olympia, Washington

Nestled in 1,000 acres of towering evergreen forest six miles outside Olympia, Washington, young Evergreen State College offers the most unusual undergraduate experience in the Northwest, or in any public institution anywhere. Along with Reed and Whitman, it's one of the three best in the Northwest. It opened in 1971 to prepare its young people to live effectively in a new kind of world. Taxpayers everywhere should demand colleges like this one that change their children's lives.

As one professor said, "I, we, came, come here committed to making a difference."

A decade later, as you will see at the end of this chapter, there were plenty of enthusiastic testimonials from both students and alumni that Evergreen was changing their lives or had prepared them both for careers and life as no traditional college could.

The campus is unlike any other. Modern concrete buildings and even the open spaces sometimes seem lost in the great evergreens. It also has more than a half-mile of waterfront on Puget Sound, and a demonstration organic farm used to teach students practical applications for the principles of sustainable agriculture.

In 2004 a new academic building, Seminar II, was opened. It is a complex of five clusters that gives a sense of community to each one by the way the complex is configured. In addition to seminar and classrooms there are lecture halls, studios, workshops, and faculty offices. The majestic setting gives a sense of being one with nature, and everything seems natural and unaffected. Relationships are on a first-name basis. Dress is casual, women wear no makeup or fancy hairdos, and the few skirts were prairie length, just short enough to reveal the same kind of hiking boots or Reeboks the men were wearing below their jeans and lumberjacks. Backpacks were everywhere. Most of the faculty women wore skirts and the men were all in short-sleeved shirts open at the throat. Mine were the only jacket, tie, and city shoes on the campus.

Evergreen would be unusual anyplace. Instead of grades there are narrative evaluations by the teachers, and by each student of his or her work. Students also evaluate their professors. For a public institution it is more than unusual; it is unique, because values are as important as learning and public service is strongly encouraged. It is a place where tolerance and civility constitute a social contract, because it is a community that values freedom. As at St. John's, there is a great deal of class discussion where ideas and points of view must be argued on their merits. "There is a good spirit here," said a dean, "our ability to argue and remain friends."

There is a group carrying a torch for every cause. A gay-lesbian alliance is just one of many groups with offices in the student union. The bulletin boards there were like soft sculptures, they were so thick with notices and calls to action, more even than in activist places like Antioch. Some appeared in every building, like the one calling for action to defeat Senator Slade Gorton because of his bad environmental record.

Evergreen appeals to the self-directed student with drive, the person who was unhappy in high school, or who wants to do things he can't do elsewhere. This is not the place for the person who can't help himself, for the person who needs a recipe, or for the passive note-taker. The Evergreen student has to be able to make

some decisions. But he has some of the best help I've seen anywhere in the Evergreen catalog. It is a model of intelligent suggestions and guidance. It tells the students that the first order of
business is to look at himself, decide what he wants, in college
and in life, and make a plan. The plan may change over time, but
its basic fundamentals won't, and they are detailed for his guidance, along with such solid tips as: go talk to faculty members,
check with academic advising and support services, visit other offices. In short, be an active, do-it-yourself consumer.

After a first-year Core program of general education, the Evergreen student has great breadth of choice. He can choose from the
menu of offerings in the catalog, or he can select from a whole curriculum of faculty-initiated and planned "coordinated studies programs." Registration is like a farmer's market with a great array
of choices. At each table in the hall is a professor or two to explain the goal and the methods of this science, humanities, environmental, or other program. Some of them build on the Core
program, some don't. The student has his pick. There is also an
All-Level Program that mixes freshmen and advanced students.

Since there are no majors and no distribution requirements,
students do design their own course of study, but it is not loose as
ashes, as it is at some no-requirement colleges. The foundation of
the curriculum is the planned offerings. Independent study is encouraged only for juniors and seniors. A faculty-planned offering
in one area may involve study in several others that the student
may think are extraneous, but he will discover he was wrong.

Like the young planners at Antioch, Hampshire, Marlboro,
and New, Evergreen students discover the interconnectedness of
knowledge. "This," observed a chemistry professor, "is a very subtle requirement for breadth. As you get into a project you find you
need to know a lot of things outside this particular area."

In its profile, Evergreen doesn't mention things like class rank
or SAT scores of its freshmen, only that 87 percent of the applicants got in and a quarter of them were from out of state. Indeed,
in a full day on campus talking to administrators, faculty, and stu-

dents, I never once heard SATs, grade point averages, or class rank even mentioned. One girl did say she'd been a National Merit Scholar. The academic dean said, "We have the best luck with misfits." When faculty members were asked what kind of kid would prosper there, several agreed with one who said, "If you want to sit and have someone lecture to you, Evergreen is not the place for you." Others said, "They're risk-takers," or "There's an enormous range of abilities here," or "Our students are idealistic and impatient with the world. They want to do good, and two-thirds of them will do some significant service before they get out, and we have programs that require it."

Although two-thirds of the freshmen had B averages or better, a lot of those were from small rural high schools. The middle 50 percent had combined SAT scores in a very wide range: 1,010 to 1,240. What the applicant said about himself or herself, meaning what indication of real desire came through, was often much more important. Indeed, one faculty member said, "A lot of students here have flunked out of other colleges." But they have to bring their GPA up to a 2.00 to be admitted.

About a quarter of the 3,200 students are older than 30, and 17 percent are minorities. More than three quarters get financial aid averaging more than $7,000 a year. The most unusual statistic is that 22 percent of the faculty are persons of color, ethnic Americans, of Asian, Pacific Island, African, American Indian, and Hispanic descent.

This is one of the rare places where older students not only feel at home but are also valued. Some professors spoke enthusiastically of their special contribution, especially in the seminars, which are the principal class form. Adults who are having successful careers often can offer authoritative, real-life observations that give the topic being discussed the shock of relevance it otherwise wouldn't have. "I have a mixed class of freshmen, sophomores, juniors, and seniors, and some adults who had degrees who added dashes of reality and real life to the discussions."

Evergreen encourages a freshman to enroll in a Core program, and after that the curriculum is pretty free form. But even the freshman Core is unusually flexible, because each year faculty members get together and decide what topics should be focused on the following year, and, depending on his interests, a freshman might choose one involving physics or mathematics, a political or environmental problem, or any one of a number of other things. Each fall at registration time the students can shop around, questioning professors about what their Core has to offer. There may be forty-eight to ninety-six students in a given Core who will be team-taught by perhaps four professors from different disciplines. The individual class groups, or seminars, are twenty-three to twenty-five. In some cases different seminars might meet together to give a broader, more interdisciplinary picture.

As a chemistry professor said, "The programs they choose are all broad, interdisciplinary ones that include elements we think are important for their education. For example, in a program on ecology, a student has to study biology, soils, chemistry, and have a seminar on the history of agriculture because it's part of the package in my program. They learn things they didn't expect to learn, and they may say, "I didn't know this was part of ecological agriculture."

But the chemist would be only one member of a teaching team. For example, in a history of science and technology program there's an economist, a political scientist, a historian, and a historian of science.

An advanced student may agree on a program-of-study contract, not unlike the plans at Hampshire, New, and Marlboro, with a professor in some broad area as listed in the catalog. At least half of the students have an internship in the field of their projects (compared to a national figure of 2 percent). Almost a third do independent study.

The contract plan has a powerful effect on the quality of teaching as well as on learning, because with each new contract with a student, the professor is faced with a new problem he has to cope with. It also means trade-offs. "I don't cover as much in chemistry as I did at Harvey Mudd. I have more time to worry if they can do something with their chemistry."

But apparently the professor needn't worry. Several faculty members told stories of employers wanting more Evergreen interns or employees because they can think and act on their own; because they're independent and have initiative. Also, a large percentage of Evergreen alumni have started their own businesses. Their testimony was in full accord with the findings of a 1991 survey of graduates and employers to prove to the legislature, and taxpayers, that Evergreen was giving them good value.

At the end of a semester, every student writes an evaluation of his work and of the teacher, and the teacher writes a page or two on the student. The students are often harder on themselves than are the faculty—which also happens at Hampshire and Marlboro. Faculty members say this is much more effective than letter grades, and I didn't run into any student who would have preferred letter grades; they were all firm believers in Evergreen's evaluation system.

There are precious few public institutions where the faculty feels as close to the students or values them as highly. Students and faculty host potluck dinners and take three-day field trips together. Also, the Core seminars and group projects provide opportunities for bonding. More than once I heard a professor say that people come to Evergreen because they want to make the world a better place to live, while at other places they were just preparing for jobs. They said they "loved" working with these kids, that they speak up, that they influence the courses and their content, and that they "are truly involved in their own education." A physics professor observed that this is the ideal place for those who want to do things they can't do anywhere else, adding, "We've done brain research here that students couldn't do elsewhere." Another said proudly, "My own kid is planning to come here."

The closest thing to a disaffected student I found was a junior changing her major to psychology who wished there'd been more general education requirements because now she has gaps to fill. All the others were enthusiastic about what the Evergreen experience was doing for them, including a couple of recent graduates who'd come back just to have lunch. They said all kinds of things:

- It has helped me figure out who I am and has taught me to analyze.
- It has made me more well rounded.
- I like the diversity, and you can do what you want here—you can start a group or you can design your own program. (a girl from Mexico)
- It teaches you how to go about learning. You learn in seminars how to present your ideas, and the more you do, the more you find you can do.
- This is a good community; there's a good spirit here. Your opinion counts.
- What it does for you is not described in the catalog, but it's to be able to think for yourself, and to think your opinion is valid.
- It teaches communication skills. The classes are small group discussions and you're asked your opinion often. There are no cookbook courses; you help design your own, often in your first year.

The National Merit Scholar, a senior from Minneapolis who had chosen Evergreen over several prestige institutions, was editor of the school paper. Was she happy with her choice now? "Absolutely! I would do it all over again. But, it's really hard here if you don't know what you want or if you have to be pushed. But what you want may change. You have to think for yourself. The person who comes here should be a self-starter or have a willingness to ask for help—and there's a lot of help available."

Here, as at some of the other colleges in this book, the students feel they're a part of the institution and take great pride in it. They may in the past have been misfits or malcontents, but now they're mover, shakers, and people who are going to cause trouble, because they see that the emperor has no clothes.

Ten years later, students were enthusiastic about what Evergreen was doing for them right from the start. A freshman girl said, "My first experience working with faculty was the most powerful. Periodically, throughout the quarter, all three professors followed up their teachings with individual student conferences. Their initiative and dedication to my learning process was both inspiring and empowering. I left each conference with new enthusiasm and confidence."

Another girl raved about the freshman interdisciplinary ecology seminars "where people throw out their ideas about what they've read and then talk about it. I've never read so many books in all my life, but I'm glad I did."

A junior said, "Faculty really take a personal interest in you. Because they write evaluations rather than grades, they watch you the whole quarter to learn your strengths and weaknesses. I think that makes a huge difference at Evergreen."

A senior made an important point with, "Evergreen is about empowerment and independence. As a student you are given a lot of choices for learning and all of them are exciting and worthwhile. The professors are knowledgeable, supportive, and fascinating teachers."

A junior girl was working with a biology prof who has a National Science Foundation grant to study a major problem, how jellyfish cope with low oxygen caused by increasing pollution. She is planning to get her Ph.D. and won two NSF Undergraduate Fellowships. She said, "I felt I had an advantage from doing all the independent projects that you do at Evergreen. We did a lot of our research on our own, but if something wasn't working or if we had a question, we went to Erik [Professor Erik Thuesen]. Erik's incredible. He was around the lab as much as we were."

Another girl, who did independent study in Nicaragua, said, "I designed my contract so that I would be doing one-on-one Spanish-language instruction and my own readings in English about the history, politics, and economics of Nicaragua, writing critiques and e-mailing them to Alice [Professor Alice Nelson]. I've never felt more independent in my life, or more responsible for my actions. I fell in love with Nicaragua."

"At Evergreen," said another girl, "you get to do things that are meaningful to you, and when you do things that are meaningful to you, they become a lot more important to you."

Alumni holding responsible jobs testified that what the students liked about Evergreen were also the things that had made them better persons.

An information systems consultant in Belgium had this advice for undergraduates: "Seize the opportunities. Along the way, you'll find that you gain the skills you need throughout your lifetime— problem-solving, communication, analytical thinking, how to learn, and teamwork. In the long run, these are the skills that serve you best."

A director of education at a community college said, "Evergreen had an impact on me [that] I still feel. The skills I learned at Evergreen in communication, setting goals, leadership, and personal ethics are with me every day."

An environmental engineer at the Los Alamos atomic laboratories in New Mexico said, "Attending Evergreen is a remarkable educational experience. I believe that Evergreen graduates have a unique perspective on life after college and end up with a strong ability to do exactly what they set out to do in life."

A media producer and Emmy Award–winner, Jeff Jacoby, offered the best advice that can be given to a college student: "Evergreen provides an opportunity to create your own challenge instead of doing what you're told to do. Take advantage of the situation. College is an opportunity to experiment and discover; to wonder 'what if,' and to push the envelope of what's possible. Don't do what you think you should do or what seems safe. Do what seems fun and pursue what challenges you."

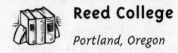

Reed College

Portland, Oregon

If you're a genuine intellectual, live the life of the mind, and want to learn for the sake of learning, the place most likely to empower you is not Harvard, Yale, Princeton, Chicago, or Stanford. It is the most intellectual college in the country—Reed in Portland, Oregon.

On the lovely 100-acre campus with great trees and expanses of lawn are slightly fewer than 1,300 students, but Reed has an unmatched record of turning out high achievers; winners of the major graduate fellowships, future scientists and scholars, and notables in many fields.

Then what is it doing in this book of colleges that take B students? A few years ago it got 800 applicants for a class of about 280. In 1994 it got 2,000 and accepted about 70 percent, but only 27 percent came.

For the class of 2008 it attracted nearly 2,500 applicants of whom 47 percent were accepted and the mean SAT was nearly 1,400. But in that group were risks—people who had indifferent high school records, even some who had dropped out. In short, the fat resumes and the top GPAs of the Ivy school achievers didn't cut it at Reed. A 2003 graduate spoke for several others when he wrote, "Reed takes risks (myself included), and lets the community self-select. I had several friends at Reed who never completed high school. The Reed admissions staff apparently is basing its decisions on potential rather than achievement." The class represented all fifty states and included 26 percent minority students.

An administrator said, "We're looking for that crazily brilliant kid." One such was a junior who'd been a turned-off D student in high school, discovered Reed, spent a year proving himself in a junior college, and now rhapsodized, "This is paradise!" (Furthermore, Reed is paying three-fourths of his way.) As another student put it, "If you took all the kids in high school who are bright but bored, that's Reed."

A phenomenal 25 percent of its alumni have Ph.D.s, a figure that only very selective Haverford and Harvey Mudd can match. One consequence is that Reed alumni are scattered through the faculties of the most prestigious colleges and universities and across the professional landscape, from designer Emilio Pucci to Apple Computer's cofounder, Steve Jobs.

An early nineties graduate on the Yale faculty said he'd run into three other Reed alums teaching in other departments. A graduate student at the University of Chicago said there was a covey of other Reedies there. Another early nineties grad, with a Ph.D. from Harvard, and now a professor of Buddhism at Amherst, said Reed was "one of the few truly intellectual colleges in the country, unencumbered by the follies of collegiate athletics and fraternities, where people who are genuinely intellectually curious can explore the ideas for their own sake."

Only one institution, California Institute of Technology, has produced a higher percentage of scientists and scholars. But in the science category alone, Reed is number one, though it is a liberal arts college. Only one college has topped its thirty-one Rhodes Scholars. What's more, Reedies have won fifty-two Fulbright and sixty-one Watson fellowships and, in the two dozen years they have been awarded, 104 National Science Foundation Fellowships. In addition to two dozen undergraduate winners of Mellon, Carnegie, and Goldwater Fellowships, two alumni have won MacArthur genius awards, two have won Pulitzer Prizes, and an amazing total of fourteen have been chosen as members of that intellectual holy of holies, the National Academy of Sciences.

Reed's title of most intellectual might be contested by Cal-Tech, which recently had a freshman class whose every member had scored 800 on the Level II math achievement test, or by Harvey Mudd, where the median one year was 790, or by MIT, where the median is consistently in the 700s. But at those schools they are specialists learning to be biologists, chemists, engineers, or physicists. Reed students are in love with learning. This is also true of tiny Marlboro in Vermont, New College in Florida, and the two St. John's colleges with their Great Books program. Such schools are Reed's closest relatives, but not its clones.

Where else but Reed would you hear a senior say, "I had the most rewarding week of my life last week working on my thesis." Or hear another say, "Everything here revolves around intellectuality; there is a deep appreciation of learning." Or still another say, "People are proud of how hard they work. It's almost a masochism; you drive yourself to the edge. Because of the drive to learn it's hard to achieve a sense of balance between social and academic needs. There are more students in the library on Friday nights than you would ever expect. And they're not cramming for an exam. They take breaks and there are chats and there are talks on issues of the day: what is power, the nature of government. There are all kinds of interesting conversations going on on campus."

Why does all this happen here? Years ago, a professor at a neighboring college gave me a sour-grapes explanation: "Their faculty isn't all that good; they just get kids with a commitment to learning." The truth is they get kids with a commitment to learning for the very good reason that that is what pervades the institution. And the faculty *is* all that good. Some kind of osmosis or magnetic vibrations work for the very distinctive colleges such as Antioch, Earlham, Evergreen, Marlboro, New, Reed, and St. John's that draw the appropriate pilgrims to each.

The word was out from the beginning that Reed wasn't the place to come for a degree or a job, but to become an intellectual novitiate. Reed has never wavered in its faith in its ideas of what constitutes a liberal education, even in the '60s when Amherst, Brown, Oberlin, and others abandoned required courses so kids could satisfy their own desires for "relevance." As Jacques Barzun, former provost at Columbia, said, "If students were competent to decide matters of curriculum they'd be in the faculty, not in the student body."

Reed also attracts people with a commitment to learning, because it takes great care to select faculty members who will feel that commitment. In 1994, for example, a few vacancies attracted hundreds of applicants, but the deans and departments didn't make the final decisions. Every lucky winner, whatever the discipline, had to convince students during long lunchtime interviews that he or she was not only on the cutting edge of his or her field, but also loved teaching and would be a friend as well as a teacher.

At Reed such rapport is vital because so much of the learning process is in one-on-one conferences with faculty members or in small discussion groups. And I've never listened to a discussion group that was sharper or more probing, even at St. John's, where it is standard fare, than those at Reed.

Every student must fulfill distribution requirements that provide the framework of a liberal education. He must take a junior qualifying exam given by his division or department before he can begin the major task of his senior year—the thesis. Just preparing for this often means an extra independent-study project.

The thesis is not just a long paper. It takes all year under the guidance of a faculty member. It must develop new knowledge and it permits the student to integrate all aspects of the academic experience, or, as the catalog says, it is "the sustained investigation of a carefully defined problem—experimental, critical, or creative—chosen from the major field. At the end of the year he submits to community scrutiny a thesis describing the problem and its attempted resolution."

In the basement of the library are a few long rows of carrels, with bookshelves rising above them, one for each senior; it is The Thesis Ghetto where they spend many, many hours. The labor and the pressure that are part of these creations are intense. More than one senior has told his or her adviser, "I just can't do it." The teacher reassures, "Everything will be all right," and it is. On Thesis Day in May, the lid blows, and there's a weeklong party. As befits all the sweat and tears and pressure, every thesis is bound and filed for public inspection in a room on the top floor of the library.

The senior must also pass a two-hour oral exam that may cover every course he's had, and on which he may be examined by professionals from outside the college. Oh yes, in addition to the thesis, one senior told me she'd written fifty-four other papers that year.

What about grades?

Grades are not revealed to students so long as their work is C or better, but they are recorded for such purposes as graduate school applications. Believe it or not, few bother to find out what their grades are. The director of institutional research who served as registrar for several years said he was always amazed at how few requests he got to see a grade.

For graduate school, a grade of B at Reed can be better than an A elsewhere. A 2002 alumnus said, "Nowhere but Reed could I have earned a total GPA of less than 3.0 and still earned a Dean's Fellowship to Northwestern Law School." He added that the average GPA that year was 2.9. But Reed students accumulate a lot of written, as well as oral, evaluations of their work along the way, so faculty members can write detailed recommendations that are much more revealing than grades. And the academic world knows there is no grade inflation here and no tougher college in the country.

The college says it doesn't want to divide students by levels of achievement. Instead, it encourages them to measure academic achievement by self-assessment of their grasp of the course material and of their intellectual growth. Their work is frequently evaluated by faculty members with oral or written comments, as might be expected at a place where so much of the learning is one-on-one, in small groups, or in independent study, and where people are on a first-name basis.

Evaluation is reciprocal and collegial, "because we're learning together," as one student said. "We talk to the prof about how the class is doing as well as how we're doing. If I feel uncomfortable, for instance, because certain people are talking too much, or if something isn't being emphasized, the prof may restructure the class. This is not arrogance but a search with colleagues."

This sense of being a community of learning gives Reed its gravity. A senior from a self-described "stuffy, conventional background" had planned to transfer after her freshman year because her mother had been leery about Reed. She herself had been shocked to see pot smoking, but then, "We'd have a reading and people would come prepared. I'd say maybe the point is this and people would turn around and say, 'That's an interesting idea.' And I thought, 'Wow!' and I was converted. Like children with blocks, we're building together—you learn so much that way. It's really fantastic."

Reed's reputation for pot smoking, long hair, and hippie attributes came under vehement attack from many students. "There are a lot of myths about all this," a senior girl said. "It's just that here people are not afraid of being themselves or of being unique, or of being intellectual. There's pot smoking here just as there is everywhere else, but people are just more open about it. At Reed it's a matter of being yourself; of individuality. Things are much more focused on thinking and learning and on experiencing that intellectually than on drinking." In two daylong visits to Reed a dozen years apart I didn't see any more green hair or earrings in male ears, or grungier outfits than I saw on most other campuses.

This is the testimony of another girl who was a student body president and who had been commissioned by IBM to design software for use in schools that would encourage girls to enter careers in science:

"With all its wonderful qualities, Reed is not perfect, and I nearly left my freshman year. Here were a lot of bright kids not knowing who they were and trying to find their identity. But whatever I did, people didn't care, only did I have integrity, was I intelligent, did I cheat, and it was really hard. I never had anyone say, 'Will you have a drink?' and I told a freshman girl worried someone might ask her to, 'Don't worry. Nobody's going to ask you or pressure you. You can be yourself.'

"Here you make your own choices. They expect you to be an

adult and that's hard, and that's why attrition is high. [About 55 percent graduate.] The adjustment is difficult. You're in charge of your own life. What kept me here was the faculty. One counseled me to find a dorm situation where I'd be comfortable. I went on a twelve-mile hike in the summer with a couple of others and I realized I'd have a hard time finding that kind of concern anywhere else."

There are no easy classes at Reed. An administrator who'd gone to Duke said it was easy to skate through there, but "you couldn't do it here." Any student I talked to would have called that a rank understatement, they were so full of how hard they had to work. But they wouldn't have it any other way. Nor does anyone avoid science and math courses for fear of getting low grades. Since 1950 only Cal-Tech and Harvey Mudd have produced higher percentages of Ph.D.s, and no place starts up as many women scientists per capita.

If things get too rough and a change of venue is needed, there is a variety of study programs in Europe, England, Asia, South America, and this country. A very large percentage of the students take advantage of them, and like the foreign study participants at other colleges, they say those experiences helped "change my perspective of the world."

For recreation and sports, the word is "informal." There are no official intercollegiate teams, but there are club teams that compete with those of other colleges in rugby, basketball, fencing, rowing, squash, soccer, sailing, and volleyball. A hundred different sports are available in the required physical-education program, with the emphasis on lifetime sports. In addition to most of the conventional ones, except baseball and football, they include Aikido, backpacking, canoeing, all forms of dance, horseback riding, rock climbing, rugby, sailing, skiing, Tai Chi, white-water rafting, and water polo, among others.

To faculty members, teaching at Reed is like going to heaven. They got their doctorates from, and taught at, all the top schools, but never before had the pleasure of teaching students interested in learning. A psychology professor said, "At Duke they wanted the knowledge delivered to them. 'Is it going to be on the exam?' It's such a thrill to work here. They learn to trust their own ideas and intuition."

A history professor who had taught at Berkeley for eight years said, "Reed students are much more active and take more risks, and share ideas and welcome the ideas of others from other backgrounds. Furthermore, it was possible to go through that prestige institution without ever writing a paper. Here they write at least one paper in every course."

Just like the students, they talked like members of a family involved in a common endeavor, one that teaches people to think critically, to present and defend their views in discussion groups and conferences, and to learn about themselves. Learning at Reed is a communal affair and that affects value systems—one reason Reed students don't cheat.

"Also," said an economics professor, "they discover how what they learn in economics may apply in other areas; they learn to recognize bullshit when they see it, and that's a very valuable skill nowadays."

Demanding as they are, these teachers aren't trying to produce ivory-tower types. A history professor said, "I don't so much want my students to get Ph.D.s and become historians as I want them to be able to rule the country."

The research experience and having so much responsibility for one's own education have a lot to do with the large percentages going on to graduate school. They have designed a project for their senior thesis and have carried it out, which gives them an edge in the job market, especially in the sciences. The high-tech companies, one professor noted, "are well aware" of the Reed student's experience.

Reed is a precious asset of American democracy. It develops people with intellectual openness and honesty; clear thinkers who are not afraid of new or unpopular ideas; men and women who have the character and the ability to make the increasingly tough decisions in an increasingly complex and troubled society. Only those willing to pay the price are either likely to come or to prosper here. But in an ideal society, everyone's education would do as much as Reed does to empower a young mind and spirit.

Reactions ten years later to their experiences at Reed were what one might expect from the most intellectual of colleges. Alumni were virtually of one voice expressing their gratitude for Reed's having been both a family and a boot camp. And as the Marine Corps ad says, they were "One of the few, the proud." Their drill sergeants were also their mentors, comforters, and friends. In fact their devotionals mirrored the ones I'd heard a decade ago, but they were more mature, based on reflection and worldly experience.

A recent graduate wrote, "My thesis adviser gives me personal and professional advice on a monthly basis."

A 1996 alumna wrote that "It was probably the hardest four years of my life, but so worthwhile." An actress summed up her paean of praise with, "Reed was very difficult in every imaginable aspect. I suffered and I grew. I wasn't fond of the place when I left, but now I look back with gratitude, respect, and longing. I think Reed is the best community I've ever known, and the world could learn a lot by mirroring our ways." But she had already said that six years out of school, she had a knowledge base in the classics that "gives me a considerable edge," although she hadn't appreciated the heavy focus on ancient Greece in the freshman Hum 110 course. But as a result she knew all the Greek dramas "like the back of my hand."

A thread that ran through many comments was the twin discovery that they were neither the freaks nor the whiz kids they'd been in high school. They were surrounded by "gloriously freaky people," humbled by the knowledge and intelligence of classmates and had to "struggle for success." One of them wrote, "I vividly recall when my first Hum 110 paper, which would have garnered me an A+ in high school was returned to me covered in red ink. It was wonderful."

Several alumna wanted me to know there was another way Reed had changed their lives. One of them was speaking for a couple of others when she wrote, "I could not imagine spending my life with a man who had not had this central experience." Another said she was joking with, "Reed 'ruined me' for anyone who did not attend Reed." Others said they could always spot "the indelible mark of a Reedie." Another alumna explained, "The one thing I know for certain is that no matter where I go I will meet and make instant friends with other people who went to Reed. They are the most creative, dynamic, active and engaged people I know."

Recent and not so recent graduates both emphasized the value of learning how to think rather than what to think, and how to write well. One wrote, "I found that thinking and writing skills can take you far in the corporate world."

Another said, "I left Reed certain that although I had no trade I could do anything."

A 2002 graduate who'd spent a year each at Bard and the University of Washington, said she did her own and then her roommate's homework at Bard but was "still bored." She wanted to be "somewhere where the students teach me as much as the professors. Good Lord, did I find the right place. At Reed, as at no other institution I had attended, the students actually fueled the discussion rather than getting in the way. And the professors seemed to mediate rather than dictate."

A 1992 graduate who said she has taught at several universities called Reed "by far the most stimulating intellectual environment. It is not for everyone, but for those it suits, Reed is a paradise."

"Where else as an undergraduate," asked another, "can he obtain a nuclear reactor license?"

A 2000 alumna in graduate school, "funky and a free thinker," said, "no one judges you based on where you come from, what you look like, or what your political views are (unless you're a die-hard Republican, and then you have to defend yourself well)." She also said, "Reed forced me to teach myself how to learn. Nothing can be more valuable than that."

A 1995 graduate said, "Listening to and engaging fellow students in conference-style classes day after day for four years clarified for me that the best ideas are often not associated with the loudest voices. That experience provided me with a confidence to speak out and act that has served me well."

A transfer from Vassar found the Reed faculty "terrifyingly brilliant" and because of the conference-style classes, the immense amount of required reading, not receiving grades contributed to a rigorous, inspiring undergraduate experience." A 1996 alumna said, "I soon got into the Reed groove of studying all the time, as if this was the coolest way possible to spend time. Like it was all there was."

A high school dropout who graduated in 1999 and got a Ph.D. from Northwestern said Reed had had "an incalculable effect" on him. But for one of his many professor friends "I would never have known that there are Ph.D. programs that will actually pay you to attend them."

A Harvard Divinity School student reported, "The difference between pedagogy of Reed and Harvard, the approach to intellectual inquiry, seemed stark to me. Harvard stressed the mastery of specific methodologies; Reed critically probed the limitations of those methodologies. Harvard invited you to label yourself (Freudian, feminist, Marxist, etc.) Reedies are too cool for labels. The first time a Harvard classmate wondered out loud how hard a grader a certain professor was or how much reading was assigned, I felt like I was back in junior high."

Whitman College

Walla Walla, Washington

Whitman, in Walla Walla, Washington, at the end of the Oregon Trail, provides not only a newly expanded campus of 100 acres in a parklike setting in a cultural center of 40,000, but also one of the three best undergraduate experiences in the Pacific Northwest. The others are Reed and Evergreen State College; each of the three appeals to a very different kind of teenager.

Whitman is for the gregarious youth, a good student who is willing to get involved in his own education and participate in a strong and active community. The kids at Whitman dress well, not outlandishly, and they are as outdoorsy as any.

They come from forty-five states and thirty foreign countries, they are achievers, and they like Whitman. As of 2005, they have included twenty-four Fulbright scholars; 94 percent of the freshmen return for the sophomore year; 86 percent graduate in four years; and over half the alumni contribute, all of which are outstanding figures.

The campus, now nearly double the size it was ten years ago, has a new $13 million campus center, a new hall of science, a thoroughly renovated and enlarged music conservatory that houses a variety of new programs and a theater. As befits a college in that region, it also has a new residential facility for the Outdoor Program, the largest club on campus. In the works are a fully equipped fitness center and a center for the visual arts.

When asked what kind of person should come here, the first thing a Whitman student is likely to say is, "If you're not willing to get involved, don't bother to come." By "involved" that student would mean in one's studies, with one another, with the teachers, and in campus life. Another student would empathetically add that academics come first here, you have to work hard, and "there's a lot of heavy lifting, but we have a lot of fun too."

A faculty member expanded on those comments with, "We're attractive to a broad spectrum, to the traditional, to the granola liberal, and to people who enjoy life; there are no monastics." Another professor added that the Whitman prospect should be self-motivated, have some kind of achievement, enjoy learning, and know how to learn. Whitman's students, he said, are socially adept, gregarious, very civil, omni-competent, and as befits Pacific Northwesterners, outdoorsy with healthful living styles.

A history professor who had taught at Princeton said, "Our students are sophisticated; they're concerned about cultural diversity, the environment, and feminist issues. They compare very well in ability with Princeton's; they're the same at the top but there's a larger lower end." In the matter of sophistication, another professor said it was a mix, but that they "are willing students who intend to work hard and who are enjoyable to work with," and develop a hunger for knowledge as they progress.

A junior from Seattle said, "Big-city kids are happy here; it's not just the nurturing environment—the town provides a safe community for breaking away from home, and there's so much going on here." This is a point worth expanding upon, because so many high school seniors think that the size of a city determines the quality of social life at a college. This is decidedly not so. At Whitman there's more going on in the way of lectures, musical or theatrical events, or dances on a weekend than any one person could take advantage of.

The Seattle junior was talking not only about the many campus activities but also about the region's vast recreational resources. For this college, with its Blue Mountains and three rivers, including the Columbia, either at hand or close by, a city is overkill. Any outdoor activity you can think of is right here. To help take advantage of each and every one, the student union runs a formal Outing Program, both to organize such activities as hiking, biking, kayaking, whitewater rafting, skiing, rock climbing, fishing, and so on, and also to teach basic outdoor skills. It's a complete resort program that also rents equipment.

Students talk enthusiastically about their relations with teachers, relations that include going on whitewater rafting or hiking trips with them or being intramural teammates. This is as it should be, because the various degree requirements dictate a lot of student-faculty collaboration. Every student has to take a large measure of responsibility for his own education, such as planning his major and doing a senior thesis, both of which means much consultation with a teacher along the way. He must pass both oral and written comprehensives in his major.

Students are made to feel they're part of the organization and have a voice in its governance, for they serve on the important college committees. It is indeed a nurturing environment. With the thesis he had yet to master weighing heavily on his mind, a senior said, "Every student has had a teacher say, 'You can do it.'" A freshman testified he had already experienced that kind of morale- and confidence-booster. A senior girl said that a math professor's going out of his way to compliment her on her piano performance was the kind of thing that characterized the warm familial atmosphere. Another added, "The best profs admit they are learning, too."

The experience obviously affects them, because after they graduate they are loath to cut the umbilical cord. They are eager to offer their services in admissions, in providing internships, and in finding jobs for new graduates. Whitman has such a broad network of alumni in professional and executive roles that it makes the job hunt a lot easier than it is for most graduates. But the real proof is that over 50 percent of alumni contribute financially; only a dozen other institutions in the country can boast greater allegiance, and none west of the Mississippi comes close.

Two-thirds of Whitman's students come from the Northwest and 15 percent come from California, with smaller delegations from other western and from midwestern states.

The admissions statistics look more fearsome than they really are. The median, or middle, grade point average is 3.83, and 64 percent are in the top 10 percent of their high school classes. The middle 50 percent of the class had SAT verbals in the 610 and 710 range (before SAT scores were recentered to make 500 the average verbal). The middle math score range was 600 to 670.

Many applicants come from small high schools in rural Washington and Oregon where few go on to college and where good grades are relatively easy to come by. A B student with a solid program in a big, competitive suburban high school where nearly everyone is going to college has usually accomplished a heck of a lot more.

Since the first edition of this book in 1995, Whitman has been getting so many more applicants, that it accepts only half of them. That should make it too selective to be in a book of colleges that are inclusive as well as life-changing. But since it is the same kind of catalytic community, I decided to keep it.

In 2003, nearly half of Whitman's 1,400 students got financial aid. The package of grant, loan, and work study averaged nearly $17,000. Merit aid was received by 45 percent and the average package was $12,000.

It is a writing-intensive college where all faculty expect papers. Also, seniors have to pass written as well as oral comprehensives and do a thesis based on original research, and there is much cooperative research as well.

Whitman has no business courses but economics majors have an in at the University of Chicago. They are also welcome at the best graduate and professional schools, the route that two-thirds of the seniors take, with the majority going to professional schools.

As freshmen, many of them have no such grand plans, but Whitman is a place that raises their sights. "Whitman," a professor said, "changes people, adds to their values, and affects the quality of their future lives. A student may come in planning to be a lawyer and go out planning to be an architect or something else entirely different because of the exposure to new things and ideas. Furthermore, he gets to design his own major to follow up on his interests."

The close-working friendships with faculty that students talked about is conducive both to opening students' eyes and to encouraging them to take a beckoning new road. A wise college policy stimulates all this by giving faculty members modest allowances for having students over to dinner or dessert or to go rafting, camping, or canoeing with them. The sums are small but catalytic. So there is, as one professor said, "a lot of neo-nannyism, but there's also a lot of pushing them out to test themselves."

Instead of competing with one another, students do a lot of collaborative learning in which members of a class may work as a team or in small groups, either on reading assignments or for an exam.

A religion professor's classes are an example of how this works and how the faculty gets students involved in their own education:

"In the freshman Core I've turned over the text discussion to students. Everyone signs up, and three work as a team, leading discussions, planning questions, and so on. There is a visible growth in the discussions and in the disagreements. I only participate as another student. This is learning by doing, making the class work."

Undergraduate research, conducted by the students and by students and faculty together, achieves a like kind of involvement and collaboration. And it has produced students who perform at the top of their class in the 3–2 transfer program at California Institute of Technology, the country's top science school.

Whitman's program ensures that students get a broad as well as an intensive experience. The General Studies Program begins with a year-long freshman core, Antiquity and Modernity; goes on with distribution requirements in the arts, humanities, sciences, and social sciences; and winds up with the senior thesis and comprehensives.

As at other colleges in this group, the students testified that the result of these enforced exposures and of working with teachers who are constantly pushing them to stretch themselves is a steadily growing confidence in their powers.

Also, because there is so much cooperative research with faculty members, students' names are often on faculty publications as coauthors, or on papers presented at professional meetings.

Such things not only foster a strong sense of community but also have a considerable market value. Not many college graduates are able to list a coauthorship on a job resume or graduate school application.

It is not surprising that Whitman produces "rabidly enthusiastic alumni" who have great success getting into graduate school or professional schools and who continue to testify that Whitman has made a difference in their lives.

Ten years later a professor was eager to testify what a happy revelation teaching at Whitman had been for him. "From the first day I interviewed," he said, "it was clear that faculty are here because teaching is their passion; the not-so-subtle message was that I should look for employment elsewhere if I did not fit that mold." He had to teach a class and was "amazed" at how interested and interactive the class was. And they grilled him afterward on why he wanted to come to Whitman to make sure he was right for the job. "I called my wife that night and said, 'I have to get this job!'"

Six years later, he said, "students have made my job a blast. I have the attitude that students can learn best when they are completely comfortable with the professor. For that reason, and because Whitman is such a small community, students have become part of my social sphere. I take students to lunch or coffee on a regular basis. I have been inducted into the fraternity I advise; I have gone on trips to New York and Africa with them. I never expected to be so accepted by or to have so many great experiences with—or most importantly, to become such great friends with—people who are half my age. Are there other institutions where I could get the same satisfaction from teaching, *and* have the student interactions I get at Whitman? I doubt it."

The students' feelings were reciprocal. A junior girl who felt blessed she hadn't gone to a big state university spoke for several others when she said, "My professors have been amazing, intellectual individuals who have a passion for teaching. Also, the relaxed atmosphere and community environment have allowed me to get to know these professors on another level. I had a class this semester that met regularly at my professor's house, and brought potluck dinners. It is not unusual to be invited to a professor's house for dinner or a special class meeting."

A sophomore thought he had everything "all figured out in high school," but Whitman had opened new doors and changed him for the better, "thanks to the incredible support from faculty, staff, and other students."

A 1999 alumna who'd had a 3.8 average in high school came to college sure it would be a cakewalk but "got walloped by freshman calculus" and flunked it. "I had a newfound fear and respect for Whitman and I knew I would have to work very hard just to graduate. And I did. I cried when I received academic distinction my senior year. I had some amazing professors who believed in my ability to succeed; they were not only great professors but great people as well. I loved Whitman. I hated it, too. Whatever I felt about it though, Whitman made me think."

A 1997 small-town alumna now in the foreign service after a masters in public administration at Columbia and the Woodrow Wilson Fellowship Program, said, "I found my diplomatic career because of my Whitman experience. Whitman encourages students not only to think big, but also to do big." A Whitman alum, Ambassador Ryan Crocker, who came to campus, was the person who got her started on her career. "As much as Whitman did an excellent job of preparing me for a professional career, its influence on my personal life is what I most value."

Addresses and Phone Numbers

NORTHEAST

Allegheny College
520 N. Main Street
Meadville, PA 16335
800-521-5293

Clark University
950 Main Street
Worcester, MA 01610-1477
800-GO-CLARK

Goucher College
1021 Dulaney Valley Road
Baltimore, MD 21204
800-468-2437, ext. 6100

Hampshire College
West Street
Amherst, MA 01002
877-937-4267

Juniata College
1700 Monroe Street
Huntingdon, PA 16652
800-526-1970

Marlboro College
South Road
Marlboro, VT 05344
800-343-0049

McDaniel College
2 College Hill
Westminster, MD 21157
800-638-5005

St. John's College
P.O. Box 2800
Annapolis, MD 21404
800-727-9238

Ursinus College
Collegeville, PA 19426
610-409-3200

SOUTH

Agnes Scott College
141 East College Avenue
Decatur, GA 30030
800-868-8602

Birmingham-Southern College
900 Arkadelphia Road

Birmingham, AL 35254
800-523-5793

Centre College
600 West Walnut Street
Danville, KY 40422
800-423-6236

Eckerd College
4200 54th Avenue South
St. Petersburg, FL 33733
800-456-9009

Emory & Henry College
Emory, VA 24327
703-944-4121

Guilford College
5800 West Friendly Avenue
Greensboro, NC 27410
800-992-7759

Hendrix College
1600 Washington Avenue
Conway, AR 72032
501-450-1362
800-277-9017

Lynchburg College
1501 Lakeside Drive
Lynchburg, VA 24501
800-426-8101

Millsaps College
1701 North State Street

Jackson, MS 39210
800-352-1050

New College
5700 North Tamiami Trail
Sarasota, Florida 34243
941-359-4269

Rhodes College
2000 North Parkway
Memphis, TN 38112
800-844-5969

MIDWEST

Antioch College
Yellow Springs, OH 45387
800-543-9436

Beloit College
700 College Street
Beloit, WI 53511
800-356-0751

Cornell College
Mount Vernon, IA 52314
800-747-1112

Denison University
Granville, OH 43023
800-336-4766

Earlham College
National Road West
Richmond, IN 47374
800-382-6906 (in state); 800-428-6958 (out of state)

Hiram College
Radefar House
Hiram, OH 44234
800-362-5280

Hope College
69 East 10th Street
Holland, MI 49422
800-968-7850

Kalamazoo College
Mandelle Hall
Kalamazoo, MI 49006
800-253-3602

Knox College
Office of Admissions
Galesburg, IL 61401
800-678-KNOX

Lawrence University
706 East College Avenue
Appleton, WI 54912
800-227-0982

Ohio Wesleyan University
Slocum Hall
Delaware, OH 43015
800-862-0612 (in state); 800-922-8953 (out of state)

St. Olaf College
1520 St. Olaf Avenue
Northfield, MN 55057
507-646-3025

Wabash College
P.O. Box 362
Crawfordsville, IN 47933
800-345-5385

Wheaton College
501 East College Avenue
Wheaton, IL 60187
630-752-5011 (in state); 800-222-2419 (out of state)

College of Wooster
1101 North Bever Street
Wooster, OH 44691
800-877-9905

SOUTHWEST

Austin College
900 North Grand Avenue
Sherman, TX 75090
800-442-5363

St. John's College
1160 Camino Cruz Blanca
Santa Fe, NM 87505
505-982-3691 (in state); 800-331-5232 (out of state)

Southwestern University
University at Maple
Georgetown, TX 78626
800-252-3166

NORTHWEST

The Evergreen State College
Olympia, WA 98505
360-866-6000, ext. 6170

Reed College
3203 Southeast Woodstock Avenue
Portland, OR 97202
503-777-7511 (in state); 800-547-4750 (out of state)

Whitman College
Walla Walla, WA 99362
509-527-5176 (in state), 877-462-9448 (out of state)

INDEX OF COLLEGES